A BOOK OF SECRETS

A BOOK
of SECRETS

Illegitimate Daughters,
Absent Fathers

MICHAEL
HOLROYD

Chatto & Windus
LONDON

Published by Chatto & Windus 2010

4 6 8 10 9 7 5

First published in Great Britain in 2010 by
Chatto & Windus
Random House, 20 Vauxhall Bridge Road,
London SW1V 2SA
www.rbooks.co.uk

Addresses for companies within The Random House Group Limited can be found at: www.randomhouse.co.uk/offices.htm

The Random House Group Limited Reg. No. 954009

A CIP catalogue record for this book
is available from the British Library

ISBN 9780701185343

The Random House Group Limited supports The Forest Stewardship Council (FSC), the leading international forest certification organisation. All our titles that are printed on Greenpeace approved FSC certified paper carry the FSC logo. Our paper procurement policy can be found at www.rbooks.co.uk/environment

Typeset in Spectrum MT by Palimpsest Book Production Limited,
Falkirk, Stirlingshire

Printed and bound in Great Britain by
CPI Mackays, Chatham ME5 8TD

To Tiziana who introduced me to the novels of Violet Trefusis.
And to Catherine who helped me to understand
Ernest Beckett and Eve Fairfax.

For the error bred in the bone
Of each woman and each man
Craves what it cannot have,
Not universal love
But to be loved alone.

'September 1, 1939'
W. H. Auden

How do I love thee? Let me count the ways.
I love thee to the depth and breadth and height
My soul can reach, when feeling out of sight
For the ends of Being and ideal Grace.
I love thee to the level of everyday's
Most quiet need, by sun and candlelight.
I love thee freely, as men strive for Right;
I love thee purely, as they turn from Praise.
I love thee with the passion put to use
In my old griefs, and with my childhood's faith.
I love thee with a love I seemed to lose
With my lost saints, — I love thee with the breath,
Smiles, tears, of all my life! — and, if God choose,
I shall but love thee better after death.

XLIII, *Sonnets from the Portuguese*
Elizabeth Barrett Browning

Contents

Illustrations

Acknowledgements

I am particularly grateful to my two dedicatees, Tiziana Masucci and Catherine Till, who guided me so sympathetically and with such perseverance during the long, interrupted quest that grew into this book.

Others who have helped me include Vivien Allen, Lucy Beckett, the late Sir Martyn Beckett, Michael Berry, Mary Rose Blacker, Simon Blow, Virginia Charteris, Judy Collingwood, Douglas Croft, Peter Dench, the late Charles Dodsworth, Paul Evans, the late Fiona Fairfax, James Fergusson, the Rev. Sir Timothy Forbes-Adams, Ken Giggal, Victoria Glendinning, the late Christopher Grimthorpe, Marion J. Hare, Felicity Harrison, Marjorie Harrison, Frances Holt, David Hughes, the late Lady Serena James, Judith Landry, Helen Langdon, Rupert Lycett-Green, Adam Nicolson, the late Nigel Nicolson, Suzanne O'Farrell, Roger Packham, John Phillips, the late Georgina Ratcliffe, David S. Rymer, Harvey Sachs, Anne Sidamon-Eristoff, the late Sir Reresby Sitwell, Diana Souhami, Alexander and Serena Sparks, Jean Strouse, Hugo Vickers, Gore Vidal, Giorgio Vuilleumier, Jane Wellesley, Ursula and David Westbury.

I am also indebted to the following libraries, galleries and institutions: Eton College Library (archivist Penelope Hatfield), Fairfax House

(Peter Brown), Johannesburg Art Gallery (Jillian Carman, Eleanor Lorimer and Thembinkosi Mabaso), Leeds Metropolitan Library (Professor Lori Beckett), The Retreat at York (chief executive Derek Thomson), Tate Library and Archive, Millbank (Lisa Cole, Gallery Records Assistant Curator, and John Langdon), City of York Library Service (local studies librarian Amanda Howard) and the Victoria and Albert Museum (Marjorie Trusted, deputy custodian, sculpture department, and Linda Lloyd-Jones).

I would like to thank Caradoc King and Robert Lescher, my British and American literary agents, for having steered the text so tenderly towards publication. The book has benefited from the enterprise of my publisher Clara Farmer and the scrutiny of my editor Juliet Brooke at Chatto & Windus; also from the attention and encouragement of Jonathan Galassi and Courtney Hodell at Farrar, Straus and Giroux. I am grateful to the eagle-eyed copy-editor Ilsa Yardley for saving me from various humiliations and for the work of my jacket designer Kris Potter.

Finally I thank Margaret, my wife, for her patience and incredulous encouragement.

A BOOK OF SECRETS

Preface

The World Turned Upside Down

High above the Gulf of Salerno, some fifty miles south of Naples, is the medieval town of Ravello. Higher still and at the end of two meandering roads from Ravello, you find yourself in a place of fantasy that seems to float in the sky: a miraculous palazzo, now called the Villa Cimbrone, which answers the need for make-believe in all our lives.

Upon Cimbrone's natural and spectacular beauty have been imposed some strange excrescences of human nature that amuse or sometimes unsettle visitors. For a hundred years the place has offered people solace, escapism, opportunities, illusions. Though the legends which fill the atmosphere suggest that many famous people were drawn there, this is something of a mirage. Instead there are forgotten names with lost identities that still haunt the gardens and terraces. Not all the characters in this book came to Cimbrone: one died prematurely before her husband, in flight from his British creditors, travelled abroad and acquired it; another, who became engaged to this widower but for mysterious reasons did not marry him, never reached Cimbrone and, living to a great age, was left homeless. For them, perhaps, it represents the promise of happiness interrupted or denied.

For the two dedicatees of this book, with both of whom I was at

Cimbrone, it has had an equally powerful significance. It intensified an early quest for love in one, but left her with a sense of incompleteness, a lack of validity. The other dedicatee used it as a shrine where she could celebrate the memory of a dead woman whom she loved but had never met.

Like the setting for a fable or fairy tale, it appears to give people what they wish — or what they believe they wish. These answered wishes are often hedged around with irony. The English aristocrat, who sought to create there a final dreamlike chapter to his life, did not pass his last year at Cimbrone but was to have his ashes interred beneath the stone floor of its temple. His illegitimate daughter, visiting Cimbrone only once to be briefly with the girl she loved, would write a novel laying bare the disastrous lure of Italian culture upon uprooted expatriates such as her never-to-be-mentioned father.

The best-known characters in this book, those who have places in volumes of political, art and literary history — Lord Randolph Churchill, Auguste Rodin, D. H. Lawrence, E. M. Forster — along with bankers and Members of Parliament during the late nineteenth and early twentieth centuries (all of them men) occupy significant minor roles in this study of 'lesser lives' (all women). These women (a mistress of both Lord Grimthorpe and the Prince of Wales, Lord Grimthorpe's abandoned fiancée who became one of Rodin's favourite sitters, a rich young American girl who married into the Grimthorpe family and died giving birth to a male heir, and the alleged illegitimate daughters of the Grimthorpes) are among my principal characters. Unlike the men, they have no settled professions and their lives are fluid and vulnerable. They exist on the fringes of the British aristocracy; and yet, for all their privileged status, they were not wholly protected from the hardship and tragedy that, in other classes and a more familiar form, were to fuel the feminist movement.

Thematically this is the third and final volume in a series that began with *Basil Street Blues* – a memoir in which I presented my years at school, in the army (as a National Serviceman) and as an articled clerk who never completed his articles. The book charted my erratic course towards becoming a biographer. If no one else employed me, I eventually decided, I would have to employ myself. The second volume, *Mosaic*, turned out to be an experiment in two forms of retrieval, exercising the powers of research and of memory, the one stimulating the other, as I attempted to recover and recreate the stories of my grandfather's wayward mistress and an intense early love affair of my own. These two books mix biography with autobiography as I seek invisibility behind the subjects I am trying to bring alive on the page. They are the confessions of an elusive biographer.

I made two journeys to the Villa Cimbrone. On the first, not finding what I wanted, the vision I had for a book I wished to write faded. On the second journey, seven years later, I rediscovered it in a different form. This is the book it turned out to be – the seeds of which had been planted unknowingly in me one evening a long time ago in London at the Victoria and Albert Museum.

PART I

1

The Importance of Being Ernest and Some Women of No Importance

In or about 1970 I was doing some research on Gabriel Enthoven whose passion for all things theatrical had led to the creation of the Theatre Museum in London. In those early days the museum was forever on the move. For some time it was lodged at Leighton House before settling uneasily for a period into the Victoria and Albert Museum where I was working. The archive was presided over by Alexander Schouvaloff, a legendary aristocratic figure with gleaming shoes, thick black hair brushed across his forehead and dark eyes that narrowed dramatically whenever someone spoke to him. It was rumoured that he had been recruited by Roy Strong who had then fallen out with him to such a degree that, in the Pushkin manner, Schouvaloff felt obliged to challenge him to a duel. The people I met were the deputy director Jennifer Aylmer, a grey-haired woman with bright pink lipstick who came from a well-known theatre family; and her assistant, a brilliant-looking young girl who quite dazzled me. I was still working there at closing time – after which we went out for a drink. My new friend often worked late and I would wait for her after the public had left the museum, wandering through the empty galleries and halls. It was during these evening promenades that I first saw Rodin's bust of Eve Fairfax.

It was a bronze bust cast in the early years of the twentieth century when she was in her mid-to-late thirties. Her face fascinated me. It appeared to change subtly depending on the angle and the distance from which I looked at it. Sometimes she appeared serene, sometimes she seemed clothed in a lingering air of melancholy and her sorrowful countenance gained a strange authority. Before long the sculpture began to exert a hypnotic effect on me and I started to make enquiries about Auguste Rodin and Eve Fairfax.

On 24 February 1905 Rodin dined in London with a new benefactor Ernest Beckett (shortly to emerge, like a butterfly from its chrysalis, as the second Lord Grimthorpe). Beckett was introducing him to several members of the English aristocracy and had been involved in raising a subscription to purchase a major sculpture, his bronze *Saint Jean-Baptiste prêchant*, for the nation. This purchase was celebrated by a banquet at the Café Royal which marked, in the words of Rodin's biographer Ruth Butler, 'Rodin's entrance into English Society'.

A fortnight before their dinner, Beckett had written to Rodin with an enthusiasm bordering on incoherence, to say how much he was looking forward to seeing 'the bust of Miss Fairfax and I know that you work to make it a chef d'oeuvre and have heard it said that you have succeeded . . . I believe that your talent is yet more grand than the great appreci-ation that it has recognised at last in all the world.' He had commissioned the bust of Eve Fairfax in 1901 to be, it was understood, a wedding present for her — he was a widower, his young American wife having died ten years previously, after giving birth to their son. He regretted that he could not afford the twenty-two thousand francs Rodin had asked and offered ten thousand francs or a delay of a year or two instead. It seems that

Rodin preferred the delay. Meanwhile, Beckett ordered a small version of Rodin's *The Thinker* and was encouraging others to contribute money to pay for his monument to Whistler in the allegorical form of a Winged Victory to be placed on Chelsea Embankment.

Visiting his studio in February 1901, Ernest Beckett had described Rodin as 'a man rather below middle height, with incisive gray blue eyes, a broad curving, downward-drooping nose, a shaggy beard, gray, with gleams of red in it'. Rodin had explained to him 'in vigorous picturesque language the sense and meaning of his great creations'. And Beckett felt himself to be 'in the presence of a man, who is not only an artist of supreme genius, but who is a poet and a philosopher as well'. What most appealed to him was the power of his sculpture – what he described as its 'full-blooded prodigal abounding force'. He called Rodin 'the Wagner of sculpture . . . with new capabilities and larger powers'. In March he had sent a laudatory article to Rodin who immediately recognised a new patron.

The article revealed Ernest Beckett as a man of great enthusiasms. More precisely he was a man of swiftly changing enthusiasms, a dilettante, philanderer, gambler and opportunist. He changed his name, his career, his interests and his mistresses quite regularly and on seeing Rodin's work, which made the work of other artists seem 'bound by the small, stiff, formal ideas' of the past, he sold his collection of old decorative French *objets d'art* and sixteenth-century pictures, and commissioned Rodin to execute a portrait bust of Eve Fairfax. She would be travelling to Paris, accompanied by a chaperone, to study the French language and would visit Rodin's studio carrying Beckett's letter of introduction. What he wanted was 'the head, the neck and the upper part of the shoulders, as you have done of the young French woman that so pleased me. I would also like this bust to have a pedestal from that same segment of marble.' Rodin's busts of men were usually done in bronze, those of women in marble – though he often worked initially with clay.

The sittings, which stopped and started and went on in this intermittent fashion for over eight years, stopped almost before they had started when her chaperone was obliged to travel back to England and Eve, who as a prospective bride could not remain un-accompanied in Paris, also had to return. She eventually found other companions to escort her to Paris and the work recommenced in April. Beckett wrote to Rodin somewhat optimistically in the second week of May that he would be 'very happy to see the bust of Miss Fairfax . . . [who] tells me that she will go to Paris in June in order to give you the final sittings'.

From March 1901 until September 1914 one hundred and sixteen letters of Eve's to Rodin survive and twenty-five from him to her. It was 'an exceptional long period', noted Rodin's secretary René Cheruy, '. . . there was a love story at the bottom of this.' Eve was in her late twenties at the beginning of the sittings. Rodin initially treated the portrait of Eve as a commission from his new patron, and the corre-spondence between the sculptor and his sitter was formal. But grad-ually, as the Rodin scholar Marion J. Hare observes, their letters 'become more personal and even intimate'. To justify spending so much time in Paris and learn some French, Eve attended a Dieu Donné school for young ladies.

Eve writes in simple French, childlike and hesitant, her limitations of vocabulary and faltering syntax seeming to hint at tentative emotions. Her letters give a sense of possibilities just out of reach, half-remembered dreams – none of which she can quite catch and make her own. Rodin, too, is restricted in what he writes – yet occasionally, for a moment, breaking free from these restrictions. It is a polite explorative conversation from a distant age, with delicate implications: oblique and unsophisticated. But where will it lead?

E. F.: I always think of you. Would you write to me?

R.: I think also that you will come one of these days and I will put myself completely at your service.

E.F.: I have been ill and the doctor tells me that I must take the electric baths . . . I am so sad that I cannot come at present but it is not my fault.

R.: I am also sad to know you are ill. Alas my very dear model, you have great spirit and your body suffers from that . . . I await you at the end of July . . . and will be happy to greet you and to finish your beautiful and melancholy portrait.

E.F.: Your letter made me so much better and gave me courage . . . it is the heart that makes the body suffer. Your great sympathy helped me a great deal . . . I am always sad to say good-bye to you . . . I think about you often . . . I would like so much to be again in your studio . . . you stimulate my heart.

An undated letter to Eve from a woman friend suggests that she may have had puerperal fever. From this suggestion a rumour arose that her engagement to Ernest had come as the result of her pregnancy, but that she suffered a miscarriage (an alternative interpretation is that this happened later and signalled the end of their relationship). There is no certainty of this and little evidence in her correspondence.

E. F.: I had wished to write something but could not find the French words to express all that I wished to say, thus the silence is always eloquent . . . I am certain that the bust will be a chef d'oeuvre and I wish so much to see it again and you also grand maître.

R.: Your letter full of kindly feelings towards me restores me. Yes, I am tired of my life . . . Give me some letters when the inspiration takes hold of you. Your French is very good for me for it shows pluck and spirit.

E. F.: Why are you sad; that causes me much pain.

R.: Your generous cast of mind and of body, your genuine grandeur, has always touched me . . . Also I am so happy to tell you now that your bust will be worthy of you . . . After your departure my memories vigorously coalesced and in a moment of good fortune I succeeded . . . Voilà the bust.

This exchange took place during 1903 and Rodin's last letter was written on 24 December 1903. In her reply four days later, Eve does not mention the sculpture itself. The question that troubles her is, if the bust is indeed successfully completed, are the sittings completed too? And will she see Rodin again? She tells him that her heart is 'full of affection' and it makes her unhappy to think that 'I cannot see you more often'. Nevertheless she asks him to write 'me a line and tell me that you are well and that I am not forgotten'.

Eve lived very intensely in Rodin's imagination and they were to continue writing to each other and seeing each other at irregular intervals until the war. They gave each other energy. Sometimes when Rodin came to England they would meet, initially with Ernest Beckett and then on their own. Back in Paris Rodin continued working on Eve's portrait, trying to define her beauty. 'I always wait for you . . .

I always hope for your visit,' he wrote in the summer of 1904. 'You are the sun and the sky in the supernatural order . . . Even when you do not speak your gestures, your restrained expression and desirable movements are of an expressiveness that touches the soul . . . I am always with you, through your bust which is not yet made as marble.'

He had finished the clay model early in 1904 and this was gradually translated into marble during 1905. A second group of sittings began in May 1905. After Eve returned to England, Rodin wrote that he was continuing to work on the bust and 'I have been thus with you without you knowing it'.

The previous month, Ernest Beckett's childless uncle, a vituperative ecclesiastical lawyer, horologist, amateur architect and mechanical inventor, died: as a result of which Ernest was raised to the peerage and became the second Lord Grimthorpe. His uncle had been a marvellously rich eccentric, a scholar of clocks, locks and bells (best known for his design of Big Ben) and a champion of 'astronomy without mathematics'. His last urgent words, addressed to his wife, were reported as being 'We are low on marmalade'. Ernest must have expected to come into an invigorating fortune. But his uncle's many controversies continued to be fought out after his death and, being enshrined in over twenty codicils to his Will, delayed probate for two years. Ernest, who had been in America at the beginning of the year, travelled to Italy for the spring and did not attend his uncle's funeral (a little later, when asked if he intended to write his uncle's biography, he replied from the Hotel Continental at Biarritz that he 'had other more congenial work to do'). It was rumoured that after the death of his father in 1890 and now the death of his uncle fifteen years later, he was immensely rich – some mentioned the sum of £7 million. The scale of his expenditure seemed to verify this. He was travelling the world, he owned houses in Yorkshire, Surrey and London and, as Lady Sackville observed in her diary on 24 February 1905, had 'done up his new house [80 Portland Place] in the Renaissance style, the mania that everyone has got in Paris now'. Unfortunately his father had left a mere £450,000 and, since he had not only a wife, but three sons, three surviving daughters and several grandchildren, his Will teemed with legacies, annuities and bequests. Ernest would have been fortunate to come into as much as £50,000. In addition to his salary as a banker this amount might have been enough for many young men, but Ernest had expensive and ever-changing tastes, as well as an instinct for losing money. He invested in Russian forestry in 1905, the year of the workers' strikes, the abortive uprising and October Manifesto; and he speculated in property in San Francisco in 1906, the year of the earthquake. He was a financial liability. In 1905, the same year in which he had become Lord Grimthorpe, his two brothers decided to remove him as senior partner in the family bank. 'I hate my title!' he said later. 'It has brought me nothing but ill-luck. I wish I could be Ernest Beckett again.' It was soon after inheriting the title Lord Grimthorpe that he seems to have finally walked away from the agreement to pay Rodin for the bust of Eve Fairfax – and walked away from his promise to marry her. Instead he bought the Villa Cimbrone at Ravello.

According to Beckett's daughter Muriel, there had previously been one or two periods of 'coldness' between her father and Eve. But this was a complete cessation of their relationship. The end came in the summer of 1905. Eve had been staying at Ernest's house, Kirkstall Grange in Leeds, during the spring. She went to see Rodin in May that year and then on 22 August wrote telling him in some distress that 'I cannot come to Paris perhaps for a long time'. She seems to have gone into a nursing home – and it was possibly then that she suffered from puerperal fever. On 3 September she wrote again, explaining that 'I have had great difficulties these past months, nearly more than I can sustain but I always have courage. Your friendship has helped me so much and that will be the saddest thing of all if I will not be able to see you. No, that cannot happen.' She proposed coming again to see him in Paris that November; but it was not until February the following year, when Rodin arrived in London, that they saw each other.

During all this time there is no record of any communication from Beckett/Grimthorpe to Rodin. But in March 1908, he suddenly offered to call at Meudon with 'two English women . . . who would like very much to meet the great man and see some of his creations'. He was pleased, he later wrote, that 'you have not forgotten me because I treasure your friendship'. Regaining his early enthusiasm, Grimthorpe (as he now signed his letters) called Rodin 'the greatest man who lives' and in his last letter to Rodin in October 1911, he offered to bring to his studio 'a young, beautiful, and rich American who . . . dances in the Greek style and I find the poses very artistic'. Eve had more difficulty in recovering her spirits. It became increasingly important for her not to lose contact with Rodin. He had written to say that he understood 'I cannot see you now'. By this he meant not that he would never see her again following her separation from Beckett, but that there would be an interval before their next meeting. 'Not hearing from you I am a little concerned,' he wrote two days before Christmas. And she, answering at once, explained that 'I have been ill and I could not write . . . I would like to see you very much dear friend . . . would you write me some words to make me happier.' What he wrote, linking her features to the sculptures of Michelangelo, the 'great magician' whose influence on his work was powerful and unique, explained why she was important to him. 'I regard you as a woman who resembles in expression as well as in form, one of the "faces" of Michelangelo.' There was no greater compliment he could have paid her (in a different fashion he was to say something similar to Lady Sackville). 'If you want me to come for more sittings tell me that and of the thought of your heart,' Eve wrote early in the summer of 1906. '. . . I am well but life is difficult and sad always, but it is the same for all the world with moments of joy. I would like to see you; that will be a moment of joy.' In November the sittings began again. 'I am so fond of you,' she wrote from her hotel in Paris. 'Then it is necessary that the bust be beautiful.'

There are ten studies of Eve Fairfax in plaster and terracotta at the Musée Rodin recording his progress. Among four translations into marble, Marion J. Hare has identified two different portrayals, one 'a subjective response to her beauty' that was finished by the end of 1905, and the other, an 'idealisation of her features' based on the sittings in 1906 that was carved in marble in 1907. Several it seems were made out of the same marble block. In one she is wrapped in the marble as if in a womb, in another she arises from it, seen from the side like the outline of a swan – and there is the impression of a struggle to emerge and peacefulness attained. The Austrian poet Stefan Zweig saw how Rodin picked up a spatula and 'with a masterly stroke on the shoulder smoothed the soft material so that it seemed the skin of a living, breathing woman'.

In the late summer of 1907, six and a half years after she began sitting for him, Rodin presented Eve with one of these marble busts, choosing the idealised version, with its unfinished aspect, serene and remote – 'the effigy of a wonderful woman,' he called it. Eve was overcome with happiness. 'It seems to me that it cannot be true that you give me my bust!' she wrote. 'You have made my heart full of joy . . . You have given me courage . . . I thank you with all my heart.'

It was a memory of their time together and 'it becomes more beautiful each day', she assured him a year later. But did this mean she would see him no more? She refused to countenance that – as she had refused before. Her friendship with Rodin, like a living branch from an otherwise dead tree, had grown and prospered, and her sittings for him were like moments of joy strung together in what seemed a life destined to be sad. Theirs was a loving friendship, an *amitié amoureuse*. It was not a sexual relationship – the marble busts, '*délicieux, dans sa grâce virginale*' in the words of Frank Harris, were evidence of that. She knew that 'Rodin liked me very much' and this gave her confidence. Ruth Butler comments on Eve's naivety in not realising that Rodin liked all beautiful women. But she does not quote the whole of what Eve said, which is recorded in Frederic V. Grunfeld's *Life of Rodin*. 'Rodin liked me very much, and I say it quite humbly. He found me refreshing because at the time he was very popular and many French women were running after him. I think I appealed to him because, unlike most other women at the time, I was not prepared to jump into bed with him at every occasion ... The fact that I treated him rather indifferently made me different from all the others.'

The words 'at every occasion' leave the reader wondering. She protests her indifference too much, too unconvincingly. Her letters are full of anxieties that he will forget her, full of plans to see him again, full of sorrow at leaving him. She begs him to send her his photograph and wishes she were able to write better French so that she could tell him what she feels – 'but you understand how I love you – the feelings in my heart so poorly expressed.' She goes to see him in September 1908, and again in March and April 1909. These are not sittings. She invites him to the theatre, tells him how happy she is in his company, goes for a ride with him in a car and apologises for being so silent during the drive '*mais nous étions trés contents parce que nous étions dans grande sympathie n'est-ce pas?*'. And surely they will have further drives together.

Then, in the summer of 1909, comes another crisis. Eve, now aged thirty-eight and still unmarried, was destitute, unable to pay her debts, bankrupt. Twice she was summoned to court and pleaded that she did not have the money to do so. She had no home (almost all her letters to Rodin come from different addresses) and only one valuable asset: Rodin's bust. In July that year she wrote to her '*cher et grand ami*' asking whether he would mind her selling it to an art gallery that was being built in Johannesburg — and, if he agreed, what she should charge for it. Soon afterwards she went to Paris and explained her embarrassing financial circumstances. Rodin advised her to charge the equivalent of £800 if it went to a gallery and £1,000 if she sold it to an individual. He also promised to give her one of his plaster studies — what she called '*la mère et son petit enfant*' — in memory of their special friendship. In October Eve sold the bust to Lady [Florence] Phillips, the wife of Lionel Phillips, both wealthy patrons in South Africa, for twenty thousand francs (that is approximately £50,000 a hundred years later). Lady Phillips presented it to the gallery and Eve, though she felt '*tellement seule*' since it had been taken away, was delighted to hear how it was admired — particularly by the children who 'throw their arms round the neck in high-spirited affection', she told Rodin.

'*Il faut souffrir si on est pauvre*,' Eve had written to Rodin. But what really pleased her was that, when she came to see him that August, he had asked her to sit for him again: and she was happy. He had told the artist Jacques-Emile Blanche that Eve was 'a Diana and a Satyr in one'. With 'those planes and bony structure' peculiar to English women and so useful to sculptors, she was a Diana in the sense of being a goddess of nature ('you shine always as the virtuous goddesses,' he had written to her in the summer of 1904). In his imagination she became a virgin goddess who might preside over childbirth (as she now presided over his plaster model of '*la mère et son petit enfant*'). But Eve as a satyr is more difficult to understand – unless it is to be seen in the more sexual light that characterises the studies he made of her during 1909 and then cast in bronze. These are more intimate, taut, realistic than the marble busts. The profile has the enchantment and youthfulness that is consistent with all his studies of her; but the front and three-quarter views reveal a more experienced woman, the image recalling some of the words and phrases that Rodin used in his letters to her: the melancholy, the courage and patience as she waits for nature to provide a cure for her heartache and give her a sense of well-being. Some sense of that well-being arose from their partnership which, as he thought of it, was a partnership with nature: 'the germ of your beauty and character that you had left in my heart to open out and blossom in its own time'.

There are letters missing from both sides of their correspondence, but what has survived shows them meeting each other in Paris or London up to September 1914. The previous year Eve had rented a small house in Rodin's garden at Meudon. During her stay there he gave her a present: '*ce beau dessin*' which she called '*un souvenir de mon coeur*' and which '*je garderai toujours avec amour*'. She accidentally left in his house or somewhere in the garden '*une petite casse pour la poudre*'. Perhaps he would bring it to England when he came or she would retrieve it during her next journey to France. By the time war put an end to their meetings, they had been seeing each other for thirteen years. He was to die in 1917 in his late seventies and she, then in her mid-forties, lived on. What began as a professional relationship had grown into something significant for both of them. For Rodin she was a *femme inspiratrice* who gave rise to some of his best late work. For her this friendship, charged with emotion and deriving from the man she hoped to marry who had suddenly vanished, was unlike any other. It was the most lasting and tender experience of her life.

What I did not know, as I walked through the empty rooms of the Victoria and Albert Museum in 1970, was that Eve Fairfax was still alive and that I might have visited her at the Retreat, a Quaker home for the elderly and destitute, in York. In any event my enquiries were postponed by other books I was beginning to write, books that often took me abroad. But I did not forget Eve Fairfax and the haunting image of Rodin's sculpture kept its place in my mind. Eventually, in the late 1990s, I recommenced my enquiries, and tried to discover more about her and Ernest Beckett, the equivocal Lord Grimthorpe. Their two families had lived not far from each other in Yorkshire and would invite one another to formal occasions: weddings, births and deaths. But the fortunes of the Fairfaxes were declining in the late nineteenth century as those of the Becketts rose. And it was less difficult, I found, to trace the contours of Ernest Beckett's life than those of Eve Fairfax because he was a public figure, while her life seemed to have slipped beyond the horizon.

He had started life under a different name. As Ernest William Denison he was born on the 25 November 1856 at Roundhay Lodge in West Yorkshire, a few miles north of Leeds where his parents then lived. On the birth certificate, his father William Beckett Denison gave his occupation as banker (his wife Helen's occupation was that of being a daughter of the second Baron Feversham). As Ernest grew up, his father's occupations swelled impressively. He became the Conservative Member of Parliament for North Nottinghamshire and, though somewhat deaf, would (according to the *Yorkshire Evening Post*) 'give an ear to any matters which his constituents thought fit to bring before him'. But his heart was not in politics – it was in banking. The son of a banker, he entered the family bank, Beckett's Bank, in his twenty-first year, becoming senior partner on his father's death in 1874 and eventually steering his three sons into banking. He was also a magistrate, deputy-lieutenant for the West Riding of Yorkshire, chairman and director of various companies and a stern supporter of church charities. He was the very model of what he wished his sons to be.

Ernest was brought up in a succession of Yorkshire estates, the most forbidding by name being Meanwood Park at Leeds. His father (known for a time as 'the Meanwood Man') also owned a London residence at 138 Piccadilly, where he would stay when attending the House of Commons. In the 1870s he rented Nun Appleton Hall from the Milner family (the home of Eve Fairfax's mother Evelyn Milner who had spent part of her childhood there). This was a red-brick mansion with a huge Gothic wing set in well-wooded parkland and approached from the village of Bolton Percy along an avenue of trees two miles long. The greater part of this house had been built in the nineteenth century on the site of a twelfth-century Cistercian nunnery, and it incorporated the old north front of General Fairfax's seventeenth-century home where he had retired, a national hero, after resigning his position in the army. William Beckett Denison seems to have taken this house to raise his social position in the county (one of his daughters would later marry into the Milner family whose old money was running out).

He sent his eldest son to Eton. Ernest was a natural schoolboy – perhaps a natural schoolboy all his life. He did well in his examinations and, more importantly, shone at games – cricket, rowing, and the arcane intricacies of the Eton Field Game and the Oppidan and Mixed Wall Games. He founded a house debating society and acted in the school's dramatic society. As a mark of his success he was elected to Pop, the select Eton Society, which permitted him all manner of luxuries such as wearing brightly coloured waistcoats. From Eton he went up to Trinity College, Cambridge, where much was expected of him. But there he vanishes. This is something of a mystery, as was to be his removal years later from Beckett's Bank and also his withdrawal from Eve Fairfax. It set a pattern. In each case there were rumours of scandal followed by silence and a spell overseas. He had arrived at Trinity College in May 1875 but did not last there beyond his first academic year. There is a mention of him as a non-rowing member of the 3rd Trinity Boat Club, but no mention of cricket or any other sport. His sole activity, apart from some acting, appears to have been speaking at a none-too-serious debating society called the Magpie and Stump, named after a local brothel. He took no degree. Instead he went abroad.

On his return to England, under the watchful eye of his father, he settled down into what appears to have been a conventional life, joining the family bank in Leeds, and establishing the foundations for an affluent career. He was to join a number of fashionable London clubs – the Reform and the National Liberal Club, the Marlborough, Brooks's, St James's, Turf. He also took up golf and shooting, and began collecting works of art for his new London apartment in Ebury Street. George Moore, author of *Conversations in Ebury Street*, met him several times and was to describe him in a letter to Lady Cunard as 'London's greatest lover'.

In the spring of 1882 he journeyed through France to Italy. 'Not at any moment have I experienced such sensations of delight, such an intense enjoyment of existence as I had at Naples,' he wrote to his mother towards the end of his tour. But 'to rush about madly guide book in hand from place to place seeing everything and taking in nothing is neither profit nor pleasure', he protests, 'though I have felt in duty bound to act as the tourist.' His eye is constantly being distracted from important buildings by the sight of pretty girls. He had been to the Baths of Caracalla on his travels after leaving Cambridge, but they were still 'completely new to me' because on that first visit he was in the company of a 'Miss P.' and 'I was looking into her eyes instead of at the Baths'. He struggles to confine himself to the strait and narrow tourist routes, with their long procession of churches and museums, but he is diverted wherever an eye-catching girl shows herself. At the Hotel Bristol in Rome, for example, he saw 'a very beautiful and very celebrated woman ... Madame Bernadocki [Bernadotti], a Russian [who] used to be a flower girl and was married to a Russian gentleman and speedily became famous in all the capitals of Europe including London where she was much sought after by H.R.H. [the Prince of Wales]. To my eyes she is of a more superb beauty than any of our professional beauties, and has a fascination in every place and in every movement.' Turning away, he feels irritated by the multitude of churches confronting him. 'I never wish to see another in the Italian style. I am tired to death of them, and do not believe there is one, not even St Peter's, as grand as York Minster.' He comes out strongly against the 'corrupt religion of Rome' and tells his mother that 'the pictures, the ornaments, the decoration, the candles, the incense and all the paraphernalia of the Roman Catholic religion continually offend one's eyes and one's taste ... For the life of me, except for the fact they substitute the Virgin for Venus, I can't see much difference between the ceremonies of the Roman Catholics and those of the Pagans. No, give me the Gothic temples and the pure and beautiful religion of England ...'

But, he tells his mother, 'I have been rather lucky in the people I have met and the acquaintances I have made in Rome especially of the fair sex, and they have made my time here very pleasant ... The Storys (the great sculptor and his family) have been very kind to me, and have asked me to all their parties, and last night to dinner.' William Wetmore Story was a wealthy expatriate Bostonian-American lawyer turned sculptor whose work had become famous after Nathaniel Hawthorne put his statue of Cleopatra into an Italian novel, *The Marble Faun* (1860). He lived in an extraordinary, seventeenth-century, yellow-marble building on the slope of the Quirinal in the Palazzo Barberini. With its liveried servants, its chain of almost fifty rooms, many of magnificent and gloomy grandeur (its mysterious upper floors lit by candles), the place had a theatrical atmosphere recalling ancient scenes from papal Rome; while Wetmore himself, tall, handsome, with a grey pointed beard, contrived the archaic look of a Renaissance princeling. Henry James, who visited him several times in the early 1870s, observed that he had 'rarely seen such a case of prosperous pretension as Story' and concluded that his 'cleverness is great, the world's good nature to him is greater'. Ernest was part of that well-disposed world. He wanted his father to buy some of what Henry James called his 'endless effigies'. Story clothed what were essentially sensuous nudes in suggestive marble costumes, making them a popular soft pornography among the Victorians (Henry James called his muse a 'brazen hussy'). He was a sculptor utterly unlike Rodin – 'almost fatally unsimple' in James's words – who led his craftsmen, amid a chaos of female-shaped marble, like a conductor leading his orchestra. Henry James was to describe Story's career as 'a beautiful sacrifice to a noble mistake'. But the twenty-five-year-old Ernest concluded rather wistfully that 'the life of an artist seems a very pleasant one'.

The Storys were leaders of an American colony in Rome and it was at one of their musical evenings the following year (1883) that Ernest met the young American girl he was to marry.

Lucy Tracy Lee, whom everyone called Luie, had passed much of her childhood and adolescence at Ondeora, the family farmhouse in Highland Falls, a large estate near the American military academy, West Point, in upstate New York. These early years were radiantly happy. There were parties and picnics and tennis and dances (at which it didn't matter if you fell over) and hilarious amateur theatricals and, above all, riding her beloved pony all over the country. But when she was aged thirteen her father suddenly died and, to help Luie overcome her grief, her cousin, the financier Pierpont Morgan, took her away for a six-week tour of England and France with his daughter Louisa (Luie's closest friend). They had embarked on the White Star Liner *Britannic* shortly before Easter 1879 and passed much of their time shopping in London and Paris. 'Cousin Pierpont', Luie decided, 'is certainly the dearest, kindest man in this whole world.'

She was a naturally happy young girl, lively and good-hearted, and she became 'an almost legendary figure of perfection to our generation', one of her younger cousins remembered. 'All the little events of her life were kept polished as precious relics.' She was an only child, perhaps rather spoilt by her mother, sometimes a little lonely and increasingly bewildered by the prospect of life before her. As she grew up, a spirit of discontent began to rise within her. So many things that had pleased her just a year or two before now bored her in this 'quiet stupid life at West Point'. In the autumn of 1881, at the age of seventeen, she began keeping a journal to record 'how the world goes with me, so that these pages may bring back some of the pleasant times as well as the bitter'. She remembered with pleasure and an aftertaste of bitterness her journey to England: 'How much better and more easily one can live in Europe than . . . in this horrid little out of the way place.' She was surprised to learn that some of the Highland Falls community thought her affected – and then she decided to take this as a compliment. 'I was, I know myself, very, very English,' she wrote in her journal, 'and did not care, or was rather pleased.' She found this stiff English manner useful when meeting people she disliked. It concealed her vulnerability.

Luie was not what connoisseurs like Ernest would have rated a profes-sional beauty. 'I do not think I have the first element of a belle,' she noted in her journal. Yet people were strongly attracted to her. Her vitality was especially winning. She was tall and athletically built, had blue eyes and long horizontal eyebrows that gave the upper part of her face a mature look beyond her years. 'They say I am old enough to be 21,' she wrote while still seventeen, 'and I certainly feel old enough to be any age that people choose to call me.' Her mouth was like a baby's, but the line to her chin gave an impression of determination — and, being highly strung and of a romantic temperament, she needed determination to navigate the difficult passage that lay ahead. Living with her mother and grandfather, and with poignant memories of her recently dead father, she seemed poised between 'happy, happy times past and the sad days to come'. Uncertainties crowded in on her. 'Oh, I wonder, I wonder, I wonder! How will all this end? Love and pain go hand in hand as do emotions and tears in a maid of seventeen, Uncle Charlie says.'

Her heart and mind appeared to be in constant conflict. She was not unambitious. 'Later in my life I may be thrown with people who will be historical,' she predicted. 'I should hate to be a wallflower.' At the same time she was possessed by 'a most uncomfortable longing for I don't know what. Something unattainable.' She was horrified to hear that some people considered her a flirt. And how was she to solve the painful mystery of men? On her seventeenth birthday, she had received her first proposal of marriage: and was revolted by the memory of it. 'If all the rest I have in my life are as thoroughly disagreeable to me as that one was I shall surely remain in the virgin state until the end of my days,' she decided. '. . . I thought it perfectly disgusting . . . I could hardly endure the sight of him afterwards.' She had one or two men friends who were 'a very good influence on me I think, but I do not mean so much morally as mentally'. Yet none of them really excited or attracted her — until she met Henry McVicker. 'He fascinated me more in half an hour . . . than any other man I think I have ever met,' she admitted.

'. . . He is good looking, almost handsome, with round black eyes and an awfully good figure, very tall and nice . . . How easily a maid of seventeen is won. He aroused all my most intense emotions . . . I was fascinated and felt that he too was just, oh so little, but still a little fascinated too! But he is so much of a flirt, I could not imagine whether he meant a quarter of what he said then or afterwards . . .' She continued seeing him until their meetings began to cause her Aunt Kitty so much alarm that she was obliged to speak very sternly to Mr McVicker, making him so angry that he left the house. And then Aunt Kitty explained to Luie that he probably did like her very much but that he was a woman-iser who amused himself at young ladies' expense. After that Cousin Pierpont, who had become like a father to her since her own father's death, told her that he felt 'quite provoked at my going out so much and at my being allowed to know Mr McVicker who . . . is a scelerat [villain]. I suppose he knows, but still no one seems to think him so . . . They say he is not nearly as bad as his sisters but – that might easily be true and he not at all moral.' It was perplexing and she felt rather angry with everyone. But she did not forget Henry McVicker. 'I wonder what he really did mean . . . To me he is a perfect enigma.'

For the first time Luie began to reflect that a simple moral compass might not after all direct her to the right man for marrying. Perhaps 'a man who has been wild and then really loves a pure, true woman, will make a far better husband than one who has never had any great temptations and has seen but little or nothing of a world which women, true women, should know positively nothing about'. Knowing and experiencing so little herself, she started observing engaged couples, trying to tell whether they were marrying for love, money or position. And she examined the behaviour of married couples such as 'a most amusing woman married to a German Baron whom she hates while the poor man adores her. She treats him horribly and he looks so very sad. It is a horrible state of things, these people who do not care one bit for each other and are yet tied together for life.'

How could she be certain of avoiding such ties herself? Was she a pure, true woman any more, with this new liking she had developed for men with a taste of excitement in their lives? 'I do not think we love people because they have few faults,' she reasoned. A year earlier, at the age of sixteen, she would not have believed it possible to be lost in such a complex sexual-moral maze. 'I wonder if life always disappoints one as mine has lately. If I could only learn not to set my heart on anything . . . perhaps we make our own disappointments . . . I do think life is not worth living and if one could give up the struggle I think it would be a relief . . . I know sometime that this dreadful longing and sorrow will be over & I shall care again for someone in the years to come but now it is all so hard . . . When I am left alone I just cry my eyes out . . . I don't think I care for a soul besides Mamma in this world . . . I feel horribly restless and wish I could get rid of that constant trying companion, Self.'

Her melancholy was intensified by the death of her grandfather who lived with them at Highland Falls. She had been very fond of him; and she had seen him die. Once again Pierpont Morgan stepped forward and suggested taking Luie, her mother and aunt off for a tour of Europe and North Africa. But this time he planned for them to be abroad much longer – perhaps for as long as two years.

This plan provoked a crisis in Luie, turning upside down many of her thoughts. 'It is a dreadful break and there will be some chains that will be very very hard to unclasp,' she wrote. The 'quiet stupid life' at West Point seemed painfully desirable to her now that she was leaving it – there was a man she had recently met whom she particularly liked and now she would never know whether he liked her. Was it possible to wait two years to find out? It seemed a lifetime. Saying goodbye to him would be awful (he came to the boat when she embarked bringing her flowers). How would she ever find the right man in England – that stiff, cold, formal country she had so admired when she was young and innocent? In those early days she had seen everything *au couleur de rose*. Now she recalled those empty words the English used over and over again – effusions of hot air over a sterile land: 'really', 'certainly', 'indeed' and 'Oh' and then 'Ah'. She had been taught French in America, but none of the other European languages. It seemed her only friends, as she travelled from one country to another, would be her favourite authors, such as Susan Coolidge, the children's author who chronicled the exciting adventures of *What Katy Did*. (In *What Katy Did Next* she went on a European tour and met a handsome naval captain whom she was destined to marry.)

In December 1881 Luie wrote a despairing farewell message in her journal: 'A week from today we sail and when I think of it, it seems too dreadful, too dreadful . . . I dread and yet am utterly indifferent to this coming week . . . Everyone and everything bores me . . . I don't think I am worth one thought or care or in fact anything. I am not of any use. There is absolutely nothing to me – and oh dear I wish I felt young.'

Once they had reached Europe and began their long itinerary, Luie's melancholy lifted a little. In Paris and London she went shopping but 'dresses by the dozen are not so interesting as I had fondly hoped and standing to be fitted is the most tedious thing one can do'. More successful were her visits to the art galleries. She listed the paintings that most pleased her: Romney's *Lady Hamilton*, Gainsborough's *Mrs Siddons* and Joshua Reynolds's *Age of Innocence* in London; Rosa Bonheur's landscape of oxen ploughing seen against distant green hills, *Dernier Jour de la Captivité de Madame Rolland* by Goupil in Paris. She seems to have been drawn to pictures with a strong appeal to the emotions.

Pierpont Morgan, who accompanied them during these first months, gave Luie many presents, filling her rooms with flowers and bonbons. He 'is perfectly lovely to us . . . He has thought of everything to make us happy . . . He is so much to me.' This was all she had once longed for: so why was she not happier? If only Pierpont Morgan had been someone else, someone her own age . . . But what awful thoughts these were! She deserved to be punished. 'I think if I were shut up in a room and endured solitary confinement I should be more agreeable after it.'

They went by train from Paris to Marseilles and sailed down the Mediterranean towards Alexandria in a 'dirty, nasty, vile, unreliable, disgusting smelling, uncomfortable & beastly boat . . . a horrid old tub called the *Alphée*'. Even so, the first few days of their cruise were extraordinarily beautiful, passing Corsica and the Island of Monte Cristo, then on between Capri and Ischia, and the exquisite Bay of Naples – 'there cannot be in the world anything more beautiful than that Bay,' she wrote. But driving helter-skelter through Naples itself she was appalled: 'in the dirty smelling town one would wish to die only to get rid of the discomfort. I never want to go back to Naples . . . A boat full of people came to the ship and sang to guitars and mandolins, but I think the songs, though musical, were most doubtful in sentiment.'

Egypt, however, was unexpectedly exciting, particularly Cairo. The people were so handsome. Their robes seemed fastened by some super-natural power (there was no sign of hooks or buttons). The beauty of these Arabs astonished her – the men were 'superb', the children in their red, yellow, blue and brown clothes so vivid and cunning. The women were all veiled, yet their eyes glowed through the enticingly thin fabric. And everywhere, through the streets and amid the orange groves, along the canals and in the doorways of the mud huts, men, women and children jostled with the donkeys, camels, sheep and goats in an endless traffic of life, which absorbed her so that she began to forget her unhappy self.

When Pierpont Morgan left the party, Luie was escorted to official dinners, Muslim processions and evenings of Arabian music by the composer Arthur Sullivan who was enjoying three months' holiday in Egypt. 'Mr Sullivan has been lovely to me and really all my pleasure has come through him,' she wrote in her journal. But he was even more devoted to a pretty young girl called Emma Colvin. Luie noted that 'English men are very familiar I think with all women, a strange thing to me; we have so little of it at home . . .'. She could not make up her mind which culture she preferred. To Arthur Sullivan she appeared delightful but also rather strange: sometimes haughty, over-fastidious and always extremely frank. She had greatly enjoyed the Gilbert and Sullivan comic operas she had been taken to in New York, but hated an *opéra bouffe* they saw in Cairo – 'a nasty, horrid piece and improper, though the music is most pretty'. And she was not pleased with the 'so-called dancing Dervishes' who twisted their necks most fearfully as they jumped in the air, all the time howling and uttering grunts and moans: 'anything more utterly horrible I never imagined.'

To her surprise, Luie became known in Cairo as 'la Belle Américaine'. A number of men told her they were 'wild about my looks' and that there were others desperate to meet her. But she protested: 'I am not a beauty.' Being praised for her beauty – while often feeling so ugly – gave rise to a strange tension within her. Perhaps it was that very sheen of unhappiness that gave her face its mysterious beauty. She wanted to be praised for other attributes: for her imagination, her aristocratic bearing and 'personal magnetism' (which in a later age might have been called her 'sex appeal').

They continued their journey on to Beirut, Damascus, Smyrna, Constantinople and Athens, spent some months in Florence and among the Italian lakes, prepared for a long stay in Paris and eventually came to Rome. If only Luie could have put all this travel into some bank, spending it in instalments between periods at home in America, it would have been perfect. But this was her sentimental education and almost in spite of herself she was beginning to look forward rather than back. Her mother and aunt had decided not to return to the United States but to settle in Rome among the American colony there – much to the disgust of their friends in Highland Falls. 'The two old girls', one of their American cousins later wrote, 'went to Rome and joined the colony of American expatriates where they lived ever after. They took on all the vices of that worthless nondescript society and became the first graceless and worldly old women I'd ever seen.'

But this was not to be Luie's fate. 'I hope in Rome someone will take a fancy to me,' she wrote wistfully. She no longer expected to fall in love and be passionately loved in return – but that is what she still dreamed of and urgently needed. Her mother and aunt understood her need well enough, but they could not speak its name – it seemed as if such natural desires in women were immoral or in any case beyond words. The time had come for Luie to escape from these widowed sisters, neither of whom could deal with what she called her 'blue and discontented moods'. She had shrewdly observed how 'a great deal of unexpected pleasures come to me, but no expected ones'. So, when shortly before her nineteenth birthday on 21 June 1883, she met the twenty-seven-year-old Ernest with his eye for pretty girls, she probably entertained no romantic expectations.

For Ernest this was a year of great sorrow and then happiness. In the spring his eldest and 'dearest' sister became seriously ill. 'She is quite sensible at times and not at others,' their mother wrote to him, 'it's curious how it is mixed up from one hour to another. I wish and pray that the crisis may be over soon and the fever break.' Ernest replied at once expressing his anxiety both for his sister and over the strain her illness was having on his mother. 'I suppose doctors can do little. Nursing, nature and God's good providence can alone save her.' But the fever mounted and before the end of March 1883, at the age of twenty-three, she died. Her name was Violet.

That summer Ernest met Luie in Rome. Their courtship, engagement and marriage were threaded through less than five months. 'Her mother and her aunt saw to it that there should be no delay, such as a wedding in America,' one of Luie's cousins remembered. Each was dazzled by the other. She had finally met someone in Europe who took 'a fancy to me'. And it was more than a fancy. Ernest felt passionately drawn to her. She thought him a marvellous proper man – but not too proper: he had a few faults, or so she hoped, guessing he may have been rather wild, seen much of the world and probably known temptation. In short, he was the man she had been looking for these last years. Her tears dried up, her blue moods faded away: she was in love. And was she not marrying into the English aristocracy? Her honeymoon was an enchantment and she felt intensely alive. The unattainable had been attained.

Ernest, too, was happy. 'A more perfect jewel of a girl I never saw,' he wrote to his mother. 'The devotion that all who know her, young, old, men & women show towards her really is quite touching. They think nobody is like her and nothing is too good for her. She is so bright, clever, sweet and unselfish that living with her is like living in perpetual sunshine. Everybody tries to spoil her & yet she is not in the least spoilt. I find I am the object of universal envy . . .'

They went up to Yorkshire so that Luie could meet Ernest's family and see the place where they would live. Set on a plateau, Kirkstall Grange was a large Georgian house built in 1752 by the architect Walter Wade as an appendage to the derelict twelfth-century Abbey. Originally called New Grange, it had been acquired in the early 1830s by the Beckett family who changed its name, made major alterations to the building, and improved the farmland and private park belonging to the estate (later known as Beckett's Park). This is where Ernest and Luie were to spend part of their married life, while in London they bought an expensive property just off Piccadilly, at 17 Stratton Street. 'My precious old boy,' his mother wrote after they had left Yorkshire, 'God ever bless you and your dear bride and give you all possible happiness this world can give darling, remembering it's only the preparation for a far happier one. You have always been such a very dear, affectionate child that I am sure you will be an equally good husband.' Ernest seemed even more pleased on Luie's behalf than his own. 'It was such a pleasure to her & to me to think that you do care for her a little,' he replied. 'She is so anxious that you should all love her, and she is so worthy of your love.' In September they went to Paris to buy Luie's trousseau – and this time she was not bored by the fittings. 'Only a fortnight to-day before I am to be tied up,' Ernest wrote ominously from Paris that autumn. 'It is a serious thought, but I don't flinch.'

The marriage took place on the 4 October 1883 at St Peter's, Eaton Square, in London. The ceremony was performed by the Archbishop of York 'in the presence of a large and fashionable assembly'. They came from Italy, France, America and Yorkshire, and included the newly knighted Sir Arthur Sullivan, the beautiful Lady Sackville and, as one of the chief witnesses, William Wetmore Story. Luie's family had taken over the whole of the Pulteney Hotel in Albemarle Street where a breakfast for eighty guests was laid and an array of glittering wedding presents exhibited for inspection: clocks and candelabra, several silver flower vases, numerous china dessert services, a gilt-mounted dressing case alongside an assortment of fruit knives, fans and vegetable dishes and thermometers, table lamps, hairbrushes, inkstands . . .

Like Lily Hamersley (who married the eighth Duke of Marlborough), Grace Duggan (who married Lord Curzon), Consuelo Vanderbilt (who married the ninth Duke of Marlborough) and the ambitious Jeanette Jerome who married Ernest's friend Lord Randolph Churchill, Lucy

Tracy Lee followed those 'Pilgrim Daughters' who left the United States for the Old World during the early nineteenth century and were to replenish the British aristocracy through their alliances. This permeation of British high society by American heiresses reached its peak in the late years of the century and became recognised as a significant component in the history of Anglo-American relations.

For their honeymoon Ernest and Luie went to Bonchurch on the Isle of Wight before settling into Kirkstall Grange where, almost exactly nine months later, on 10 July 1884, Luie gave birth to their first child, a daughter, whom they named Lucy Katherine but who liked to be called Lucille. There was a slight atmosphere of disappointment in the family that this first child was not a son and a suspicion, in later years, that she (who needed 'a firm hand') was not quite so favoured as Luie's second daughter, 'my little pet' Helen Muriel, born in 1886.

The importance of having a son was emphasised by changes in the family name – changes, inexplicable to foreigners and indeed to most British people, that seemed to emanate from a comic opera world. Ernest's great-grandfather had assumed the surname and arms of the Denison family out of respect for his wife (or rather the expectations of his wife – she was a celebrated Denison family heiress). But their son relinquished the name Denison after his father's death, leaving the rest of the family in some confusion as to what they should call themselves. Ernest's father somewhat hedged his bets by inserting a hyphen and becoming William Beckett Denison and finally, by royal warrant, assuming the single surname Beckett, the surname of his ancestors. The position was further complicated by Ernest's uncle (his father's elder brother) who, being raised to the peerage and created a baron at the beginning of 1886, chose the forbidding Dickensian name of Grimthorpe. Ernest then followed his father's example, expunging

Denison and replacing it with Beckett. So the family at Kirkstall Grange was now the Honourable Ernest Beckett, his wife Lucy Tracy Beckett and their two daughters, Lucille and Muriel (both Denisons at birth but soon growing into Becketts). Since the first Lord Grimthorpe had no children, the baronage would pass to his younger brother William Beckett and then to William's eldest son Ernest — hence the importance of producing a male heir.

This requirement was made more dramatically urgent in 1890. On Sunday 23 November that year, Ernest's father William Beckett instructed his butler at the family home in London, 138 Piccadilly, to put his luggage in a cab and have it sent to Oxford Street, indicating that he intended to spend the night there. He then set off himself in the opposite direction from his luggage telling no one where he was going. Some said that he was looking forward to seeing a granddaughter in Dorset; others that he was determined to inspect Lord Lonsborough's new house at Brockenhurst; and there were those who believed that he was visiting Lord Wimborne to discuss financial matters. But he saw none of these people. Alone and luggageless, he took an early afternoon train from London and arrived at Wimborne a little before three o'clock. Enquiring of a porter what time the next train for Bournemouth left, he was told there was one in five minutes and another in an hour and five minutes. It was a sunny if rather boisterous day and he decided to take the later train so that, it was claimed, he could look at the 'interesting old Minster' in Wimborne. A little later he reached the central square of the town and, a witness reported, 'he was standing still as if undecided which way to take'. On his arm was folded a mackintosh and in his hand he carried an umbrella. 'He did not appear to be under the influence of drink,' the witness volunteered.

Then, as if suddenly making up his mind, he hurried off across a field to Oxley Farm and, after some unaccounted-for time there, walked rapidly along Canford Park Drive towards the station. The railway track ran through Canford Park along a high embankment. Near an ornamental bridge stood a signal box with steps leading up to the line which the signalman used to reach the station quickly. It was by now almost time for the four o'clock train to arrive and William Beckett, climbing up the signalman's steps, began walking hurriedly back along the line. With the high wind in his face and because of his deafness, he did not hear the train approaching behind him. As it drew level his hat flew off, he raised his hands to his head and the umbrella and mackintosh, like a mast and sail, filled with the rush of air, flung him violently under the second carriage. His body rolled beneath the wheels, he was dragged along the bridge for some sixty yards and, in the words of _The Times_, 'cut to pieces'. The train driver had noticed nothing, but the signalman alerted two railwaymen who found portions of his mutilated body strewn along the line. No one recognised who he was, but a policeman noticed the name 'W. Beckett Esq. MP' on the collar of an undercoat. In his dress coat pocket they found an envelope with a lady's name and address (not disclosed in the newspapers) written on it, together with a one-hundred-pound note. There was also a ring, a timepiece, a five-pound note having a recent stamp of the Bachelors Club on it – and, some way off, the umbrella. William Beckett was aged sixty-four.

Ernest was enjoying what the _Yorkshire Post_ called 'a well-earned holiday' in Algiers and could not get back for the inquest. The jury was taken up on to the ornamental bridge and, encountering a fierce gust of wind, almost perished themselves. They returned the obvious verdict of accidental death. But behind the fatal accident lay a mystery. Why was William Beckett there? A rumour wafted round the community that he had been visiting his mistress – the envelope with a lady's name and the terrific bank note (worth £8,000 today) seemed to lend colour to this story. Later there was an attempt to extort money from the Beckett family, which Ernest successfully resisted.

William Beckett's fragmented body was gathered together, taken to the Railway Hotel and put by the undertaker into a shell, which was carried by train to the Beckett family residence in Piccadilly and then conveyed to Yorkshire. The funeral took place on 6 December at a remote little stone church at Alcaster, a mile and a half away from Nun Appleton Hall. No invitations had been sent out except to close members of the family, but no restrictions were imposed on people wishing to attend. The terrible nature of his death had caught the public imagination and the railway companies arranged for special trains to take sympathisers from other parts of the country to this remote destination. At Bolton Percy station over a hundred carriages waited to drive them to the burial ground. This thin black line of carriages, a cavalcade stretching over half a mile, moved slowly between fields of thick snow while from the opposite direction a family cortège with the hearse carrying William Beckett's remains set off from Nun Appleton. Men and women of all ranks and opinions assembled for the simple service: bankers and railwaymen, politicians, churchmen, country gentlemen, friends and servants. Heads bared, they formed an aisle down which the coffin was carried in silence to the church. The nineteen-year-old Eve Fairfax was also there with her mother. Ernest had arrived back via Paris and was accompanied by his wife Luie. But his elderly uncle, the first Lord Grimthorpe, sent apologies for not risking the bleak weather to attend his brother's funeral.

Ernest Beckett was now the heir presumptive to the Grimthorpe title; but Luie had recently suffered a miscarriage while she was visiting her mother in Rome. 'The Dr says I am doing perfectly well and should be on my sofa in a few days — I don't suppose anyone has had an easier fausse couche but it is tiring,' she wrote to Ernest. She reassured him that this did not mean she could not bear him another child: a boy. 'There will be no weakness or liability . . . Don't let anyone worry you into thinking so.' Being apart from him and feeling vulnerable, she declares: 'I have loved you so my darling these last few days and feel no woman ever had such a sweet, dear husband as mine.' Her one regret is that he does not write to her as much as she would like. 'I am quite sure you would not have failed to write when you knew I was ill – I have been so cross with the postman, & servants all day, for every knock at the door I hoped was a letter from you.'

On her recovery, Ernest arranged for Luie to be painted by the Royal Academician, Edward Hughes. It is a studio portrait staged against a back-drop of trees, showing Muriel charmingly perched over her shoulder and Lucille, standing next to her mother, carrying some flowers. A sympathetic and celebratory picture: Luie in her décolleté evening dress is seen as having regained her figure. She looks young and happy.

Her letters to 'my beloved darling' suggest that these first six or seven years of married life were untroubled. In the autumn of 1884 they travelled to America, staying for the most part in New York. 'People have been so exceedingly kind and hospitable', Ernest wrote, 'that now I shall be almost as sorry to leave as Luie. Every night during this last week a dinner is given in our honour . . . All the best people in New York have called upon us.' In a letter to his mother, Ernest suggests they were being lavishly entertained 'as a bait to make us stay. I am not exaggerating in the least when I say that Luie receives more attention than any woman in New York. We have opera boxes sent us nearly every night . . . And the papers are continually saying nice things about us. Luie seems to thrive on all the love & admiration that is showered upon her . . . and I feel a different man altogether. I think all this agreeable society does me good. As it is such a contrast to the life I have led for so many years.'

But though 'in every way this visit has been a pleasure & success',

Ernest added, 'I feel as if we ought to be home again before the year's end.' There is an indication that Luie would have preferred living in America. But Ernest missed the Yorkshire hunting and the shooting. And there were other considerations. What he admired most in America was the ostentatious display of wealth. There is a revealing passage in one of his letters in which he describes a visit to the spectacular house of William Henry Vanderbilt 'the richest man in the world', he writes with schoolboy enthusiasm. 'It is known positively that he has £50 millions.' Ernest is dazzled by the marble entrance hall with its mosaic pavement and also by the many opulent rooms – one hung round with red velvet and gold into which precious stones have been worked, another lined with mother-of-pearl and bearing Japanese curtains, and a third of carved wood with its ceiling painted on canvas 'by one of the best French painters who charges £1,000 for a single picture'. But most wonderful of all was the picture gallery 'with the best collection of modern pictures in the world, a perfect enchantment. One small picture cost £1,200. Mr Vanderbilt has excellent taste in pictures and he has always the pick of the market.' Ernest seems interested in the price of everything and the identity of nothing. He was drawn to wealth but he also needed power. He met many powerful and wealthy people in America, but he met them at one remove as Luie's husband. His own best chance of advancement lay in England.

At the age of seventeen Luie had dreamed of being 'thrown with people who will be historical', and when Ernest was elected the Conservative Member of Parliament for Whitby in November 1885, her dream appeared to be coming true. Whitby was traditionally radical, but Charles Stewart Parnell, the influential Irish Member of Parliament, had called on all Irishmen in England to vote Conservative, and although the Liberals won the General Election, Ernest was returned with a majority of 340 votes. Standing on the slopes and looking out to sea, with the crowds gathered below on the sands at Whitby, he resembled a classical orator in a natural amphitheatre. In his election address he had called on voters to 'reject the Feeble and Futile policy of the late [Liberal] Government through five years of failure and disgrace', condemned the 'waste of men and money in unjust and unnecessary wars', defended the Established Church as 'a strong bulwark against infidelity' and appealed for the maintenance of the Imperial Parliament's jurisdiction over Ireland.

In the summer of 1886 Gladstone, who had formed a third Liberal ministry, introduced a Home Rule Bill for Ireland, which was defeated on its second reading and, Parliament being dissolved, a new General Election was called. This time the Liberal Party was split in two by the Irish question, and the Conservatives won. Lord Salisbury became Premier and Ernest quadrupled his majority at Whitby. 'I regard myself as your representative and not as your delegate,' he told the electors. 'Fishermen, sailors, miners and working men of every sort and condition have joined with landowners and professional men to make up my big majority. And why? Because from the bottom of their honest English hearts they believed their country was in danger [and were] determined to maintain the union between England and Ireland. I have received my orders and shall stand by my guns.'

He liked making political speeches – and his audiences enjoyed them too. He flattered them nobly and made them feel important. If necessary, he discovered, he could speak with ease and fluency for over an hour, enriching his rhetoric with fine-sounding biblical quotations, interspersing it with clever topical jokes and producing a swell of reverberating invective. On the Irish Home Rule Bill he declared: 'It sweats difficulties at every paragraph, every provision breeds a dilemma, every clause ends in a cul de sac, danger lurks in every line, mischief abounds in every sentence, and an air of evil hangs over it all.' He castigated

Gladstone as a man 'who had been tinkering at Ireland for twenty years, and under his treatment the last state of Ireland was worse than the first. And this was the man who had got the amazing effrontery to come forward and ask to be allowed to have a free hand to boggle at the job he had so much mismanaged before.'

For the first year Ernest enjoyed his time as a Member of Parliament in the House of Commons. It reminded him of his happy debating days at Eton and Cambridge. But soon he began to grow impatient with the limitations of the party system. He wanted more than laughter and applause. He looked round for someone with whom to align himself. He had been polite to Lord Salisbury but his praise was always lukewarm and he calculated that, his health being poor, Salisbury had little political future. There was only one man whose verbal sword-play excited him and that was the maverick figure of Lord Randolph Churchill (son of the seventh Duke of Marlborough and father of Winston Churchill). In the early 1880s Randolph Churchill had formed a small group called the Fourth Party which attacked everything the Liberals proposed and, sidestepping the guidance of the party whips, set out to force reforms on the Conservatives. Ernest quickly joined this small band of ambitious malcontents. Churchill's brilliant speeches were making him the most popular politician in the country and the Conservative success in the 1886 election was largely credited to him. 'He carries the Conservative party and its fortunes,' Ernest declared. 'No man has done so much to mould it into its present shape. In all its words and works it bears the impress of his hand. It is popular mainly because he won popularity for it.' Few people doubted that Randolph Churchill would one day be Prime Minister. Nevertheless he was considered a dangerous figure within the party. He was, however, given high office in Salisbury's new administration until, at the end of 1886, in the face of Cabinet opposition to his budget, he suddenly astonished everyone by resigning both as Leader of the House of Commons and Chancellor of the Exchequer.

In his biography of Lord Randolph Churchill, his son Winston Churchill describes Ernest as an intimate friend of his father who 'stood by him, worked with him and rendered many political services in the years that followed his resignation' — services, he adds, 'which were not extravagantly beloved' in the high places of his party.

Luie, who took a careful interest in her husband's political career, seems to have had some doubts about Randolph Churchill. 'You are the only person I am sure who can get together a Randolphian party,' she wrote to Ernest early in 1889, 'but you must be sure he will lead you to Austerlitz & not to Moscow — or that at all events intends to!!' But then, thinking perhaps this was too inconsiderate, she added: 'He is an Englishman & gentleman therefore it will be safe to trust his word.' Yet she was pleased with Ernest for distrusting Gladstone's word, and also told him she was 'very glad you had a fine dig at Ld Salisbury'. She welcomed, too, the distance he kept from Salisbury's nephew, Arthur Balfour, who was attempting to act as mediator between Randolph Churchill and Lord Salisbury. There was something she did not like about the self-aggrandisement of these top dogs in party-political life. 'The Balfourian worship is as odious to me as Gladstone worship,' she wrote to Ernest, 'and I only hope there will never be Randolph worship. It turns men into automatons and takes away their reasoning powers . . .' Perhaps she feared that Ernest himself might be drawn too far into this mechanistic political life.

Ernest's reasoning powers told him that Randolph Churchill's star would indeed rise again. He was a natural successor to Disraeli and nothing could stop him. 'Raised by his genius far above the common herd, he has that penetrating insight which is the imperial prerogative of genius to possess,' Ernest declared in one of his speeches, 'and his eye like that of the eagle hovering in the heavens, discerns things clearly which are hidden from the view of ordinary mortals.' Why then did his party distrust him? Ernest's answer was clear: 'When the Tory party gives birth to a genius they always stare and blink and rub their eyes and fidget about uneasily and ask each other anxiously what manner of man is this? "Is he a spirit of health or a goblin damned? Brings he airs from heaven or blasts from hell?" They begin foolishly by suspecting and trying to suppress him, and not being able to do that, they end wisely by trusting implicitly to his guidance. So will it be with Randolph Churchill.'

Ernest saw in Randolph Churchill a version of himself, a superior version to which he aspired. Churchill was said to have been 'too proud to care for any but the first place' and he believed that you should never resign until you were indispensable. But in becoming indispensable to the Conservative Party, he had also become what Salisbury called a boil on its neck. He was admired but not liked by his colleagues. They were disturbed by his cleverness, his individuality and the way he came out with opinions that were entirely his own. These were all qualities that appealed to Ernest, who invited him to speak at Whitby and to stay at Kirkstall Grange. Churchill had the extravagance and charm of someone who has been much spoilt as a child. He could be petulant, rude and capricious when thwarted in what he wanted. What he wanted was power over men and the love of women.

And so did Ernest.

It was strange, with such important work to occupy him in banking and politics, how often Ernest disappeared abroad. During another of his visits to Rome in the late 1880s he was taken by William Wetmore Story's son, Waldo Story, to a ball where he met Josephine Cornelia Brink, a voluptuous, nineteen-year-old girl from South Africa whom everyone called José. She was one of the five children of a prominent legislator who, dying at the age of fifty-five, had left his family near Cape Town in financial difficulties. His widow, 'the golden-haired Mrs Brink', found José the most spirited and unruly of her children. When Lady Robinson, an Irish aristocrat and wife of the Governor of the Cape Colony, Sir Hercules Robinson, offered to bring her up at the official Cape residence, Mrs Brink readily consented. The Robinsons treated her like their own daughter and introduced her at dinner parties and country-house weekends to smart society. Tall, fair, with great vivacity and 'a gorgeous figure', she was an immediate success, receiving impetuous offers of marriage and, on travelling to England with Lady Robinson, being presented at Court to Queen Victoria. 'You will have much joy and much flattery as well as much temptation in your life,' Lady Robinson advised her. 'Snatch at every ray because they may never return again.'

José seemed determined to follow this advice – even after her mother joined her in London. It was when she was visiting Rome as the guest of Lord and Lady Dufferin, the British Ambassador and his wife, that she met Ernest. José's picture appeared in many newspapers and magazines, and Waldo Story used one of these photographs to help him create a marble statue of her entitled *Victory*. Seeing her at Story's studio, Ernest entreated her to write to him after they were both back in London. She did so. He replied inviting her to lunch at the Savoy Hotel and enquiring whether she might come without the formality of her mother's consent. She had no intention of doing otherwise and met him in a private suite there. 'So much in love were we with each other that it seemed quite natural when he took me into the bedroom adjoining his suite and with love and fondness I let him unclothe me,' she wrote. This was the beginning of her first serious love affair. 'I want to teach you what love means,' she remembered Ernest telling her.

To assist with this tuition, Ernest took a small flat in St James's Street, between Piccadilly and Pall Mall, where they continued meeting.

He let her know he was married – though she must already have been aware of this. But he does not appear to have told her that, by the late summer of 1890, Luie was again pregnant. He said she was ill and that if she died he would marry José – that at any rate was what she recalled. And probably it explains her decision not to accompany her mother back to South Africa to prepare for one of her other daughters' marriage there. José was no longer under the protection of the Robinson family and her own family threatened to stop her allowance if she did not return immediately. However, she had recently inherited a legacy of six hundred pounds and this may have emboldened her. But how long would this money last her in London? Where would she live and what would be her future? She had found a wonderful little house called Leinster Lodge in Bayswater, overlooking Kensington Gardens – should she risk taking a long lease on it? She put these questions to Ernest who, according to a short Life of her by Daphne Saul, 'made himself responsible for the down payment, which she declared she could not afford, and also for the rent of £150 a year'.

In an early unpublished autobiography, José writes of her time at Leinster Lodge as being extraordinarily happy. The house, its garden and stables, were encircled by a high brick wall. Her bedroom was situated on the ground floor with the drawing room, reached by a Jacobean staircase, above it. A conservatory opened on to the back garden, and the kitchen and servants' rooms lay somewhat obscurely in a 'wonderfully ventilated' floor below stairs. José was looked after by a cook, a parlour maid, a housemaid and a lady's maid, while the horses and brougham were under the care of her coachman. She rode most mornings in Rotten Row, but her social life as Ernest's mistress was restricted. No longer could she be invited regularly to 'At Homes' and for country weekends. When she saw people it was usually at small dinner parties she and Ernest gave at Leinster Lodge.

On Sunday 3 May 1891, in the family home at 138 Piccadilly, Luie gave birth to a son, Ralph William Ernest Beckett. Six days later she died. She had suffered from a bronchial attack the previous month, gone into premature labour a week before the birth and caught influenza, which developed into pneumonia after her son was born. Losing a lot of blood, she fainted and lay unconscious for two days before dying on the Saturday afternoon. She was twenty-six years old.

Her death was, in the words of one Yorkshire newspaper, 'of a peculiarly pathetic and painful nature'. When Ernest was in London, Luie had often stayed at Kirkstall Grange and it was in Leeds, and also round Whitby where she stood on election platforms with her husband, that she was best known and most missed. People knew she was ill but had felt confident that her natural vitality would pull her through. What they called 'her sunny disposition and gentleness' had made her a popular figure in the county, and her charitable work was every-thing that could be desired from the wife of a prominent politician. Her funeral in the churchyard of St John the Baptist at Adel on Friday 23 May was attended by her two young daughters, her mother, members of Ernest's family and also the Fairfaxes. But what gave the procession its unexpected poignancy were the number of children, almost outnumbering the adults – children from St Chad's Home for Waifs and Strays and the Mill Street Mission in Leeds, charities she supported – as well as what the newspapers called 'the poorer classes of the people' in whose welfare she had been so active.[1]

---

[1] In memory of his wife, Ernest donated £3,000 to the building of a new Church of England home for waifs and strays in Hollin Road, Far Headingley. It is now part of the Weetwood Primary School. The Beckett coat of arms is above the entrance and there are three foundation stones with the initials of Luie's three children, Lucille, Muriel and Ralph.

2

Ernest Goes Abroad

'It is doubtful whether he will be seen in the House of Commons again this Session,' the *Yorkshire Herald* wrote of Ernest. Following his father's death, he had been made a senior partner in the family bank in Leeds. The welfare of his three children was partly handed over to Luie's family in Rome. Then there was José in London.

He could not marry her, he explained, until a decent interval had passed following his wife's death. He then set off for South America. But José was still waiting when he returned the following year. Their liaison was by now known to Ernest's family, which was strongly opposed to it – particularly his two banker brothers, Gervase and Rupert Beckett. José and Ernest began quarrelling and eventually agreed to break off their relationship. Determined to start a new phase in her life, José persuaded a mutual friend to introduce her to the famous actor-manager Beerbohm Tree. Much impressed by her face and figure, he engaged her to play a small part in Oscar Wilde's new play, *A Woman of No Importance*, when it went on tour in 1893.

It seems unlikely that José was very popular with the other actors. She refused to travel with them in third class railway carriages, sending her lady's maid to keep them company while she occupied a first class compartment. She also put up at superior hotels (with her maid who, being more popular, was given a walk-on part in the production). Once, when Tree's wife Maud Holt fell ill, José took her role – that of the cynical libertine Mrs Allonby. She played it well because 'it was the part of a coquette'. Some of Mrs Allonby's lines suited her perfectly: 'It's such a strain keeping men up to the mark. They are always trying to escape from us.'

One weekend that summer, when the company reached Eastbourne, José went up to London for a dinner party given by her brother-in-law who had recently arrived in England and was staying at the Langham Hotel. There she met John Joseph Lace, a rich, handsome man in his early thirties, with a fine moustache and brilliant solitaire diamond ring glittering on the little finger of his left hand. It had been presented to him, he told her, by Cecil Rhodes. José replied bluntly that she disliked seeing men with rings on their hands – at which he took it off and moved it on to the third finger of her left hand. Was he joking or serious? José believed she was still in love with Ernest and told this new admirer about him. But this had the opposite effect to what she expected. There seemed no resisting his passion for her. He was so flattering – it was exactly what she needed after Ernest's unsettling treatment. Before the weekend was over he had proposed to her and she had come near to accepting him. The following weekend, on 12 August, they were married at a London register office in Hanover Square with José's maid as witness. They celebrated afterwards with a splendid lunch at the Savoy.

But though they were married they had not consummated their marriage, José having made it a condition that they should not do so until they had gone through a church ceremony. This, at any rate, was what she later told Ernest. It was a curious arrangement and seemed to indicate a profound uncertainty as to what she wanted, and what she thought the consequences of this marriage would be. Had she started a brilliant new chapter in her life or ruined an unfinished one? The change in her circumstances was bewildering, almost frightening. Might Ernest have come back to her – might he even now come back to her? She and Joseph spent that weekend together at Leinster Lodge, then travelled to Eastbourne where they persuaded a reluctant Beerbohm Tree to reduce her twelve-month contract to six months.

Early that autumn Joseph was obliged to hurry back to South Africa on urgent financial business. When *A Woman of No Importance* returned to the Haymarket Theatre in London for a second run, Ernest came to see it – kept coming to see it and seeing José after the performances. He told her that now his wife had been dead for over two years he could at last marry her. Perhaps she read more into what he was saying than she should have done. Or perhaps he was tempted to say more than he really meant. She was the perfect mistress – and it seems unlikely he really wanted to marry her. But he always gave in to his moods and his moods were always changing. He was not insincere: he was consistent yet never constant. 'And faith unfaithful kept him falsely true.'

A proposal was what José had longed for and now dreaded. What should she do? Ernest Beckett was the man she loved. She could not let him go. What she did was to prevaricate, telling him that in his absence she had become engaged to marry John Joseph Lace. Ernest was shocked. He insisted she break off the engagement, insisted so strongly and with such perseverance that she had to confess she was married to John Joseph Lace. Ernest was appalled, incredulous. How could she have done this to him? But when she swore that their marriage was unconsummated, he told her it had to be annulled – and she cabled her husband asking him to release her.

It was as difficult escaping from men as it was keeping them up to the mark. Instead of agreeing to her request, John Joseph Lace took the next boat to Southampton where he was met by José's mother and one of her daughters imploring him not to see his wife who certainly did not want to see him. The three of them travelled by train up to London and by the end of the journey he had persuaded the two women that José really must see him. And so she did see him and he convinced her that it would only be fair to experiment with a trial marriage for three months at Leinster Lodge (which was still being paid for by Ernest) before making a final decision. It quickly became evident, however, that there was no future in the marriage. Before returning to South Africa, Joseph agreed to sue for divorce (not mentioning Ernest's name) on the grounds of José's desertion. He was, in José's words, 'a man in a million'.

José and Ernest were now free to live together – but not to marry since her divorce was not made final until 23 November 1894. In May that year José became pregnant and on 25 February 1895 she gave birth to a son at Leinster Lodge. On the marriage certificate 'Joseph Dale-Lace' appears as the name of the father (the Dale being his mother's surname which he had attached to his father's name). Her name is given as 'José Dale-Lace' and her maiden name recorded as 'Lange-Brink' (Lange being her mother's surname which she had spelt backwards for her acting name, 'Valdane Egnal', in Beerbohm Tree's company). The names she chose for her son were Lancelot Ernest Cecil: the first was a tribute to her ex-husband's Arthurian behaviour; the importance of being Ernest was to signify the actual father of her child; and the third was a family name. But whatever names she played with on the certificate, her baby, born three months after the final divorce decree came through, was illegitimate.

Ernest rented a house for them on the Thames and, in the words of Daphne Saul, 'settled a sum of money on her and agreed to pay for the boy's upbringing and education'. But still he had not married her.

One reason for this must have been the entry of Alice Keppel into Ernest's life. They met in the winter of 1892–3. Her name and that of her husband George Keppel first appear in the guest book at Kirkstall Grange in 1893. Alice also began visiting him alone at 138 Piccadilly, into which Ernest had moved after the death of his father on the railway line. According to Raymond Lamont-Brown, author of *Edward VII's Last Loves*, Ernest 'showered her with presents of money and gowns, all of which were a godsend to the Keppels' strained budget'. By the late summer they were lovers, by the end of the year Alice was pregnant and in the early summer of 1894 she gave birth to a daughter. She was called Violet, the name of Ernest's favourite sister, 'dearest Vi', who had died in 1883.

Alice was running the risk of social ostracism but, with the help of a complaisant husband, she managed everything with perfect discretion. The Keppels went on visiting Kirkstall Grange until 1898 (but not in 1895 while the Prince of Wales was staying there for the Doncaster races and Leeds Music Festival). Alice's affaire with Ernest was like a rehearsal for her role as royal mistress, which began in 1898.

Violet never mentions having met Ernest, her presumed father. If everyone is to be believed, she was his fourth child, her illegitimate half-brother Lancelot being born some eight months later. Ernest was now in a predicament. If he had not married José before Lancelot's birth, why should he marry her now? She had had a good innings, a good run for Ernest's money: it was unreasonable of her to expect anything more. Besides, how could he give up Alice who was so wonderfully discreet and refreshing? With her the awkward matter of marriage never arose and besides he had known her less than half the time he had known José. It was seven years since he and José first met in Rome and, now that she had given up her South African husband for him, she seemed to have become less of a necessity to Ernest. In any event, he refused to marry her and in 1896 she returned with their son to South Africa. The following year she married John Joseph Lace once more – this time in a church at Cape Town. In the early twentieth century, while travelling in Europe, José and Joseph met Edward VII and a rumour spread through South Africa that José had been the King's mistress and Lancelot was their son. She found herself curiously unable to deny it. When the Royal Academician, Hal Hurst, painted Lancelot's portrait, José asked him to add in the background of the picture a shadowy image of the King – and this ghostly silhouette kept the story alive.

John Joseph always treated Lancelot[2] as his son. The Dale Laces were to become celebrated figures in South Africa, and Northwards, their spectacular residence, later a National Monument, is now part of the Johannesburg College of Education. 'Living with José is hell,' John Joseph admitted, 'but it is worse hell without her.'

What was worse for Ernest was the prospect of living without both José and Alice – and also without his mother who had died in 1896. His political hopes, too, had collapsed when, early in 1895, Randolph Churchill died. What was Ernest to do? He decided to go abroad, as he so often did at moments of crisis, and this time, as if measuring the extent of his dissatisfaction, he travelled from east to west round the world.

'The glory and the charm of life on the tropical seas – the soft, warm, sweet air, the brilliant sunshine, the sparkling waves reflecting in their clear depths the unutterable blue of the heavens, and at night the silver

---

[2] He was awarded the Military Cross for gallantry in the First World War and died at the end of the Second World War in London.

glow of the moon,' Ernest rhapsodised. '. . . What can be better for those who, for a time, wish in this age of over-pressure to know what real leisure means than to pass idle days lounging reading or thinking or taking a stroll watching the porpoises gambolling in the waves or the flying fish flitting from wave to water or last, but not least in some quiet corner engaging in a game of whist or poker? . . . To anybody suffering from work or worry I could recommend no more efficacious and agreeable remedy.'

He was abroad for over eight months. Sailing in fair weather down the Red Sea and across the Indian Ocean to Bombay, he could put his worries far behind him. Then travelling through India and along the North-West Frontier, he grew absorbed by what he saw: 'the intense glow of colour everywhere . . . none of it mild or modified or shaded down, but bold, blatant, defiant colour that struck you full in the eye, seized upon you and would not let you go'. Above a tide of jostling people in the streets 'wheeled and circled vast numbers of kites and crows filling the air with harsh croaking, screaming and whistling, pouncing down directly . . . and doing their scavenger work with skill and thoroughness'. Beauty and poverty, poverty and beauty, were all around. 'One of the most pathetic sights is the child-mother, with an old face on a small, frail, youthful, unformed figure, and carrying on her hip a child half as big as herself.'

The novelty of everything, its sheer unfamiliarity, invigorated him. On board a steamer from Bombay to Karachi, he describes how 'by night buckets of water have to be thrown over you as you lie in bed; also at times there arises a peculiar quiet, deadly wind, which it is death to breathe'. Having reached the Northern Frontier, he began his expedition by riding over a hundred miles through country seldom seen by Europeans to Kalat, the capital of Baluchistan. 'The roads are merely tracks, and the accommodation such as you

could take with you on camels, naturally presented irresistible attrac-
tions to anyone fond of riding,' he wrote. He was accompanied by

an escort of police levees commonly called 'catch-em-alive-
ohs', gentlemen of a most truculent appearance, though really
'the mildest-mannered men who ever cut a throat' . . . armed
with carbines and curved scimitars attached to their sword
belts. They were men of fine physique, with long flowing locks,
dark eyes, hooked noses, and big black beards, or beards of a
most villainous red, dyed that colour to conceal the grey
approaches of age . . . We passed a few shaggy savage-looking
shepherds attending flocks – as shaggy as themselves – of sheep
that were almost indistinguishable from goats . . . we galloped
merrily, attended by our 'catch-em-alive-ohs', their hair flying
in the wind, and their arms swinging and rattling against their
horses sides . . . We had left civilisation, with its cares and
conventionalities, its duties and restrictions . . . we were to live
alone with nature and with the children of nature.

This is the setting for a boy's adventure story, a spellbinding novel by
Rider Haggard or Conan Doyle, and Ernest seems to become a boy again
as he travels, looking at everything with a fresh eye and welcoming the
shedding of a politician's, a banker's and a gentleman's responsibilities. He
was to ride twelve hundred miles along the North-West Frontier. The
lives of the villagers among these arid mountain ranges appeared to him
enviably simple and straightforward: a conservative ideal. 'Their place in
the community is fixed, and the duties they owe to it are defined by
immemorial custom, and rendered with cheerful obedience; and so generation after generation passes through life into the grave and gate of death,
knowing nothing of the fever and the toil and the fret that make men

moan in modern England, rich as she is in all the blessings that freedom, progress, and an advanced civilisation can bestow upon her.'

One of his more comic encounters was with the Khan of Kalat who, having 'a very exaggerated idea of the influence and importance of members of Parliament', greeted him with a nineteen-gun salute, a band playing 'God Save the Queen' 'in various keys', and a military parade most of which was hidden by clouds of dust. 'I believe such infantry has never been seen since Falstaff drilled his troop of "ragged rascals",' Ernest reflected. These manoeuvres were followed by an audience with the Khan himself, a shy young man dressed in utmost magnificence and with a tuft of feathers at the front of his turban which blazed with many jewels. He was attended by a line of grave and reverend seigniors posted along the walls of the chamber and by a Prime Minister who was meant to act as interpreter but who had little to do because the Khan replied to whatever Ernest volunteered with 'a sickly smile or a nod of his head'.

Ernest's political views appear controversial. He is opposed to what he calls 'the over-education of the natives' and the liberty of the press. The over-educated Indian 'is subtle, ingenious, plausible, with a remarkable skill in metaphysics and mathematics . . . Many of these highly educated men, unable to find employment in Government offices . . . turn their attention to journalism and produce the scurrilous prints which spring up like deadly fungi in every part of India, and corrupt the surrounding atmosphere.'

He launched an even more provocative attack on the English missionaries in India. 'The conversions are very few, and the natives who are converted are by no means a credit to Christianity,' he explained. 'Missionaries too often make the mistake of living in India as they would at home. Natives expect extreme asceticism in their ministers of religion . . . they do not think it right that one who claims to be the messenger

of God should live in a comfortable house with a wife and children apparently enjoying the good things of this world. Their ideal is far different.'

On later parts of this journey the traveller, with his vivid and
observant eye, increasingly gives way to the glass-eyed politician. In
Burma he is still alive to the landscape and the people: 'its glorious
vegetation, its jungles and orchids, its pagodas and monasteries . . . its
comely women, crowned with flowers, and clad in white jackets and
short pink petticoats, its yellow robed priests, its enormous bells, and
glittering golden palaces'. But then his focus changes, his style falters
and runs dry. He has begun to think of his return to England and
what he should say after he gets back. And what he says is over-
whelmingly banal. 'As for Singapore, and Penang, and the Strait
Settlements, as for Hong Kong and China, as for Japan [where he met
the Prime Minister] and the Far East generally, its peoples and its policies, its aspirations, and its openings for trade and commerce . . . the
political situation is decidedly interesting and not unimportant.'

Back in England he was to give several lectures on his travels,
which were aimed at repositioning himself in politics. He represents
this travel not as a holiday but as an education in foreign policy. 'I
can honestly tell you that I don't think my time has been wasted,' he
tells his audience. 'In many respects it has been better employed than
if I had remained in the House of Commons . . . Foreign affairs are
taking a far larger share in the thoughts and the discussions and the
debates of the English people, and I think you must all admit that
foreign affairs can be best studied in the foreign countries themselves.'
He is careful to say flattering things about Britain's diplomats. 'The
more I travel and the more I see of the representatives of England
abroad the more I am satisfied that our affairs are in the most capable
hands.' But they could be improved. Ernest quotes a Chinese official
who tells him: 'We prefer the English nation to other nations but we

don't always know what you wish ... Russia has a fixed policy, Germany and France have fixed policies, but the English have no fixed policy; it seems to change from day to day: if we knew what you wanted we should be glad to back you up.' And this was important, Beckett adds, because China was a country of 'first-rate business capacity, and of indispensable industry – people who have only to waken from their sleep of centuries and to adopt modern ideas and modern methods to play a very great part in the world, to create an economic disturbance which will be felt in almost every household in Europe'.

Ernest knew that, because of his allegiance to Lord Randolph Churchill, he had been branded as untrustworthy by the Conservative Party. He did not improve his position early in the twentieth century by making a special ally of Randolph's son, Winston Churchill (Ernest had been made one of Randolph's executors and was to appoint Winston as his father's biographer). At Ernest's luxurious apartment at 17 Stratton Street, the two of them brought together a small group of dissatisfied Tories and revived the idea of a Fourth Party. For a couple of years Ernest became the leader of this group – regarded by the Cabinet as one of those guerrilla bands 'ripe for revolt and greedy for reward'. To his colleagues in the House of Commons he was never the team player. He is referring to himself when he says in a speech at Whitby: 'In the last two Parliaments I have seen young men of ability, full of energy, anxious to serve their country, anxious to get on, who were ready to give all their time and their energies to political work, and it has been rather disheartening to notice how they have been discouraged Parliament by Parliament.' Between the lines of his speech he is suggesting that there might have been less trouble with women in his life, trouble which dismayed his colleagues, had he been given political advancement and his time and energy been properly employed. Being disheartened there, his heart had strayed elsewhere. For this he blames the rigid political system. There is a bitterness as well as disenchantment in his peroration. 'For 15 years I have been a member of the House, and only three years of that time have I been in Opposition,' he says. 'What is expected of a supporter of the Government is that he should suppress himself, that he should become a mere mechanical perambulator through the division lobbies; he must efface himself; he must have no opinions of his own; a man who ventures to think for himself does not recommend himself to the favour of the leaders of the party. Therefore you have to lead a more or less mechanical existence, or to place yourself in an attitude of criticism towards those whom you would rather support. That is the position of a great number of the Conservative party.'

So what was the solution? The Conservative Party could not get rid of him – his seat at Whitby was safe and he had become popular there. The answer, he is suggesting, would be to give him an appointment in the Foreign Office where his energies would be focused abroad, or to move him to a senior position in the diplomatic service.

Under Lord Salisbury's and then Arthur Balfour's premierships, Ernest was to wait over twenty years for political promotion that never came. He remained a talented, unruly, intermittently brilliant but often absent backbencher all this time, doing occasional work on committees until, being raised to the peerage on his uncle's death, he was obliged to exchange the House of Commons for the House of Lords (his brother Gervase taking his place as the Member of Parliament for Whitby). Like Winston Churchill in these early stages of his career, Ernest was to be remembered as a man who scattered his energies in too many directions and kept bad company. 'And thus he flitted across the stage,' a political colleague wrote of him, 'a graceful, ineffectual figure.'

At the time when he became involved with Eve Fairfax, Ernest was seen as an ageing playboy with a romantic past: 'the perfect lover and generous to a fault' in Rodin's words (spoken before the bust of Eve Fairfax was cancelled). Getting married, joining the bank and being promoted to senior partner, then becoming a Member of Parliament – all these things, his family hoped, would have steadied him. But his wife had died, the business of banking did not suit his erratic temperament and he was grievously underemployed as a politician. Approaching fifty, it was surely time for him to marry again and settle down. Eve Fairfax must have seemed a perfect choice. She had no money, it was true, but Ernest had little need of money – or so everyone believed. The truth, however, seems to have been that, by the summer of 1905, he was in desperate financial trouble. His creditors were closing in on him, hearing rumours of his extraordinary wealth on the death of his uncle and his elevation to the peerage. The crisis is alluded to in a letter from his daughter Lucille in which she mentions £700,000 as being insufficient to pay off a debt. On 13 July 1906 she writes from Rome, hoping that he has been successful in 'warding off the worst and that you have got some arrangements with creditors which leaves you at least in peace'. She implies that some of his financial difficulties have arisen from his investments in art and that it would be safer if he would 'turn your mind seriously to politics'. But it was too late for that.

He must have been paid to leave Beckett's Bank, and he sold his houses in London and at Virginia Water. He also sold Kirkstall Grange with its extensive outbuildings and the surrounding estate to Leeds City Council for £48,000 (Kirkstall Grange becoming the Leeds

Education Authority's Training College and subsequently part of Leeds Metropolitan University).[3]

Ernest also unburdened himself of much of his art collection (one or two pictures to Leeds Art Gallery);[4] and served a writ on José seeking to retrieve the money he had settled on Lancelot on the grounds that her child was not after all his son. These proceedings were eventually dropped. Most of the next ten years he passed abroad, beyond the reach of British creditors. His letters to *The Times* reveal him at one time or another in Capri, Paris, Florence, Montevideo and elsewhere. 'I leave this week for South America,' he wrote to Rodin on 17 January 1910. He is always on the move. Occasionally one of his adventures would be reported in *The Times*. In the first week of April 1908, while travelling from Marseilles to Naples, the German steamship *Hohenzollern* was grounded off the coast of Sardinia owing to one of its passengers – the notorious Admiral von

---

[3] Ernest had at first offered the mansion house with its 264-acre estate for £240,000. He was opposed by the ratepayers who issued a pamphlet exposing the 'scandal' of such an exorbitant price. The matter became the subject of an acrimonious debate, and Ernest appealed to Winston Churchill (recently appointed President of the Board of Trade) to help him get Government Board approval ('I leave it to you, dear Winston, to do what you think best'). Churchill succeeded, helped by Ernest's last-minute gift of forty acres to be used as a public park. 'I am glad it is all right,' he wrote to Churchill, '. . . A friend in need is a friend indeed.' Today, Beckett Park is open to the public and covers ninety-two acres.

[4] Though Ernest was often described as a generous patron of the arts, it is difficult to find pictures that he owned in public collections. In 1913 he gave a naval picture in oils called *The Wooden Walls of England* to Leeds Training College. It was, he said, by a Yorkshire artist, but was unable to recall his name (though he did remember he had paid £1,600 for it). A picture with this name, painted in 1891 by John William Buxton Knight (of ships in Plymouth Harbour) was presented to the Tate Gallery in 1931. In 1896 Ernest donated a bust of Napoleon by Joseph Gott (after Canova) to the Leeds Art Gallery; towards the end of the twentieth century the gallery bought a male nude by Rodin, *The Age of Bronze*, in the form of a cast that had originally been owned by the Beckett family.

Tirpitz. Tirpitz's plan was to achieve world status for Germany through enlarging the German fleet so successfully that it threatened Britain's navy – vital for defending the empire. This had led to an arms race between the two countries that was part of the build-up to the Great War.

'He [Tirpitz] was a tall man with a greyish beard, a somewhat severe and formal expression, and an unmistakable air of authority,' Ernest wrote,

> . . . The admiral and captain discussed with complacency the state and growth of the German navy . . . until they parted for the night their heads full of the days to come when the pride of place hitherto held by England should be seriously challenged, if not altogether overthrown by the might and power of Germany . . . [Next morning] a peculiar soft bump was felt, followed rapidly by two more accompanied by an uneasy sliding, quivering, rocking motion of the ship. The engines stopped suddenly and everything remained absolutely still. We rushed on deck . . . close to us grey walls rose out of the water, protecting from the sea a picturesque town of white-walled, red-roofed houses . . . It was Alghero, a small unvisited town on the north-west coast of Sardinia. How on earth did we come to be there? . . . The fact was that, without giving any notice to the passengers, the ship had been permitted to deviate widely from her course in order to land Admiral Tirpitz at his country seat in Sardinia . . . and the captain had run the ship aground.

Stranded there for four days and nights while, urged on from time to time by cheerful messages from the Admiral's residence, they were joined on the lumpy waters by several Italian fishing craft, a torpedo boat, a cruiser and miscellaneous vessels (all of them providing entertainment for the Sardinian audience on shore). Various prolonged and humiliating attempts were made to work out their salvation. Eventually violent hands were laid on their luggage and the passengers were transferred to another boat, which delivered them safely to Naples the following week. All this enabled Ernest to do what he did best: use a personal anecdote for a political purpose – mocking the pretensions and alleged competence of German seamanship. Looking round for some good words to give a ship bearing the illustrious name of *Hohenzollern*, he concluded: 'There was no band on board and the cooking was excellent.'

The focus of Ernest's life had now moved to the Villa Cimbrone. It was a vision: a magic place to which, he believed, he would always return. For what he sought on his travels, what answered his dreams, he would bring back to Cimbrone, hoping to make it the centre of his life. He had found enough money to buy it some time between 1905 and 1907, though he later told his son Ralph that it had been only a farmhouse with a few acres of barren land costing no more than 'the price of a cow'. This exaggeration obscured the fact that he had more money available abroad than in England. He certainly spent lavishly on the property, extending and remodelling the Gothic building and constructing a belvedere at the top of the parapet wall overlooking the Gulf of Salerno. He also added a new wing with a spacious drawing room decorated with Turneresque watercolours.

Shortly before the war, D. H. Lawrence's friends, the expatriate American painter Earl Brewster and his wife Achsah, together with their daughter Harwood, arrived at Cimbrone. In an unpublished autobiography Achsah Brewster put down her impressions of Ernest's renovations and the miscellaneous erotic objects picked up on his travels round the world. The place was, in its fashion, like the depository of William Wetmore Story's great studio in Rome, which had so impressed Ernest when young and made him envy the illusory life of artists. Here are 'statuosities' that greatly irritated Lawrence and a picture that brings to mind E. M. Forster's pagan 'Story of a Panic'.

'How entrancing everything looked to our uncritical eyes,' Achsah Brewster remembered,

the spacious halls, sweeping gardens, views as wide as if we had been translated to heaven above all earthly contacts. Our hearts were light, it was spring time . . . the sun soaked through our bones . . . The gardens hung fragrant from terrace to terrace, among pools and statues and groves, over tilled fields. Wide terraces and roof-tops open to the sky, pergolas and arcades opened from the rooms.

My room was off the music-room, with green glazed tiles and a fireplace carved of grey, volcanic stone. The window opened on to the large sunny terrace where we always lingered. Above the bed, spread over with Kashmir silk embroidery in rich, solid design, hung a six-foot canvas of a Rubens, a nude nymph under a tree overtaken by a goat-hoofed faun . . . I shut my eyes.

. . . Lord Grimthorpe's suite lay between the salon and library, adjoining a sun-parlour with a marble Ariadne stretched on a panther. Along the hall were bronze females, replicas from Pompeii. The library was stored with Greek amphoras and vases, good and bad statues, elaborately shaded floor lamps, and books, books, blessed books, broad couches and embracing chairs. An isolated salon was in the entrance garden where a fountain dripped over a Verrocchio 'putto'.

. . . We went from the library to a stairway grilled off on one side by a wrought-iron inwoven design of rare beauty. Then we emerged into the dining-hall with its Arabic traceries of windows open to the breathless view of the Avoccata, Mariore, Minore and the sea and sky. This part of the house was covered with honeysuckle in spring, the fragrance blew in from the open windows, and bees hummed. That beautiful dining-hall with its long refectory table

. . . a Pietà statue placed on it! There were two upright paintings by
Andrea del Sarto in reds and greens, hieratic in treatment.

In the afternoons the Brewsters usually ate below in the crypt,
with its vaulted roof and stone pillars leading to an orange garden
where, in summer, immense salvers of fruit were heaped – musk
melons, peaches, pears and purple, white and pink figs. A copy of
Donatello's *David* stood further off among the roses and a stone pine
avenue led out to the belvedere. At the end of the pine walk was a
Roman temple, open on all four sides and, higher up, a broad conifer
grove planted with larches, firs, cedars and blue spruces – and higher
still stood a quadrangle of horse-chestnuts.

Britain's ageing Casanova, Frank Harris, whom Ernest had befriended
and, during the winter of 1909–10, invited to Cimbrone to write his controversial *Life of Oscar Wilde*, held strong opinions on the garden. He would
stroll in this garden of an afternoon, taking the air and becoming engrossed
in conversation with the head gardener, Nicola Mansi. He was a renowned
horticultural scholar assisted in his work by many under-gardeners who
would form an intense ring round the two men. Frank's eyes would blaze
as he pointed aggressively to various plants and statues. At a suitable
distance his wife Nellie, seeing the head gardener waving his hands with
much energy and excitement, feared they might be fighting – until both
of them would smile and begin quoting Dante to each other. 'Our
wonderful gardener knew Dante by the yards,' Nellie reckoned. For Harris's
birthday, coming down from their cathedral-like bedroom, they found
the baronial hall filled with flowers and they drank 'the best champagne
and wines', Nellie remembered. 'How happy we were there. There was a
great terrace that seemed to look over the whole world – Frank worked
and we danced and life was a wonderful thing.' But Harris himself, once
a reckless social climber, was less delighted. Describing himself as being

heavily 'pregnant with four or five books', he had come to feel that Ernest, who had expressed confidence that he 'would come through' (though deploring the fact that he was writing about Wilde), tended to waste his time by introducing him to members of the aristocracy who seemed to believe they were helping him simply by allowing him to shake their hands. 'I can't get away till Tuesday,' Harris complained. 'I've done my best but Beckett insisted I must stay for it seems Royalty – the Duke and Duchess of Connaught – are coming tomorrow – what good I'm to get out of that God alone knows . . . I'm tired of this rot – this society rot all false and insincere . . . I hate the people.'

Two of Ernest's three children, Ralph and Lucille, had married before the war and would sometimes visit Cimbrone. Lucille especially loved the place and it was she who made friends with the Brewster family. In Achsah Brewster's memoirs there is a mention of Ernest staying there shortly before the war with 'a young, fair-haired Englishwoman, Mrs Green' whom she describes, in inverted commas, as his 'ward'. In June 1915 Ernest made a Will in which he appointed Mrs Florence Green as his executor. Having made provisions for his three legitimate children, he left 'the residue of my property both real and personal after payment of my debts funeral and testamentary expenses and legacies to my godchild Mrs Florence Green absolutely'. Two years later he added a codicil to this Will, transferring shares in various companies to her and 'my property in Italy known as the Castro Leone Estate in the Province of Salerno'. He gave her some additional money 'to enable her to build a house at Castro Leone' and drafted a request to his son Ralph to pay her a yearly sum to bring her income up to £400 a year free of tax. In the event of Ralph selling the Villa Cimbrone, he directs him to pay her £2,000. This codicil is devoted entirely to the security and interests of this mysterious woman 'in fulfilment of the promise and undertaking made to Mrs Florence Green at the time of her marriage'.

There is no sign of Florence Green or any husband among the guests at the Beckett family's weddings or funerals in England and no knowledge now of an estate in Salerno called Castro Leone. In Ernest's Will she occupies a place of equal significance to his children – more than a ward or godchild would naturally occupy (these would appear to have been honorary titles). She is clearly not a woman of independent means or living under the protection of a husband. She may have been Ernest's illegitimate daughter or his last mistress – and possibly, in one of these roles, an obstacle to Eve marrying Ernest.

In 1916 Ernest returned to England to see his unmarried daughter Muriel who was ill. He was 'present at the death' on 16 June that year when she died of 'general tuberculosis'. This was especially cruel: for he seems to have caught tuberculosis from his daughter. Beginning to feel ill, he did not return to Italy but travelled up to the Nordrach-on-Dee Sanatorium at Banchory, a few miles south of Aberdeen. This vast and isolated sanatorium incorporated a German approach to treating tuberculosis, with its unswerving routine of rest, milk, meat and more rest, and an emphasis on brisk, fresh air supplied through large, perpetually open windows. Somerset Maugham, who went there at the end of November 1917, observed the macabre way in which, lined up in their deckchairs along the veranda, 'the tuberculars fall in love with one another'. He later turned this observation into a short story in which a man and a woman agree to marry despite their knowledge that this may shorten their lives. Their romance, however, is used to illustrate Maugham's view that suffering does not ennoble us but makes us 'petty, querulous, and selfish'. It was here, on the afternoon of 9 May 1917, that Ernest died, aged sixty, of pulmonary tuberculosis. In a last codicil to his Will, he asked that he be cremated and his ashes preserved in an urn to be sent after the war to the Villa Cimbrone.

3

All About Eve

She had grown up in a world of horses. Her father (an Old Etonian and Lieutenant-Colonel in the Grenadier Guards) was a slim and wiry figure, reputed to be 'the best looking man in the army', who devoted most of his life to 'the pursuits of a country gentleman'. In short: he was a keen rider to hounds, a useful oarsman and a fine shot. But he pursued nothing with more diligence than hunting. There was no separating him from his celebrated mare, Bella Minna, and it was wonderful to see them racing over the pastures as the hounds settled to their work. He was a considerable landowner, his fox coverts being well-stocked and many famous hunts starting off near these strongholds. It was difficult to persuade him to talk of much else – his political views were so unpronounced that even his nearest kinsmen and closest friends could not be certain what they were. But his opinions on how to improve the hounds, how to weld together the old and new schools of hunting and maintain the goodwill of owners and occupiers of land over which they galloped were often quoted at the Yorkshire Club. When he put by the horn, sounding so cheery and challenging in the brisk morning air, he called up many bright and happy hours. These were splendid days. His jaunts and jollities could find an honourable place in the pages of his contemporary, the novelist Robert Surtees. No one, it was said, not even Captain Slingsby himself, had more beautiful hands or a steadier eye, or showed more devotion to the sport than 'Colonel Fairfax of the Blues'. It was a sad day when, on 19 February 1879, the gallant Colonel handed over the mastership of the York and Ainsty Hunt to Captain Slingsby and was presented by members of the hunt with a group picture of themselves.

Thomas Ferdinand Fairfax was only forty-four when he died of cancer in February 1884. Much of his land had to be sold to pay off gambling debts. Eve was aged twelve. There was a provision made for her in his Will guaranteeing her £4,000 on reaching the age of twenty-one or marrying under that age with the consent of her mother. But although the gross value of Thomas Ferdinand Fairfax's estate was calculated at over £25,000, when all his debts were paid the net value was nil.

If there was a more adventurous rider to hounds in Yorkshire than Colonel Fairfax it had been his wife. She was a brilliant horsewoman – everyone agreed she had one of the finest seats in the county. She was seldom seen off a horse. Her exploits in the saddle delighted readers of the *Yorkshire Post*. They relished episodes such as the time when 'she jumped her horse over a stream but the moment she touched the banks, they gave way. The horse fell back into the ditch, rolling upon his rider and passing her below him in the mud and water. He struggled furiously in the stream, and the spectators held their breath with horror, for no one dreamed but that Mrs Fairfax was dead. A moment later however she emerged half-drowned, suffocated and exhausted. In spite of the condition she was in, she sprang on her horse again, forced it to take the stream in which she had so nearly found her death; and, wet as she was, went on after the hounds as if nothing had happened!'

Eve was named after her mother: she was Evelyn Constance and her mother Evelyn Selina. They came to dislike each other and this similarity of names sometimes irritated them. 'I wanted a petite dark girl — and look what I've got!' Eve heard her mother exclaim as, tall, fair and self-consciously awkward at the age of thirteen, she entered a room full of staring guests. Evelyn preferred her sons, Guy and Bryan. Guy, who was a year older than Eve, was packed off to Eton, and Bryan, the youngest child, dispatched to Winchester. Little money was wasted on Eve's education; and once she was in her 'teens she stayed at home with her mother. Guy turned out a steady churchman, a staunch Conservative and solid cricketer. He listed his recreations as 'all sports and fox-hunting'. His father would have been pleased to see him described as 'a brilliant man to hounds and as good a heavyweight as could be found anywhere in England'. Bryan, who went from Winchester to the Royal Military College and served in the Durham Light Infantry, settled down after the war as the owner of a prolific stud farm.

Eve was as enthusiastic about all sports as were her brothers — there was really no alternative in the Fairfax household. She was judged to be 'the champion of the ladies' at cricket and, sometimes got up in a faultless costume of white flannel, or adding brightness to the scene when prettily attired in a scarlet petticoat and gypsy bonnet, would display 'great agility' in the field and was admired for her vigorous 'late cuts and fast runs'. In a match against the men all playing left-handed and led by Ernest Beckett, Eve was the highest scorer and the women handsomely routed the men. On a horse, any horse, she was as comfortable as the rest of her family. When young she would ride her pony, summer and winter, the eight miles across open undulating country with wide horizons, small woods and farming villages, to her school, and stable it at an inn near York. On her route back she often stopped

to have tea with the Archbishop. Later, when she was invited to balls
or dinner parties, she rode out carrying her evening dress in a saddlebag.

Her mother became increasingly fierce and eccentric after her
husband's death. It was said that she used to go to bed with a piece of
string tied round her toe and hang it out of the window. Each morning
the gardener used to pull the string to wake her up. But however early
she started the day, she had little time for Eve and did not trouble to
have her presented at Court when she was eighteen or nineteen. 'I
had a funny bringing up – not bothered about much,' Eve recalled in
old age. In the late 1880s she became friendly with 'Prince Eddy', the
Duke of Clarence, who was garrisoned at York. He was suspected of
being Jack the Ripper and had made several visits to the Fairfax family
home – Eve, it was said, sometimes 'walked out' with him. (He was
the Prince of Wales's eldest son, and second in line to the throne but,
when Prince Eddy died at the age of twenty-eight, his younger brother
became King George V.) Prince Eddy insisted that Eve be presented at
Court – 'all girls of our sort were at that time but mother didn't
bother,' Eve told a friend. After Prince Eddy's death 'I arranged that a
dear friend Lady George Gordon Lennox would do it – so she took me
and we sailed into Buckingham Palace. She had the entrée as her late
husband had some job at Court . . . I was 24 instead of being 18.'

Her mother's interest in Eve was confined to her marriage. But
she did not marry. She was handsome but, even in her mid-twenties,
still something of a tomboy. Perhaps, too, there was some pleasure to
be enjoyed from thwarting her mother. Everything would change for
Eve after her mother's death in 1901 at the age of fifty-three. In her
Will, Evelyn Selina Fairfax made her elder son Guy her executor and
trustee, leaving £3,000 absolutely to her younger son Bryan and a
further £3,000 for Guy to invest and pay the income to Eve – an arrangement that was to cloud their friendship (one of the difficulties being

that their mother's estate was valued at less than £1,500). She also left her 'trinkets and ornaments of the person except my Diamonds unto my daughter'. The diamonds went to Guy Fairfax with the rest of the estate.

Within a year of her mother's death Eve became engaged to marry Ernest Beckett. He presented her with his family pearls and it was then that he commissioned Rodin to make a sculpture of her head and shoulders. They had known each other for several years as friends, but this was now a love affair. She kept his letters for almost sixty years as evidence that she was loved and then, at the age of ninety, sent them to Ernest's daughter Lucille. 'What wonderful love letters!' Lucille wrote. She could hardly believe such a man of the world who 'had been more than a little intimate with some of the most famous society women of his day, could possibly have written such pure and tender letters of love. What an extraordinary character – never hardened or made blasé by life, he remained eager and enthusiastic about every-thing to the end . . . I am happy to have them – on the other hand they make me very sad . . . Why you didn't marry each other in 1904 will always remain a puzzle to me – there was nothing to prevent it and loving you as he did, it seems quite unbelievable. Perhaps at heart you felt he was too old? Over 20 years is a big difference.' In fact there were fewer than fifteen years between them.

In the last years of her life, Eve let it be known that Ernest had proposed to her and she had refused him. But it was she who kept his letters, not he who kept hers. What evidence remains suggests that Ernest walked away from the engagement, leaving her with a melan-choly that shows through her letters to Rodin. She had to tell him that, owing to 'money difficulties', Ernest could not pay for the bust – 'rather an awkward job for me,' she admitted.

It was important for Lucille to think well of her father. She had not always done so. He had persuaded her to marry Count Otto Czernin, a man she did not love – a marriage which, despite their four children, she later sought to annul (both Eve Fairfax and Alice Keppel had attended the wedding ceremony in 1903). Lucille wanted to eradicate this hostile memory of her father and refashion his character so that it resembled what she believed to be essentially her own. She willingly surrendered to the belief that it was Eve, and not Ernest, who had ended their love affair. These letters from almost sixty years back, showing Ernest in his most romantic vein, gave Lucille a sympathetic father she could cherish. 'A *1000* thanks – it was too dear of you to give them to me,' she wrote to Eve in February 1962. 'For I am so like him as a character with faith in life and in people and the eagerness for everything that comes – even at my age [seventy-seven].'

Eve in her later years would not tolerate the notion that she had been Ernest's victim. In her prideful and imperious imagination there was only humiliation to be incurred through having been proposed to by Ernest Beckett MP and then rejected by Lord Grimthorpe – whether she had been sacrificed to financial needs or set aside for another woman hardly mattered. Far more invigorating, once he was dead, was to take the initiative and manoeuvre herself into more dignified territory. Otherwise she was merely 'damaged goods', someone who had lost her chance and lived on in the shadows of life – an embarrassment to everyone.

'We will discuss it further when we meet,' Lucille promised. The pact they were to make, a story they told others, suited them both. For his daughter, Ernest became a singular man hounded by ill fortune – had his wife lived he would have risen high in politics and served his country nobly. As it was, he created at Cimbrone an aesthetic palace, Lucille believed, almost Buddhist in its atmosphere, where he could pursue the esoteric religions that were to be her inheritance. 'You may be sure that, next to yourself,' she wrote to Eve, 'no one could treasure them [his letters] as I do.' But they did not survive her death.

Those years before the Great War were the most emotionally active of Eve Fairfax's life, though they left much turbulent wreckage in their wake. She had told Rodin that she wished to be an actress. But she took no bold step such as José had done – perhaps her insistence on high social position made such a step impractical. In any event, she contented herself with amateur performances mostly in the Yorkshire Pageant Plays. These were open-air, sometimes processional shows celebrating great moments in the country's history and performed by townspeople and local children. Eve favoured queenly roles – Eleanor of Aquitaine, Margaret of Anjou, Queen Elizabeth ('no mere imitation,' Professor Hubert, writing in one of the Yorkshire newspapers, described her, 'but a perfect representative of the Royal Sovereign'). She also played in charity productions at Yorkshire theatricals including *A Woman of No Importance* and was praised for her 'wonderful elocutionary power'. In later life she was reputed to have been so exemplary as Lady Bracknell that people told her she had missed her vocation.

In her early forties she was still an attractive-looking woman – possibly more so than she had been in her early twenties. Romantic rumours inevitably clustered round her. She formed a close friendship with Sir William Eden, the amateur painter adept at turning compliments into insults. When, in the mid 1890s, Whistler sent him a letter of thanks for the hundred guineas he had been given for a little portrait of Lady Eden ('You really are magnificent . . . I can only hope that the picture will be even slightly worthy of us all'), Eden decided to take offence and lose his temper. The two of them brought out the very worst in each other, their differences leading to two battles in the Paris courts on the competing claims of owner versus creator over works of art (made famous in the early twentieth century after the publication of Whistler's book *The Baronet and the Butterfly*). The Baronet (father of a future British Prime Minister, Sir Anthony Eden, who, it has been suggested, lost his wits in a similar aggressive style over the Suez crisis in 1956) was a wealthy, sometimes generous, often irascible, self-tormented character with romantic leanings, which for a time pointed rather peremptorily in Eve's direction. 'Just answer "yes" – no arguments please!' he wrote when declaring his affection for her with an offer of financial help. He showed his love, too, by treating her to convoluted analyses of her character: 'though intelligent, you are not intelligent enough, dear Eve – or perhaps you are too intelligent. At any rate you are not stupid: for if you were, you would not be admired, if not loved by yours truly William Eden.'

Among some single pages of letters to Eve that have survived her years of wandering are statements of passionately incomplete love. 'Charlie' begins his letter from Lower Berkeley Street to 'my own darling' and, poignantly omitting the most vital words, assures her that 'whatever happens to either of us in life we shall be always and for ever to the end dear one'. A learned professor writes of the temptation to 'give up my liberty to you' and explains why, in the interests of scholarship, he must not do so: 'for a short period of (I admit) intense joy, I should make myself miserable for the rest of my life.' The Beckett family was sure she had an affair with Ernest's womanising brother Gervase, a Soames Forsyte character (a successful businessman with poignant leanings towards the arts) who, on his wife's death, married his regular mistress with disastrous consequences. They liked to believe that she had also been involved with the youngest Beckett brother, Rupert. 'All Becketts make bad husbands,' Eve said.

Her air of superiority suggested in some people's minds that she was a virgin and they were happy to congratulate her, and themselves, on prolonging this condition. 'It is an inexpressible pleasure to me to know that I have left you as I found you as pure as you were as a child, and have not taken any advantage of your loving trust and confidence in me,' one hesitant suitor propounded. '. . . I love your fine natural mind. You really hate wicked things & all the naughtiness attending them in speech, writing and other ways.'

These men, it seems, were wary of Eve as if conscious of something vengeful in her. She is no longer the tender, vulnerable figure who was engaged to Ernest and who sat to Rodin. She was perhaps an example of Somerset Maugham's belief in the damage suffering inflicts on people. When the Duke of Grafton proposed to her hoping she would accept him, not for his title or money, but simply for himself, she replied 'Rather a tall order' and brusquely turned him down. She allowed herself brief infatuations for people who were securely out of reach – an actor, for example, whom she saw playing Jesus Christ at the Oberammergau Passion Play. But she was careful not to expose herself to more suffering. It was the men who must take that risk. The Duke of Wellington (a one-time suitor of Alice Keppel's daughter, Violet Trefusis) described the feelings Eve provoked in many of her admirers. She had invited him to come and see her privately: but he would not. 'What would be the use?' he replied. 'Either you would let me get to know you very intimately, or you would not. If you did not, I should suffer, to no purpose. If, on the other hand, you did, I should soon fall entirely into the drama and light literature of many nations . . . I know that you could make a fool of me very quickly, if I were rash enough to come within striking distance; so I mean to keep some hundreds of miles between us. I quite recognise that you could give me pleasure that not one in a million could give. That makes me want you; but it also warns me not to want you.'

Remaining unmarried, Eve presented her friends with something of a puzzle. There was talk that she was the daughter of a royal duke and, perhaps inevitably, whispers of an illegitimate child. Echoes of these rumours still lingered in the air when, over eighty years later, I began my researches into Eve's life and met a younger generation of men and women belonging to the families who had known her in Yorkshire. I was highly sceptical of these stories – they were characteristic, it seemed to me, of the gossip that often follows someone who has grown into a local legend. Apart from the speculation over her relationship with Rodin, I heard a rather vague story of a son who had been dispatched to South Africa – which had its confused roots, I suspected, in José's son. I was surprised when Eve's solicitor, Charles Dodsworth, told me matter-of-factly that he had seen the birth certificate of her child. Then, among the papers of Ernest's grandson Christopher (the fourth Lord Grimthorpe) I saw a photocopy of this certificate. I have it before me as I write.

The date of birth is given as 7 March 1916, the name of the mother is Evelyn Fairfax and her occupation listed as being 'of independent means'. But could this really be my Eve Fairfax? She would have been forty-five – not impossible, of course, but rather old to give birth to a first child in those wartime days. There were few people who could be less accurately described as being 'of independent means' – though this is the description Eve would most likely have given. The child was born at a nursing home with royal connections, at 15 Welbeck Street, in London. The matron, Clara Nelson Smith, who was 'present at the birth', had been awarded the Royal Victorian Medal by Queen Alexandra following an operation there on His Serene Highness Prince Francis of Teck (the brother of Queen Mary). The Prince had died and his Will was sealed to avoid a scandal (setting a precedent for future royal Wills). The matron, who was in charge of the files, had been honoured for her discretion. This was a perfect setting for the birth of Eve's illegitimate son. Yet I was still reluctant to accept it as authentic.

Then I looked at the mother's address on the certificate: 64 Gloucester Place. This was the home of Eve's friend Maud Hope (the Hope and Milner families were connected by marriage). John Francis Mordaunt is the name on the birth certificate. The first two names lead nowhere with certainty, though the first Fairfax to be recorded in the family tree, born in York in the eleventh or twelfth century, was John Fairfax; and Francis may have been chosen to recall Prince Francis of Teck (certainly Eve would have been happy to make this link). Mordaunt is unusual. Examining the family tree of Eve's mother, I see that her father was Sir William Mordaunt Edward Milner, and his father Sir William Mordaunt Sturt Milner, and his father again Sir William Mordaunt Milner — indeed, there are Mordaunts everywhere in the family reaching back to the second baronet, Sir William Milner of Nun Appleton who, in the early eighteenth century, married Elizabeth Mordaunt, daughter of the Hon. and Rev. George Mordaunt. It may not excite today's reader, but this alliance entitled the Milners to quarter the arms of Mordaunt, Howard and Plantagenet — which would have appealed to Eve. This arcane world with its distinguished blood of ancestral vintage is where she sheltered from the actual world around her. I am finally convinced that John Francis Mordaunt was her son.

No father is named on the certificate. But among the Grimthorpe family papers, with the birth certificate, is a letter sent to Christopher Grimthorpe by the Hope family, which identifies the father as Désiré Defauw, a Belgian violinist and concertmaster. As a refugee in England during the war, he led the Allied Quartet (sometimes known as the Belgian Quartet) with Lionel Tertis (violin), Charles Woodhouse (piano) and E. Doehard (cello), which was centred in London but also toured the country. Lady Cynthia Asquith, who met them all in 1918, has left a vivid glimpse of Désiré Defauw her diary: 'The first violin, Defauw – a ghastly sight in a yellow wig – fell in love with me, said dancing with me was enivrante [intoxicating], toyed with the tangles in my hair, which he compared to flames, and even went so far as to ask me to bite off a piece of chocolate for him! I have never seen people so happy as those four men – they did admirable stunts . . . Defauw did some excellent ones – an acrobat, a cock, an elephant, and so on . . .'

Désiré Defauw was almost fifteen years younger than Eve and aged thirty at the time of John Francis Mordaunt's birth. He was to enjoy a successful career abroad after the war, his 'Concerts Defauw' becoming famous throughout Europe before he went to the United States, conducting major American orchestras and being appointed musical director of the Chicago Symphony Orchestra. He died in the United States in July 1960. I can find no reference to a son named John Francis Mordaunt in any published writings about him. And there is no record of a child of that name having died in England in the years immediately following his birth. He disappears.

Eve worked for the Red Cross during the First World War and in a bookbinding company during the Second World War. Otherwise she had no employment except as a companion, not paid but paid for, of a few grand people such as the Ladies Scarborough, Helmsley and Wenlock (the latter, being deaf, was equipped with a massive trumpet and a typewriter with which to carry on conversations at greater distances – conversations which spoke of such amazing exploits that she decided to treat the trumpet and the typewriter as diabolically inspired). Some of these ladies would leave Eve trifles in their Wills and her brother Bryan was to bequeath her almost £8,000 when he died.

While it was thought she was going to marry Ernest, Eve continued to give her home as being Bilbrough Manor, which then belonged to Guy and his family. That was still her official residence when, on 30 May 1908, the *Yorkshire Gazette* published a bankruptcy notice as having been served on her. At a meeting of her creditors on 26 June, a deficiency of £225 in her affairs was reported, which she attributed to 'living beyond her income'. But she had no income. She was described as a spinster and a descendant of General Fairfax 'of Cromwellian fame'. This must have been a humiliation for her family and it was her younger brother Bryan, who had served in the army in South Africa and met the art patron Lionel Phillips, who helped her sell the Rodin bust to the Johannesburg Gallery for £800. She would sometimes stay with Bryan at Whitwell Hall in York, and very occasionally with Guy at Bilbrough Manor, but she was not encouraged to remain with her family and began to drift apart from them.

She filled her time with various ladylike occupations. She played an aggressive game of croquet, was a shrewd bridge player and embroidered curtains and cushions with birds, centaurs, swans – and on one occasion the clever design of a backgammon board. Though she picked up information about literature, she was never a great reader.

In 1909 Lady Diana Manners gave Eve an enormous empty volume in which to record her life. It was sturdily bound in leather and bore a device embossed at the front with the letters E. F. surrounded by a pattern resembling a wreath. As a frontispiece there appears a contemplative picture of Eve as Queen Margaret of Anjou in the York Pageant that year, wearing a crown and gazing serenely into the distance. On the title page is inscribed: 'Eve Fairfax. Her Book' and the date: AD MDCCCCIX. Below this has been inserted the engraving of a young damsel, or damozel, plucking thoughtfully at a bow having loosed her arrow into the forthcoming pages while, with a pencilled caption in

Greek lettering, the reader is advised that this is Artemis (or Diana). There is also space for the book's provenance: 'Given to her by Diana Manners'. At the corners of the page, paying tribute to biblical Eve, are decorations depicting blushing apples on a leafy stalk, a serpent coiled round a flourishing tree, a device showing two enjoined capital Ds (the second in reverse), and finally what appears to be a faint smile or perhaps a crescent moon on its back.

Eve Fairfax, too, had, as it were, been cast out of Eden. Her engagement was over, she had been declared bankrupt, obliged to sell her most treasured possession, the Rodin bust, and was now homeless. In 1909 she was close to her fortieth year and, with half her life presumably over, her future seemed imprisoned by her past. Diana Manners chose as an epigraph to Eve's Book a quotation from Shelley's prophetic lyrical drama, *Prometheus Unbound*: a work of radical optimism in which Prometheus, the champion of mankind, is released from incarceration in 'a ravine of icy rocks' where Aeschylus had bound him, and united with Asia, the Spirit of Love. Shelley creates a benign and hopeful world in which goodness and free will bring light out of darkness. This is what the epigraph, Demogorgan's lines from Act IV, promises:

> To suffer woes which Hope thinks infinite;
> To forgive wrongs darker than death or night;
>   To defy power which seems omnipotent;
> To live and bear; to hope till Hope creates
> From its own wreck the thing it contemplates;
>   Neither to change, nor falter, nor repent;
> This, like thy glory Titan, is to be
> Good, great and joyous, beautiful and free;
> This is alone Life; Joy, Empire and Victory!

This is followed by equally aspirational quotations from Dante's *Inferno* and *Purgatorio*; from Alfred de Musset in French and Maeterlinck in English: all with a similar message – that life is not over until it is over (and perhaps not even then) and that wisdom needs to be constantly changing from childhood to death.

Eve's Book was intended as a diary, but she made it into something more bizarre: partly a social calendar, partly a volume of autographs, partly an eclectic anthology. It is an *omnium gatherum*, a vast *vade mecum*, following no order and having no chronology, theme, agenda, prescription. It becomes the reverse of a visitors' book: it is the visitor's book, a book of collected hosts and their guests pinned like butterflies to its pages. For Eve herself it would serve as a book of memories, opening up dense pages of compliments and compensations in her prolonged, singular peregrinations. To read it for very long feels like holding one's breath under water.

Many poems or lines from poems were added along the years. People likened her to Shakespeare's Cleopatra ('Time cannot wither her nor custom stale / Her infinite variety') and one contributor quoted from Donne's Elegy IX, 'The Autumnal': 'No spring, nor summer beauty has such grace / As I have seen in one autumnal face.' Other quotations are more indistinct and disturbing – for example, two lines from Humbert Wolfe: 'There was a thing to do; and it is done now; / The high song is over.' The poets who were fellow guests in the houses where Eve arrived carrying Her Book penned their own poems:

> There on the Norfolk tow-path,
> Where the River Waveney rolled,
> I stood like the child Pandora,
> Suddenly old.

These were the last lines of 'Zany' by Dorothy Wellesley. The last lines of Edith Sitwell's 'To Eve' also touch on lost youth:

> The moon for ever seeks in woodland streams
> To deck her cool faint beauty; thus in dreams
> Belov'd, I seek lost suns within your eyes;
> And find but wrecks of love's gold argosies.

Edith's father, Sir George Sitwell (who had appointed Eve his son Sacheverell's godmother) wrote a version of *Paradise Lost* and *Regained*, which he also dedicated to Eve.

> Oh Eve, to thee a happier chance shall bring
> The Dragon's fruit without the Dragon's sting.
> Adam shall find his Eden in thine eyes,
> And whisp'ring Love lead back to thy lost Paradise.

Laurence Whistler contributed a long poem, which set out to answer the question put in its first line; 'Man, what is man?'

> Forged in four seconds of distracted fire
> Unkindly cast into the world to cool
> In the cold wind of loneliness – until . . .

. . . until, after death, loneliness again envelops him:

> And even in the grave, I dare say, lonely
> Till the dark figures of the trees break through –
> Woman, you make us at your pleasure – only
> That our poor bones may be embraced by yew.

There are several entries in foreign languages – a Hungarian folk song, a German quatrain and Leon Montenaeken's short poem on the vanity and the shortness even of a long life.

> *La vie est vaine:*
> *Un peu d'amour*
> *Un peu de haine –*
> *Et puis – bonjour!*

> *La vie est brève:*
> *Un peu d'espoir,*
> *Un peu de rêve –*
> *Et puis – bonsoir!*

The bleakness of these poems is offset by continual dewdrops of flattery. One contributor mentioned 'my overwhelming love' but neglected to say who he was. 'So honored to add my name in this Book of Memories,' added an indecipherable American. People found it increasingly difficult to come up with something generous and appropriate – 'Satan finds Books for idle hands to write in,' cautioned Sophia Kennedy. Perhaps the most inappropriate cliché of all for someone virtually homeless and so sharp-tongued was delivered by Ernest Beckett's niece Beatrice who had married William Eden's son Anthony Eden. 'No place like HOME!' she wrote. 'Eve makes the final cosy touch.'

Opinions differed as to whether it was better to fall back on quotations or attempt something personal. A few people escaped this choice by contributing drawings or watercolours, most noticeably Chloë Preston who filled several pages with excruciatingly cute paintings of Dutch Dolls, grotesquely sentimental children, wide-eyed dogs and a spotted cat with a pink scarf.

Sybil Hart-Davis (one of Gervase Beckett's lovers – their son was the well-known publisher Rupert Hart-Davis) quoted Walter Pater to the effect that we are all under sentence of death – adding, however, that 'we spend the interval in song'. Ethel Thomas used Emerson's words on love ('Love and you shall be loved. All love is mathematically just'). Gwladys Chaplin left a message possibly for biographers: 'Be to my virtue very kind. / Be to my faults a little blind.' And there were lines from Meredith on swallows and swans, by William Blake on happiness, Queen Christina of Sweden on weakness, and Nietzsche on the shortcomings of men. But no one quoted Andrew Marvell who had spent two years (1650–52) teaching General Lord Fairfax's daughter languages at Nun Appleton where he wrote many of his lyric poems and stored up memories for some of his later work. 'The quiet country existence of Nunappleton released in him the tastes which he could most happily express,' wrote Vita Sackville-West in her short biography of Marvell, 'and the two years he spent there were, poetically, the most fruitful of his life.' This would have pleased Eve more than other people's poetry.

Breaking suddenly into verse Sir Hedworth Williamson sought to denigrate himself in contrast to other contributors:

> Of talent too modest, of genius too cold
> Like Berners to write, or like Rodin to mould;
> But you can win flowers from climate most harsh,
> From a barren old Moore, or a watering Marsh . . .

Lord Berners had contributed a few bars of music, an Allegro Spirito written 'under the influence of drink': George Moore's signature next to the date (11 November 1915) was considered a sufficient tribute and Eve went to the trouble of pasting in a congratulatory card from Rodin.

One of the oddest passages in the book (stranger than the lines from Richard Savage's dramatic poem 'The Bastard' and the quotation from a letter by Mary Queen of Scots on the morning of her execution) was provided by Edward Marsh (one of Harold Nicolson's discarded lovers) who copied the Last Will and Testament of a lunatic who died in an asylum in Illinois – underneath which, Marsh's knighthood being absent, Eve has added 'for me. Sir Edward Marsh'. Perhaps these entries illustrate the panic that filled some of the contributors when Eve slowly approached them with her monstrous and forbidding volume. Sir Hedworth Williamson, while praising Eve, ended with a vigorous curse upon Her Book:

> . . . and Eve of lost Eden, I will you no evil,
> But heartily wish your old book to the Devil.

Eve was to carry this portmanteau of a book from place to place for over fifty years. Though the pages blew from it like leaves from a tree, it increased in bulk and irregularity as she stuffed into it all sorts of photographs, letters, bits and pieces. So it began to resemble a huge and dilapidated saddle of a horse, a chaotic artefact that was a part of Eve's personality: her pride and her penance. Like an extraordinary tramp, she travelled the country between Castles, Halls, Granges, Manors, Priories, Abbeys weighed down by its heavy load like a figure from *The Pilgrim's Progress*. Ernest Beckett's daughter Violet Trefusis gives a picture of her in her novel *Pirates at Play*.

> Poor Francie . . . was one of those popular elderly girls whose happiness was purely vicarious . . . It had taken her the best part of ten years to realise that popularity could become a substitute for love . . . Of course she never got married . . . Much in demand

for week-ends (Francie is such a good mixer) the only tribute she exacted was a caricature or ribald verse in her visitor's book, which was her most valued possession. It was a stout tome bound in green morocco; the addresses of nearly all the stately homes in England figured in it; neatly cut out of the writing paper and placed above a view of the house, there would follow the signatures of her fellow guests, some laboured doggerel on the hunt ball, or a frieze of the local 'meet' done in coloured chalks borrowed from the nursery. There were also a few meticulous watercolour sketches of salmon flies, and half a dozen dance programmes with tiny white pencils attached . . .

The Keppels were among the many families that signed in. The heads of these families often bore the names of places: Chesterfield, Devonshire, Norfolk, Plymouth, Southampton, Wellington, Westminster, Windsor, Zetland. Other signatures were hyphenated, the most endearing of which was Gregory Page-Turner (Adrian Bookholding Jones disdained the hyphen). Perhaps some jokers were making fun of Eve. Archbishops, generals and foreign royalty filled up the pages and there was a picture of the Prince of Wales fondling a baby kangaroo in Australia (1932). Rosamond Lehmann copied down a page from her novel *Invitation to the Waltz* describing the seventeen-year-old Olivia Curtis running into the sunlight, Hilaire Belloc added a poem and so did Vita Sackville-West's one-time lover Geoffrey Scott, while John Betjeman, Harold Nicolson and Somerset Maugham contented themselves with signatures. There were plenty of actors' autographs from Ellen Terry to Michael Dennison. Then I come across a Concert Programme dated 22 July 1915 given in the Lord Roberts Memorial Workshops at Norfolk House. Tertis and Rubinstein are playing with several other musicians including Désiré Defauw. A piece of blue paper has been inserted which reads: 'DEFAUW (on music programme)'. This concert took place a year before the birth of John Francis Mordaunt and was possibly Eve's first meeting with Désiré Defauw.

And there is one name, probably entered in the mid 1960s, which also catches my eye: Mordaunt Milner – which may indicate that Eve's son had been absorbed into her mother's family. So, amid all the chaos and oddity, the poetry and applause, this is a book of secrets.

At the age of eighty Eve seems to have come to the decision that Her Book had finally grown too cumbersome and unwieldy for her to manage. She wrote to Johannesburg asking whether the art gallery there would like to add it to her Rodin collection. The curator replied that he would be delighted and Eve sent it with a somewhat apologetic note: 'It is really a very small part of my life – the gay side – and I am afraid it is all rather a muddle as I had some loose leaves put in at one time which seemed to upset things. They are all my friends, great and otherwise . . . I don't know if the book is suitable for your museum but I hope and think you and others will find amusement and interest in it.'

The book had become an encumbrance to her and a torment to others. But once it has gone she misses it as if she has lost some essential part of herself. It represented much more than 'a very small part' of her life: it was an anchor that she dragged from one harbour to another; it was also her daemon. In its absence this prodigious object gained the affection of those who had dreaded seeing Eve bent over or beneath its substantial bulk as she approached them. Without it she was no longer quite the legendary figure she had been. She was diminished.

After half a dozen years without Her Book she wrote to the Johannesburg art gallery asking whether she could have it back. Maybe

she had hoped to be paid for it; maybe the gallery had expected something that was attached more closely to Rodin. In any event, both sides
were happy to see it returned – the art gallery photocopying a few
Rodin items before letting it go. In her mid-to-late eighties Eve could
no longer drag this hefty property around with her. Instead she would
solicit items that she could take back and give to it, like a mother bird
feeding its young.

She seldom stayed anywhere long. Between the wars people had lent
her their London flats and country cottages from where she set out
on her peregrinations. Sometimes she stayed at a large unheated house
in the village of Acomb on the outskirts of York. It had been bequeathed
to the spinster daughter of a one-time precentor of York Minster on
condition that she look after a pack of collie dogs – duties that Eve
occasionally took over in what she called 'that doggie place'.

In her seventies, she still sometimes rode side-saddle through the
streets, a striking figure in her top hat and veil, a long dark skirt, jabot
and black coat. And she would make appearances at the Snow and
Summer Balls in the Old Assembly Rooms in York. One of her
favourite staging posts was the Yorkshire Club, a big, rather dismal
and somewhat Gothic, red-brick, late-Victorian building with white
stone dressings, overlooking the river on the approach road to Lendal
Bridge. There she sat, a frail but powerful figure, as if enthroned, her
luggage cast around her, her face plastered with white make-up
invaded by irregular dots of rouge and a bright cherry-red mouth,
and wearing enormous earrings. The staff treated her with a mixture
of reverence and exasperation. This was principally a men's club, a
watering place for gentlemen visiting their Yorkshire estates. But Eve
managed to find a hideout in one of the attics until this became known
and she was invited to leave.

Afterwards she found a room above a stuffed-birds shop at Petersgate, and then again at the top of a house over a woollen shop at Stonegate: both districts of York. She suffered painfully from arthritis during her nineties and had great difficulty going up and down the stairs – throwing down her sticks first with a terrible clatter and then sitting on each stair as she descended. She went upstairs backwards.

Like an itinerant refugee, she still made her way round the country. Her stamina was extraordinary. And she grew adept at calculating how long she could stay before her hosts became too irritated – and how soon she could return. Arriving for a long weekend, she stayed six months with her cousin Lady Serena James at St Nicholas, Richmond. 'Those whom the gods love die young,' she announced, 'and I am eighty-seven.' She was eighty-eight by the time she left. She enjoyed telling people that 'I shall be immortal in art galleries all over the world after my friends are dead.'[5] In all moods and weathers she was protected by the aristocracy: she was one of them and they looked after her, arranging for cars to take her from one place to another, telephoning the next batch of hosts on her itinerary to make sure she was met when travelling by train. She was not always polite and saw no reason to be grateful. Why should she be? After all, was she not a direct descendant of the famous parliamentary general, Lord Fairfax, who had defeated Charles I's troops at the Battle of Naseby? The answer, strictly speaking, was no: Lord Fairfax had no direct descendants. But she was of the true blood and belonged to one of the two branches of his family. She spoke of His Lordship as if his ghost were following a

[5] There are examples of Rodin's busts of Eve Fairfax at the Fine Arts Museum of San Francisco (*La Nature*), the Victoria and Albert Museum in London, the Johannesburg Art Gallery in South Africa, the Galleria Communale d'Arte in Rome, and several versions at the Musée Rodin in Paris.

few paces behind, shadowing her, giving her special status and authority. She was imperious, abrasive, amusing, lively, entertaining, cross and sometimes raucously snobbish.

Men liked her more than women did – she flirted with them but treated women dismissively. She was sometimes rude with servants too, but children liked her. They liked her rudeness, which sounded funny when she insulted adults in her old-fashioned Yorkshire voice – dropping the gs in huntin', shootin' and fishin', and pronouncing her rs as ws when she referred to the presents people had given her as 'Wubbish!'. When she gave presents she would frequently take them back. But there were genuine presents for children in the huge over-flowing bag she carried round with her: it was a bag of treasures, a medley of biscuits, embroidery, sixpences, underclothes, everything . . . But sometimes she would frighten them, particularly at night when they heard the awful tapping of her sticks and the crack of her bones as she found her way up to one of the bedrooms, her legs so bent she was forced to move sideways like a crab, clutching for support with hands that had grown into arthritic claws. She was the very image of a witch – except for her face. All her life she remained 'fair of face' as a genuine Fairfax should be and in some ways that face grew more remarkable: full of vitality and mischief-making.

For her hundredth birthday a lunch was hosted by Lord Savill at the Yorkshire Club. Friends travelled there from all over the country, seeing one another, many of them, after intervals of many years and with gasps of amazement at their being still alive. Eve appeared very much alive. She gave a short, fluent and amusing speech but complained that she had not been offered enough wine.

Following a stroke, the last seven years of her life were passed in the Retreat, a Quaker hospital in York, founded in 1796, which specialised in treating infirmity and providing mental health care. The heads of three families paid for her: Lord Grimthorpe, the Duke of Wellington and Lord Linlithgow. Visiting her there towards the end of 1971, her friend Serena James came away very distressed. 'She was sitting in a small room surrounded by obviously mentally sick ladies,' she wrote. 'She herself seemed more alert — she implored me to take her away, suggested a taxi . . . She is undoubtedly very unhappy.' She asked whether Eve could be moved from this small annexe to the main building where she might be able to play cards and 'would see some men'. The following February she was transferred to 'more congenial surroundings' in one of the central wards.

She seemed for a time more settled. Some days there were echoes of her former self. During a pause in a Christmas Nativity play, her voice boomed out: 'I can't hear the bloody fairy!'

When the young historian Hugo Vickers visited the Retreat in March 1977, he was escorted to the Charlotte Ward and advised to 'look helpless' until a nurse brought Miss Fairfax to him. Eventually she arrived in a large, high-backed wheelchair wearing a mauve dress. 'She moved and reacted very well. We shook hands and I introduced myself,' he wrote. 'She asked a lot of questions about me, where did I come from, what did I do, was it my first visit to York . . . did I have brothers and sisters . . . Eve asked my age. "I'm somewhat older," she said . . . Lunch arrived and she fed herself without problems. It really is remarkable.'

Hugo Vickers was writing a biography of Gladys Deacon, Duchess of Marlborough, and wanted to see whether her name appeared in Eve's monumental book. A nurse heaved it to him. 'It was quite amazing,' he wrote. He turned the pages and there it was, Gladys Deacon's signature, accompanying a quotation from Baudelaire. At the end of his visit Eve said to him: 'It hasn't been a silly life, it's been a useful one. Anyone who saw the book could see that.'

When Hugo returned the next day he was told Eve was asleep. They wheeled her through in her geriatric chair but she did not wake up. 'She looked absolutely like a wax-work,' he wrote. '. . . They said she sometimes spends as long as three days like that. So I had been very lucky the day before.'

She was suffering from senile dementia as well as arthritis and needed constant observation. Sometimes she claimed to be Queen Elizabeth I (the part she played at one of the York Pageants). She could not stand unsupported but often forgot this and had several falls. The nurses aggravated her – they did not come when she called them. She was often disorientated, not realising she was in a psychiatric hospital, and was frequently upset, confused and outspoken. At night two nurses had to raise her several times from her bed to prevent incontinence.

She died of bronchopneumonia at half past three in the morning of 27 May 1978, five months short of her one hundred and seventh birthday. There was a memorial service at St James's Church at Bilbrough. She had made a Will with various dukes and barons as her trustees, but since she had no money it was not proved and she died intestate.

The Times obituary of Eve Fairfax, on 12 June 1978, described 'this grand old lady' as representing 'a fascinating chapter of history starting in the reign of Queen Victoria and ending after man had successfully walked on the Moon'. But she belonged to neither world. Without money, a husband or recognised children, she lost her position in late-Victorian and Edwardian times; and without employment her nomadic existence led nowhere in the twentieth century. She was like someone waking from a dream and not knowing what is real or imaginary. In Her Book, she copied out a speech made in 1944 by Dr Temple, the Archbishop of York, arguing that 'the burden of work' was often 'a curse' and that, in spiritual terms, unemployment had its blessings. Perhaps this was the basis of the claim she made to Hugo Vickers that her life was 'useful'. It was, in the words of the Rodin scholar Marion J. Hare, 'a genteel tragedy'.

Her Book, with its great empty spaces, its undergrowth of clichés, its photo parade of men and women on horses, of children and flowers, dogs, prime ministers, and then the dark floating passages of poetry, is truly her autobiography. I look through it one last time and enter her world again. Among the crowded signatures there are few revealing facts. But I sense that I am closer to Eve. She carried this great book so far, valued it so highly – and now it rests in my hands. While I slowly turn its stiff and crackling pages I feel I am about to come across something unexpected and significant. This is the excitement and mystery of research. I trawl through many famous names that have signed up to the statement that she 'will never be forgotten by . . .'. Yet she makes no appearance in their biographies and autobiographies. She is a legendary character in a small world, all shadow by the end – the substance vanishing with time. It is as if her story is written here in invisible ink, which appears faintly when you breathe on it. In an interview she gave to the *Star* shortly before going into hospital, she was asked if she had any regrets and replied: 'Yes, only one, and that is I never married. I was very popular in my time and had many offers. Maybe, if I had married, I would be better off today.' Then, without being asked a further question, she adds that she knew various people in South Africa, and 'had relatives there, including Sir George and Lady Milner, of Cape Town'. If I were a novelist I could arrange for her son Mordaunt to meet Ernest Beckett's son Lancelot in South Africa and carry on their adventures there.

Prising open two pages that had become stuck together, I suddenly come across Ernest Beckett who, signing himself Grimthorpe and recording the date as 15 May 1915, two years before his death, copied down a devastating verse from Swinburne's poem 'Dolores' written in reversed dactyls.

> For the Crown of our life as it closes
> Is darkness, the fruit thereof dust;
> No thorns go so deep as the roses
> And love is more cruel than lust –
> Time turns the old days to derision
> Our loves into corpses or wives,
> And marriage and death and division
> Makes barren our lives –

4

With Catherine at Cimbrone

My researches into Eve and Ernest, as I had begun to call them, took very different courses. Early on I wrote to someone I had known at school. Rupert Lycett Green was married to John Betjeman's daughter Candida – they had spent their honeymoon at the Villa Cimbrone (and both their families appeared in Eve's Book). Rupert replied that the best person to help me was his sister Catherine.

Catherine Till was the same age as me. She had her own reasons for research into the Grimthorpe family, I was to discover, which followed an adjacent course to mine. Our two lines of enquiry stretched ahead of us, never colliding, but appearing to meet at an ideal point on the horizon.

Pond Farm, where she lived, was a stone farmhouse on the top edge of a sloping village green at Newton-upon-Rawcliffe, a windswept hamlet not far from Pickering in the North Riding of Yorkshire. She is not altogether alone when I arrive: Romney, a medium-sized dog (a lurcher) and Crackers, her multi-coloured cat, live very contentedly there. Next door is Basil, her horse. Catherine, who is a valiant motorist, drives me to see anyone in Yorkshire who might have useful information. I meet people who had known, or whose families had known, both Ernest and Eve. I visit houses where the Becketts and Fairfaxes lived, and cemeteries where they were buried. But nowhere on our journey could I find what I most wanted to see: Eve's Book – though everyone knew of it and had elaborate theories as to where it might have come to rest. Then one day at a Yorkshire racecourse someone makes off with Ernest's grandson Christopher Grimthorpe's hat. In the hat left behind, he finds the name 'Sparks' and when he catches up with Mr Sparks (who is also searching for him) he discovers that Alexander Sparks is the husband of a great-niece of Eve's. So he speaks of my interest in her famous book. My search is at an end. For Alexander and Serena Sparks have Her Book – and six weeks later I am turning its pages at their house in Wiltshire.

When I first met Catherine she was completing a mass observation survey for a government department on psychiatric morbidity in a crime-stricken area of Middlesbrough. She is also in regular correspondence with a man on Death Row in Florida and twice visits him in jail for a charity before he is finally executed. By conventional standards this is a most irregular career, not harnessed at all to money-making (she is far from being well off). But to my mind her work is all the more admirable.

Like Eve, Catherine spent her very early years at Bilbrough Manor which her father, David Lycett Green, bought after his marriage to Catherine's mother Angela. As a child Catherine was unaware of her mother's long and passionate love affair during the 1930s and into the 1940s with Ernest's son, Ralph Grimthorpe, the boy Luie had died giving birth to. Ralph, who married Mary Archdale in 1914, turned out to be in some ways very like his father. When he spoke to you, whether you were a woman or a man, it seemed as if you were the only person in the world to whom he wished to speak.

Hurtling round the Yorkshire moors in her brave car, Romney

lurching around on the back seat, Crackers left guarding Pond Farm, Catherine informs me that she is not after all the daughter of Angela and David Lycett Green, but of Angela Green and her lover Ralph Grimthorpe. Catherine had got into the car at the beginning of our journey as my old school friend's sister, but gets out of it an hour later as Ernest's illegitimate granddaughter. This has been a hectic research trip and I need time to catch up.

Over the next couple of days Catherine tells me about her early years. Owing to the war, she saw little of David, her legal father. 'One vivid memory', she tells me, 'is walking in the snow with him trailing animal and bird prints.' Her adult life was also to become a trail, following prints that might lead her to a secure identity.

Before the end of the Second World War, Ralph's wife petitioned for a divorce on the grounds of his adultery and Ralph married Angela after her divorce from David. Catherine and Rupert, then aged ten and eight, were unaware of the scandal that swirled round the county families of Yorkshire and was aggravated by David and Ralph being masters of foxhounds (members of one pack not speaking to members of the other for several years). Soon afterwards the children went to live half the time at Ralph's home, Easthorpe Hall, a fine eighteenth-century house near the village of Amotherby. Ralph talked cricket to Rupert and horses with Catherine, and when David Lycett Green asked them what they thought of him 'we said we very much liked him', Catherine remembered. 'I can still see the rather sad, wistful expression that crossed his face. Perhaps it was then, for the first time, that I felt the tug of divided loyalties.'

This tug of loyalties was made more acute when in 1948 David married again. His new wife, 'a very striking woman', had two children of her own and turned out to be an awkward stepmother. Even her compliments undermined Catherine's confidence. ('She once told me I had a good complexion and must take care of it. I felt like Masha in *The Seagull* who, when complimented on her hair, remarks "everyone says that to a plain girl".') Shortly after their marriage, Catherine told me, David Lycett Green had a coronary and became more or less an invalid for the last twelve years of his life.

In 1950, at the age of fifteen, Catherine went to the Villa Cimbrone for the first time. 'I always loved the villa, particularly that jagged outline of mountains above Maori,' she told me. 'I loved wandering through the rooms, occasionally to evade my mother's wrath, mainly to open drawers and make discoveries.' On one of her early visits she discovered a diary Ernest had written at the beginning of the 1880s before he met Luie. 'I thought he was insufferably pleased with himself,' she recalled. The diary was full of trite generalisations such as 'Fringes and flirtations go together. Where you don't see the former you seldom find the latter.' It was a wonder to the teenage Catherine that any woman could find a man with such a ridiculous moustache attractive. But the adult world was full of such mysteries. Ernest's diary made it clear that an innkeeper's beautiful daughter in Naples had fallen in love with him. This was the sort of episode that often overtook him on his travels abroad.

It was not simply the fun of bathing and being with Ralph's family and knowing that her mother loved the place, it was the haunting beauty of Cimbrone that cast a spell on them all. Catherine seemed inexplicably happy. Yet still she went from room to room, looking in cupboards, opening drawers, as if trying to find a solution to her divided loyalties.

Back in England she went through 'all the foolish fanfares' of being a debutante. To the horror of her mother, the irritation of Ralph, she fell in love with an impossible Polish man called Jan. Ralph had a tremendous row with him and Angela's vituperation was so extreme that it had the unintended consequence of preventing Catherine from ever again confiding in her. To get over this infatuation she was sent once more to the Villa Cimbrone. Though she would never have a romance at Cimbrone, it became a Promised Land where strong feelings about absent lovers were intensified. She resumed her search through drawers and cupboards. What was she searching for? I ask her. 'I feel sure that for everyone much in childhood is known without being known,' she answers. What she did discover was a bundle of love letters from her mother written to Ralph during the war. Her mother had sometimes opened and read the letters sent to her children, but now Catherine reversed this process as if taking over parental seniority herself. Soon she came across an early letter that confirmed her silent suspicions. She shows me a photocopy. In it Angela writes that she could never leave Catherine because she is in love with her father, Ralph. Catherine later realises that this letter, overflowing with love for Ralph, is not proof that Ralph was actually her father. It is a strategic document, drafted with the intent of strengthening Angela's position before she leaves David. The letter makes no claim or protest – it repeats something she has obviously discussed with Ralph. She wants to make doubly certain that Ralph will take responsibility for Catherine, after she joins him – which he does.

Carrying on her search, Catherine also found a letter from Ralph to Angela saying that Catherine is the most beautiful baby he has ever seen. She is filled with sudden happiness.

Catherine could never raise the matter with her mother: they were not on such intimate and sympathetic terms. Closeted in their bedrooms, she and her brother Rupert discuss it (they are by now close companions). Examining pictures of both families for similarities, they take their pick. Rupert remains a Lycett Green and Catherine becomes a Beckett.

Catherine's parentage lies at the very centre of her worries. 'I felt I belonged nowhere,' she tells me, 'and I judged both Angela and Ralph quite harshly.' It seemed to her she was doomed to make a mess of her life. As if to delay this fate, she prolonged her adolescence. She wanted to marry and have children, but not until this problem was settled and she was acknowledged to be Ralph's daughter, Ernest and Luie's granddaughter, without any shadow of guilt or sense of betrayal. But how could she be certain? Her instinct pointed in one direction; reference books told another story. We sit in her drawing room at Pond Farm: Catherine needs official recognition of what she feels is the truth. The evidence may still lie hidden, she believes, at the Villa Cimbrone.

When I got back to London, I began to wonder why the solution to Catherine's paternity might be at Cimbrone. Apparently the Grimthorpe family had unintentionally left all sorts of papers there when, in the early 1960s, and shortly before his death, Ralph sold the place to an Italian family, the Vuilleumiers. There were still secrets to be found at the villa.

We make a plan. She will write to the Vuilleumier family and arrange for us to stay at the Villa Cimbrone for a week as their guests, explaining that we wish to go through the Grimthorpe archive, which is in their care. I will pay for the air tickets and the hire of a car. Catherine will use her international skills as a motorist and also act as my Italian interpreter.

The night before we set out I have a strange dream. I am in a hotel and when I go to unpack my suitcase I find a number of clothes that do not belong to me. Among them is a small black computer with a red button that says 'Press me' (rather like the 'Eat me' and 'Drink me' from *Alice's Adventures in Wonderland*). I press it and hear a woman's voice thanking me for finding her clothes. 'Where are you?' she asks. I tell her and she instructs me how to return the clothes to her (which apparently I am obliged to do having pressed the magic button). I must go to where she lives, travelling by exactly the same route as she used. I am dismayed by this, particularly since I don't know the final destination of my journey. But I recognise that there is no appeal – I must go. I begin packing her clothes together with my own but do not think they will any longer fit in the suitcase. I wrestle with them until the hotel fire alarm suddenly sounds – and I wake up to the ringing of my alarm clock.

We meet at Gatwick in the last week of April 2000. I am innocently dressed in grey flannels and a change coat on which, I suddenly notice, a great blob of ink has appeared from a leaking pen in an inner pocket. Is this an honourable mark for a writer or a sign that my vital strength is ebbing away? Should I flaunt it or wear a patch? I see Catherine ahead of me and join her. She is carefully dressed in a light green outfit useful, I judge, for climbing mountains or trekking through a desert. It is, I decide, a guerrilla outfit. She has advised me on the phone to leave my suitcase half-empty so that we can fill it with precious papers from Cimbrone. She is accompanied by an extraordinary piece of luggage, beige and formless, resembling at some angles a small bear. I offer to carry it and she very readily agrees. But how can it be half-empty? Is it half-full of lead? I grapple with it, unable to tell where its front is, where its ceiling, its back. It seems to have wheels but they are inside – one would have to gut it to reach them. We stagger along the queue creating waves of impatience behind us.

Once we have taken off, Catherine produces some photocopies of letters that help to bring the story she has told me at Pond Farm up to date. She has an ingenious theory that having two fathers whom she loved in confusing ways and with pangs of disloyalty was like a man having a wife and a mistress — indeed it may have led, she suggests, to her emotionally untidy past. During her twenties there was almost always some intense involvement with a man, bringing her much pain and pleasure.

At the beginning of 1966, when she was thirty, she travelled to India, Thailand and Cambodia, meeting at an Italian Embassy dinner in New Delhi Raja Ranbir Singh, 'a Raja without a state'. Ranbir had spent much of his life outside India, being educated at Balliol and passing the war in Switzerland 'seducing women and learning exquisite French'. He was sixteen years older than Catherine and she was greatly impressed by him. 'He had absolutely no common sense,' she says with a smile, 'and a violent temper.' He liked nothing better than parading his knowledge. It was like 'listening to an encyclopaedia'.

That autumn she joined some friends she had met in Kathmandu and drove up to Nepal. They were like pioneers along the hippy trail. It was an unforgettable journey: the splendour of Afghanistan and the wild beauty of the Bamian valley with its huge statues of the Buddha still standing there. She took voluntary work teaching English to Tibetan refugee children at a rat-infested hill station in the Indian Himalayas. 'I loved it all,' she says to me, 'apart from the rats. I particularly loved the Tibetan children. It was, perhaps, the happiest time of my life.'

Unlike many other English travellers, she never fell in love with India. But she saw Raja Ranbir again and fell in love with him. 'I suppose I was flattered that, among a stream of women, he only wanted to marry me. He was striking to look at but vain, always glancing in the mirror. It took time for me to realise that he needed reassurance for his looks and for everything else.' And perhaps Catherine needed reassurance too and maybe they could reassure each other. It occurred to me (though I did not say anything) that those Tibetan children she had taught and loved at the hill station had suddenly, urgently, made her want to have children of her own. They decided to marry and were to have three remarkably good-looking daughters – she shows me their photographs. Ranbir, by a previous marriage, had two sons aged fifteen and twelve (both of whom went to school at Harrow). He had more or less driven their mother out of their lives while they were still very young and they did not to see her again until they had grown up. Catherine formed a bond with these sons which, to some extent, excluded their father. 'His behaviour towards me grew more and more obsessive. It took me several years to admit the failure of our marriage and leave him.'

She sought sanctuary, with her daughters, for a time at Porlock in West Somerset before Christopher Grimthorpe gave her a cottage in the remote village of Westow, a few miles north-east of York. The threats and endless telephone calls from Ranbir began to subside. 'We were happy,' she says. 'I started work for a degree with the Open University, studying sociology and the humanities. My degree has been of little practical use at my age, but it is a source of satisfaction.' It is a rare badge of conformity.

She has covered these years of turmoil on our short flight to Naples and we are approaching the airport as she sketches in her second marriage. In 1974 she met Patrick Till, a country solicitor who, 'with uncharacteristic spontaneity, immediately decided he wanted to marry me'. He was, like her, passionate about horses and fox-hunting, and like her lacked perhaps some degree of self-confidence. But that was all they had in common. He was good to her daughters and had three sons of approximately the same ages. 'I should have refused to marry him or, having done so, I should have tried to make the marriage succeed,' she says. She does not blame him for leaving her. 'But I found the process painful. Once again I felt an outsider.'

We land and, in the seething chaos of the airport, with what Catherine calls 'a miracle of efficiency' and I call simply 'a miracle', we find our car. It is a miracle, to my way of thinking, because, though we have bundles of papers mentioning it, there appears to be no car-hire company in Naples with the name we have been given. This is an opportunity for Catherine to try out her Italian as I look on with what I hope is a severe expression. She speaks with energy, breaking into incapacitating laughter every two or three sentences (in which everyone else joins – while I struggle to hold my fierce glare) at the sound of her downright English pronunciation. There is an atmosphere of bewilderment like a thick fog over everything: then suddenly, and without explanation, the sun shines through and, amid more laughter and congratulations, we are handed the keys. Our car is parked so close to other cars that I can see no likelihood of entering it except perhaps through the roof. But difficulties like this bring out Catherine's strengths. With the skill of a contortionist, she fights her way in and begins experimenting loudly with the gears until the car, like a frightened animal, jumps backwards, almost knocking me to the ground. But we are on our way.

Not knowing what direction to take, I suggest that we stop to read the signs. This seems to Catherine rather a tame suggestion. I remember that she has driven across Nepal and give a slight shudder. I have a map, a small map, but unfortunately it covers the whole of Italy and our fifty-mile journey (it turns out to be somewhat longer) is hardly visible. Reading the road signs, which Catherine politely allows me to do, is like deciphering a complicated code, since the directions appear mainly to indicate restaurants. We attract a line of hooting and gesticulating motorists behind us before taking the Salerno road south which, rather unnervingly, is also the road north to Rome. Unfortunately Catherine has made an enemy of the Italian gears. 'Am I in second or third?' she shouts to me, and I bend down, still holding my map, to find out. But we successfully reach the autostrada; fling indiscriminate coins at the guard-cashier; then rev up and sail on.

'Where are we now?' Catherine answers her question decisively. 'There is Vesuvius!' she cries, taking both hands off the wheel. But there is no hint of how to reach Ravello and we decide to stop at a motorway station and buy a local map. There is no motorway station. My hand moves frantically across the map of Italy and I occasionally call out a name. 'NOCHERA IN!' I cry. Catherine turns to correct my pronunciation. 'Nocera Inferiore,' she says. I pretend to take no notice. Eventually we do find a motorway station and Catherine, having overlooked the door, forces her way into and eventually through a closed glass panel. I sit in the car like a dog, like Romney, guarding our luggage, watching helplessly and unhelpfully. Catherine disappears, then returns triumphantly with a map and, after I have studied it, I tell her that we have come too far and must somehow return if we are to avoid touring the south of Italy.

We charge down the road, come off the autostrada, perform a fabulous U-turn, rejoin the autostrada, fling more coins at the guard, and are on our way again in the opposite direction. Suddenly we see a sign to Ravello, turn and turn again and lose ourselves in a maze of indistinguishable streets. Are we in Agni or Pajani? Catherine murmurs. I say nothing. We ask a girl with a dog: neither of them admits to knowing anything. We head for the mountains, go back, go on, go almost mad. Suddenly there is another signpost to Ravello. We are on course again. But it is a topsy-turvy course. We climb, veering one way, then another, sometimes (it seems to me) on two wheels. Catherine encourages the poor car as if it were Basil, her horse. She is enjoying herself. At one hazardous point she asks me whether I would prefer to be crushed against the rock face or fall to my death into the valley. I choose the rock face. 'Do keep reminding me', she reminds me, 'that they drive on the right in Italy.' Much of the time we compromise and drive in the middle. I shout out my reminders, clutching, white-knuckled, the side of the door.

One of the advantages of geared cars, Catherine suggests as she spins the wheel, is that they are narrower than automatic cars and this enables her to whiz through corridors and squeeze past obstacles. Can it be true? She is very game and I feel that we are more at risk from her occasional spasms of doubt than her fierce determination. So I let out extravagant cries of encouragement as we hurtle along. 'Brilliant!' I cry as she accidentally sounds the horn. 'We've done it!' I shout again as we overtake a stationary lorry behind which we have been impatiently waiting in the belief that there is a red light ahead of it. Sometimes I wish there were a red light ahead of us, several red lights. But we continue in good spirits and I notice that Catherine is more confident in the mountains. When I say 'we go right here', she answers that it doesn't matter – and she is correct. From now on all roads lead to Ravello. We enter by an unexpected route, pass unexpectedly through a tunnel, turn unexpectedly left, proceed without much expectation and arrive at a car park where there is some incomprehensible paperwork to complete before we slide into a space and the car, with a final backward lunge (as in *The Wages of Fear*), almost topples down a precipice.

We decant the luggage. Though we are high up, we must go higher, much higher. There are some forty steps from the car park to the square in Ravello and then, moving diagonally past the drinkers, children, worshippers, we stagger up and along winding passages, corridors, alleys, mountain pathways, bridges, gangways, kerbs; by churches, houses, restaurants, shrines; and under arches, over stones, sometimes accompanied by music, fading music, fewer people. If this seems exaggerated (and it is), that is because I am toiling with Catherine's badly behaved baggage, which wants to go downhill fast – particularly down the one hundred and sixty-three steps that lie above the forty we have already conquered. I gasp and pull, pull and gasp, urging Catherine to go ahead and alert the good people of Cimbrone that, like Hannibal, I am approaching. But she will not desert me. So she is witness to my laboured and humiliating progress as I have been witness to her intrepid zigzag motoring. At last we pass through a large wooden portal: the entrance to the Villa Cimbrone.

The gardens stretch peacefully before us and far below the mirrored sea, with a thin intermittent layer of stationary clouds (or are they islands?) under the hazy sun. To our left is the villa with its courtyards, terraces, cloisters, balconies. This, for the next week, is to be our place of research. The people who visit the gardens each day are now leaving and we make our way against a current of parents and children, courting couples, tourists. Catherine begins talking to one of the Vuilleumier family and we are led through a small courtyard, past a gate and a door marked private and up some stairs to our rooms. Mine is mainly pink and green, Catherine's blue, and both look down through orange and lemon trees to the bay below.

We meet the family that evening on one of the terraces and I present a copy of my *Lytton Strachey* to Giorgio who, since his father's recent death, has become head of the family, though his mother still lives there and, somewhere deep within the building, I believe, her mother too. I am handing over my book partly to establish my creden tials as a 'gentleman-scholar', and partly to make a link with the Villa Cimbrone, Catherine having shown me beforehand a brochure with its claims to be a regular meeting place for the Bloomsbury Group. I take out my pen and on the title page write 'at the Villa Cimbrone', signing my name – this is my passport to speak on Strachey here seven years later when I will meet Violet Trefusis's young admirer, the mysterious Tiziana. My book is admired from a distance by the family. They surround it with amiable gestures and sounds, though not liking to approach too close. I hope this will encourage the habit of giving during our negotiations. We are to hold our first formal meeting the next morning.

Catherine and I then descend the one hundred and sixty-three steps along the alleys and passages, and ask an old gentleman which restaurant he would recommend. He points to one, raising his fingers to his lips to convey the deliciousness of the food.

Catherine does not want to talk about the next day's meeting and I see that she is worried by the prospect. So we talk a bit about ourselves. 'I am more interested in him than he is in me,' she notes in a journal she kept of our travels. But this is not quite true. In Yorkshire I was continually questioning her and think she needs a rest from this bombardment. But Catherine interprets this as being due to something lacking in herself. I do not understand this until she later gives me her journal to read. She is someone of immense courage and dash on the outside, and much uncertainty within. It is to address this imbalance that she is here.

We walk back up to the villa, stopping to look at the lights in the valley. It is quite cold. We come to the great wooden door – it is bolted, so we press every bell we can find. Alfonso, a very amiable man of all trades with a hefty moustache, lets us in and says he will bring us both breakfast in the morning. Since the Villa Cimbrone is not yet open as a hotel we had not expected breakfast; we decide to eat together on Catherine's balcony at 8.30 and discuss tactics before beginning our negotiations.

I wake at 7 a.m. and look around. It is a misty morning but the room is bright and pretty. There are tiled floors, enormous chunks of furniture and a brilliantly white modern bathroom. Just before 8.30 I knock at Catherine's door. It is her birthday, which 'I would be glad to forget' she says. The room is full of cards people gave her before she left. Birthdays are a symbol of what worries her, but these happy cards seem a promising sign. We go on to her balcony overlooking the sea – a wonderful, dreamlike view. As we stand there, Alfonso opens some shutters further off and appears at a window to our right. Catherine shouts a greeting to him and he disappears. Ten minutes later he is at the door with our breakfast as he will be every morning: good strong coffee, delicious croissants, jams, honey and marmalade.

Over breakfast Catherine says she will be angry if the family insist on holding on to Lucille's family papers. They were left accidentally and, except for those that specifically refer to the Villa Cimbrone, should be returned to England. I say that we should set an example by giving the family whatever photocopies we have that might be of genuine interest to them. For instance, I have brought a copy of Ernest Beckett's Will and would be happy for them to have it since there are many references to the Villa Cimbrone in it. I will ask them about Beckett's companion Florence Green and her house at Castro Leone. And if they have any Beckett letters I will ask for photocopies.

Before the negotiations begin we make our way along the belvedere, passing its line of battered Roman statues as if inspecting a parade of wounded soldiers. Then we explore the layers below, descending every so often a flight of stone steps with wooden banisters from one level of the garden to another. The sun has now emerged through the mist, making trembling patterns on the ground as its light penetrates the trees. Many of these trees and plants come from North Africa and the eastern Mediterranean. There are cypresses, junipers, yews, an azalea walk, hydrangeas. From the deep valley and hills come distant echoes of people working. Every so often we turn a corner and come across some Beckett eccentricity, my favourite being a naked statue of a rather plump biblical Eve reclining in a dark grotto. This was possibly made in Rome, I like to think, by Waldo Story with the voluptuous José as his model. When D. H. Lawrence came on this same walk with Earl Brewster in 1927, he also walked through these woods, past pools where irises grew, and, seeing this grotto with its life-size marble statue, remarked that she was 'too pale' and needed 'a touch of colour'. Snatching up a handful of dark brown earth he began energetically rubbing it on Eve's face and then, liking the effect, gave her 'a complete mud-bath' transforming her into 'a black lady'. Since Lawrence's act of vandalism, iron bars have been fixed to the entrance of this grotto excluding Eve from Ernest's Eden and, effectively, imprisoning her.

We go back to the library where we have arranged to meet Giorgio. There are two or three hundred books here from the Grimthorpe days — English, Italian and many French classics, mostly in collected editions, well-bound, untouched. On a circular table at the centre of the room a few modern novels have been left by guests. Giorgio arrives, we go through double doors on to a large patio and begin our discussion.

I show him Ernest's Will, read out very slowly the parts mentioning the Villa Cimbrone, and ask him about Castro Leone and Florence Green. He has never heard of either and refers us to a local historian in Ravello who might know something. I then hand the Will to him expecting him to keep it but he goes and makes a photocopy of it. The hum of his photocopying machine becomes a familiar sound over the next few days. He also shows us some white envelopes, which contain press cuttings from the *Yorkshire Post*, *The Times* and the *Morning Post* during the late nineteenth and early twentieth centuries — mostly reports of Ernest's speeches during general elections. I read while Catherine talks of the Grimthorpes' lives. I fear that talking about the careers of these Yorkshire bankers and Members of Parliament is out of place and a waste of time. But I am wrong. There is nothing Giorgio likes to hear about more than the lives of the English aristocracy. It is as if, having taken over the house early in the 1960s, the two families have been miraculously entwined. Giorgio values all these brittle, yellow press cuttings, these notices of weddings and deaths, these reports of election results in a far-off country, not for their commercial value or even their content, but simply as evidence of their connection. The very sound of these aristocratic names is music to him. He wants to hear more; he wants to hear again what he has already heard. He is spellbound by what, in her wonderful Yorkshire-Italian, Catherine tells him.

He asks why, if the family did not want this material to become part of the Cimbrone estate, did they leave it here? There is so much: books, furniture, and these papers — it cannot be wholly accidental. And why, after such a long time, are we coming to ask for it? I answer that there is a difference between furniture and papers. Furniture is part of a house — the transportation of such substantial stuff is impractical. They must treat these tables and chairs and even the books in their bookcases as a legitimate bonus. But papers left in cupboards and chests of drawers are essentially different. They are so easily left by mistake. Have we not all done something like this one time or another? I explain that, while writing my memoirs, I had returned to my grandparents' house where I grew up and was shown by the owners books I had read as a child, also my father's 'Book of Lights' which were designs for Lalique glass lights from the 1920s and 1930s, and my great-grandmother's 'Book of Ferns' a vast calf-bound volume arranged and pressed by her while in India during the 1870s. All these had been found behind a curtain in an attic by the people who bought the house after my family left. The new owner, who was something of a horticulturalist, had grown especially fond of the 'Book of Ferns' but let me take it away, together with the other books. It was not an easy decision for him, but he acted with generosity, recognising that they were accidentally left there and rightfully belong to me. Catherine, I say, is looking for the same generosity and sense of justice. In return she promises to let them have anything she finds in England that ought to have its proper home in Italy. That, in short, is our case. Our difficulty is that we don't know what there is at Cimbrone – and nor, I come to suspect, does Giorgio.

Our meeting goes on until the early afternoon when I am introduced to Giorgio's mother, a small, sturdy, smiling woman in her late fifties with short-cut auburn hair, who greets Catherine warmly as 'one of the family'. We are to resume our talks in the evening after a late lunch in Ravello and a siesta. This was to be the pattern of our work, a pattern sometimes varied at short notice.

One afternoon when there is a pause in our work on the patio, we meet the local historian. He is sympathetic but cannot help us over Castro Leone, though he is at work on some bulky papers and will contact us if he comes across anything this year, next year, some time . . .

Another day we have lunch with Gore Vidal. He lives on the promontory below and beyond the Villa Cimbrone in a spacious and fantastical cliff dwelling cut into the precipitous rocks and perilously clinging to them. Poised above the sea, it is set over several acres of descending terraces where grapes, olives and lemons grow among the cypress trees and umbrella pines. Visiting writers have likened it to Prospero's kingdom, though it reminds another visitor this year, the American novelist Erica Jong, of Hitler's eagle's nest at Berchtesgaden. But it has a gentler name, La Rondinaia (the swallow's nest) and was built for Lucille (who, Gore says, still haunts the place). And probably this land, it occurs to me, was once called the Castro Leone and is the place where Florence Green was intended to have her villa. Everyone had told the architect who built this spectacular house that it would quickly become detached from the cliff face, tumble down the mountain and with a great splash enter the sea. So Lucille procured some dynamite, which she exploded in a cave below the house: and behold, the house still stood. It was, everyone agreed, a miracle.

Lucille was a believer in miracles. Travelling down Oxford Street in London one day in deep despair on the top of a bus, she was visited by a revelation, which she set out to elucidate in two books, *Unbound Worlds* (1955) and *Neti. Neti* (*Not This. Not That,* 1959). In these books she sought her own 'theory of everything'. Mixing philosophy with astrophysics, adding a portion of ancient and modern religious dogma, some measure of infinity, a sprinkling of quotations from Jung, the Buddha and the astronomer Fred Hoyle, she concocted a terrific brew to keep despair at bay. La Rondinaia, which defied all pessimistic predictions, is a temple to her faith.

As with many religions, the path to this temple is not easy. The true pathway begins at a gate at the back of a hotel in Ravello, a gate with a bell, which one must ring to gain entry to the vertiginous path. There are other gates with bells along the way. We ring them and we hear the voice of Howard Austen, Gore Vidal's guard and companion, instructing us to keep to the strait and narrow mountain path. We pass through the last gate, enter the garden where two lion-like cats patrol the grounds and are guided by Howard to the house where Gore greets us with glasses of champagne.

Arriving there four months later, Erica Jong was to call this 'one of the most beautiful spots on earth' – though, standing on the balcony, the author of *Fear of Flying* suffered a dizzying attack of vertigo. She sees what we see: the seventeenth-century canvases, the Graeco-Roman head of Zeus, the first-century mosaic floor mounted as a wall piece and the sitting room with its framed pictures of Gore's 'old pal Princess Margaret'.

We walk slowly to Ravello and have lunch in a restaurant on the edge of the town. Gore is greeted there as a great man, a 'maestro'. They do not know the difference, he tells us, between one writer and another, but since he has done a television advertisement for vodka (he absolutely forgets which vodka) his reputation has risen steeply. The only other writer invited to do this was Salman Rushdie. Gore asks about him and his relatively new wife Elizabeth, and I hear myself calling Salman my 'foul weather friend' meaning that I see more of him, and am closer to him, in his days of peril than in easier times.

Gore strikes me as an American version of Winston Churchill. He is in his mid-seventies now and not in good health, but he remains full of bulldog energy. He likes high-class gossip, is well read both in the classics, in modern literature and politics, enjoys drinking and tends to dominate the conversation. He also seems vulnerable and, being interested in power, is conscious of his career and the careers of his contemporaries. He says that when he was young, Bernard Shaw had an immense reputation in the world: but where is it now? I believe he is reflecting on his own future reputation and wondering whether he has spread his interests too widely, too thinly. Catherine is amused by the way we congratulate each other (and therefore ourselves) on having come through without having gone to university. He realises that he cannot go on living in such a remote place and wonders whether he might leave it to St Alban's School, his alma mater, as a place of study like Bernard Berenson's I Tatti and Harold Acton's La Pietra. He suspects the Vuilleumier family have their eye on the property and he doesn't want them to have it. They are peasants, he says. There was a fire at the Villa Cimbrone the previous December, and who can say how it started? We have in fact seen the black marks, like strange inky shadows, at the top of the house and been told that the top floor was gutted. Giorgio informed us that some of the Grimthorpe papers have been singed. But Gore is contemptuous. How can papers have been singed? Either they are burnt or not burnt. In fact Giorgio has brought us envelopes which are blackened and unopenable (our hands are also black by the end of that session).

Catherine is growing dejected by our slow and erratic progress at the villa, her nerves jangling during the intervals between one instalment and the next. She imagines Giorgio putting his arms into a chest of these family papers in the burnt-out attic and pulling out bits and pieces at random. If only we could look through the trunk ourselves. She longs for the day when she can walk from room to room searching drawers and cupboards. Is she not trusted because she is illegitimate? When she holds a letter in her hands that has a genuine connection with the Grimthorpes (some letters, for example, from Lucille's sons), I see that more than once there are tears in her eyes. After the first day or two, I do not think she really expects to come across evidence of her paternal origins. But if she can gather some original Grimthorpe letters and return them to the family, this will give her satisfaction. No one then will be able to deny that she is a genuine messenger, someone who has carried out a family task that has been entrusted to her. Between these sessions, at restaurants in Ravello, she sometimes introduces herself as Lord Grimthorpe's daughter who is staying at their old home, the Villa Cimbrone. I worry that waiters and maîtres d'hôtel might be embarrassed by this. But I am wrong again. They are delighted. They talk of the great benefit the Grimthorpe family has brought to Ravello and see that we have good tables, excellent service.

At our next meeting I suggest to Giorgio that if he were to make photocopies of all the Grimthorpe archive in his possession then one batch could be held at the Villa Cimbrone, the other in Yorkshire – and there would be less danger from fire. He replies (via Catherine's hectic translations) that he cannot take such a decision himself but must consult his mother to whom, he says, Lucille gave these papers. But when his mother comes in, he adds that it is a matter for the whole family and his two brothers must also be consulted. It strikes me as the Spenlow and Jorkins gambit, which Dickens uses to such effect in *David Copperfield* – the final authority always lies with someone who is absent. He finds this sudden interest in the family papers curious. Catherine explains that people often become more interested in the past as they grow older.

We are held in a force field between two different cultures. Giorgio's attachment to this archive is, in its way, as magical as Catherine's though less deeply imprinted. But the case for a photocopying comprom-ise is a powerful one, and we agree in principle that this should be pursued in due course. It may mean nothing, but we have played the long game as well as we can. Are there treasures here that will one day be discovered? I believe there are not. But there is a possibility that Lucille left Ernest Beckett's love letters to Eve Fairfax here. So I, like Catherine, leave with a sense of something unknown and unsatis-factory. As for Catherine, it has been in some ways a sad quest. She feels that the Villa Cimbrone is part of her. The fire takes on a symbolic meaning: Cimbrone's precious days, and all they stand for, have been consumed and are gone.

We go out on our last evening to an expensive restaurant in the Hotel Palumbo, both feeling very tired. We order a bottle of wine and Catherine asks me what the label says. I put on my glasses and examine it closely. It says 'Drink the lot!' I tell her – and we both break into idiotic laughter.

On our last day the Vuilleumier family give us a splendid lunch.

Four generations of them are seated round two tables in what on one side is a cellar-kitchen with a blue-and-white tiled stove, and on the other a dining room with the sunlight streaming on to the cliff face and through the windows. A woman I take to be Giorgio's grand-mother has surfaced from her lair — an ageless woman — along with his two brothers (who sometimes visit to make complaints, Giorgio's mother amiably tells us), and also his sisters and their children at the junior table. We are given a delicious meal of many courses: pasta, salad, local vegetables, fruit and cheese. Catherine is busy translating all over the place. She notes in her journal that I was 'in sparkling form', making everyone laugh, even those who understand almost nothing of what I am saying. She wonders whether I am happy to be leaving Cimbrone and ending our expedition. This is not so. I want us to leave on the jolliest of terms, presenting myself as a clown at the Grimthorpe Castle and demonstrating that we are not enemies. And indeed they behave very kindly, arranging for our baggage to be taken down to the car park and giving us lemons and (to Catherine's dismay) bottles of lemon liqueur.

I am anxious lest we miss the plane. Catherine has no such worries. She aims the car down the mountain and we surge along at terrible speed, taking at the last second all the correct roads. We get there finally with the last drop of petrol and in perfect time. Catherine makes a point of this, indicating that I needn't have been so anxious. I explain that it is only perfect timing because our plane has been delayed. She maintains that we would have caught it anyway — and she is probably right.

By the time we reach Gatwick and then Victoria we are both exhausted. We have become comrades, but Catherine observes that I keep my distance (most of her friends call her Katy but I still call her Catherine). Would she be surprised to know I see her as a female version of Don Quixote, while I, her cautious travelling companion, am the shrewd and credulous Sancho Panza? Our adventures have been full of hope: hope singed but somehow not extinguished.

It seems to me that Catherine becomes more herself the further she travels away from Yorkshire, where she is most at home. A postcard will suddenly arrive from her in Azerbaijan, Kiev, Chernobyl and several stopping places along the Silk Road. She joins an international group riding small horses through Mongolia where a gentleman from Singapore threatens to kill her. There are other occasional setbacks. 'I forgot to tell you that my car, which you liked, was written off,' she tells me. 'Fortunately no one, not even Romney, was hurt.'

Christopher Grimthorpe's wife Skip has advised her to forget the unsolved puzzles of the past and concentrate on her future. It is wise but perhaps impossible advice. The guilt and ambiguity of having two fathers are branded upon her and she cannot forget or ignore this. In recent years the quandary could have been settled by a DNA test. Why then has the Grimthorpe family, who are her friends, not encouraged this? I believe it is because any such simple solution at this stage in her life, far from solving the problem of her dual identity, might aggravate it. Caught between two fathers, she is in no-man's-land and has lost her natural confidence. She sees her past as being pitted with mistakes, though to my mind her adventurous life has been very far from a failure. But this view, like Skip's advice, Catherine finds hard to accept.

Illegitimacy is a word with several meanings. Ernest's wife Luie was to die in her twenties producing a legitimate heir to the Grimthorpe title. Eve Fairfax was illegitimate in the sense that, not marrying Ernest, she lost her legitimate place in society. Her Book is a unique testament to the enduring pride that kept her afloat. And then there is Ernest's extraordinary illegitimate daughter Violet who, exiled from England, was to compensate for her outcast state by claiming the King of England as her father. Such fantasies were a balm for the pain of lost love. But fact and fantasy are held in subtle equilibrium in the best of her novels, which may yet find a legitimate place in European literature for the name Violet Trefusis.

PART II

5

Excitements, Earthquakes and Elopements

It was a surprising invitation. Would I fly to Ravello in the summer of 2007 and give a lecture at the Villa Cimbrone, as part of a festival there? It was seven years since I had been there with Catherine.

Due to illness I had not been able to travel abroad for two years. But I was gradually recovering and, to escape the prison of ill health, regain some freedom and self-confidence, I said yes. I vividly remembered the Villa Cimbrone. It was like a castle reached, as in a fairy story, by two steep and wandering paths leading from the square at Ravello and finally opening on a dream garden that overlooked the Mediterranean far below.

The festival, lasting from June to September, was now 'in its sixteenth edition' and the 'keynote' in 2007 was to be 'La Passione'. I was curious as to my own place in this programme. It seemed to have its origins in a film-and music evening dedicated to Greta Garbo 'whose visit to Ravello in 1938 was the occasion of a famous liaison with the conductor Leopold Stokowski'. The word liaison, combined with the theme of La Passione, brought into the frame the Bloomsbury Group whose members, I was surprised to read, frequently visited Ravello. The programme promised 'films based on famous novels by

Woolf and Forster . . . and an exhibition in the Villa Cimbrone
featuring the writer Violet Trefusis, daughter of Alice Keppel and
possibly of Ernest Beckett, the second Lord Grimthorpe, who had
owned the Villa Cimbrone'.

The person responsible for this literary part of the festival,
'Bloomsbury in Ravello', was Tiziana Masucci, the Italian translator of
Violet Trefusis's novels. I could picture 'Professor Masucci' very clearly:
a stout and serious scholar – elderly and with a pince-nez perhaps,
somewhat bent, as if weighed down by the awful labour that fell on
her declining years of academic endeavour. My incredulity was heightened by some lines from Edward Fitzgerald's translation of *The Rubáiyát
of Omar Khayyám* that appeared in the Cimbrone brochure imagining
the moon rising over the garden while the author speculates on the
shortness of life. These lines had been attributed to D. H. Lawrence.
But did Lawrence actually stay at the Villa Cimbrone? Had Forster,
Strachey or Virginia Woolf ever gone there?

I began my research by looking through Virginia Woolf's
published letters and diaries. In the spring of 1927, travelling through
Rome, Palermo and Syracuse, she told her sister Vanessa Bell that
she was 'rapidly falling in love with Italy . . . Undoubtedly I shall
settle here – it surpasses all my expectations . . . if I had my way I
should live here for ever.' All her friends, she decided, should do so
now they were getting old – they could form 'a death colony' there.
But I could find no mention of Ravello. I was beginning to regret
having accepted this speaking engagement. But then Tiziana Masucci
invited my wife Margaret Drabble to come out to Ravello with me
and I felt grateful for this kindness. Maggie had endured an appalling
eighteen months or more spending long hours in the hospital
and looking after me between operations. These few days in Italy
would be an unexpected treat, a small thank you for all she had

done – and besides I would feel more secure with her there. So I continued my research.

I decided to turn my attention to an enemy of Bloomsbury, D. H. Lawrence – and found him at the Palazzo Cimbrone. In March 1926 he was walking through the Cimbrone gardens with his friend, the painter Dorothy Brett (with whom, over a couple of nights, he had unsuccessfully tried to have sex). The Palazzo Cimbrone itself he thought 'a bit too much of a good thing'. The hot sun and cold wind among the mountains unsettled him. It 'feels earthquaky', he told his friend Koteliansky.

A year later, while in Florence, he was asking the American expatriate painters Earl and Achsah Brewster who had leased Cimbrone from Ralph, the third Lord Grimthorpe and his sister Lucille, to invite him back there. Yet he was uneasy. 'Ld. Grimthorpe's house was so full of junk,' he wrote to Richard Aldington shortly after leaving, 'one felt one might turn into an antique (pseudo) along with it all.' He wished that Brett's sorrel horse had been there 'to kick over a few statues'. Cimbrone was crowded with fakes and misattributions as if some practical joker had been let loose to wander the grounds by night. The best fun Lawrence squeezed out of his time there was imagining an auction that he and the Brewsters might hold in the piazza below of all Grimthorpe's old junk – his furniture and pictures. How it would cleanse the place! Meanwhile he worked there on *Lady Chatterly's Lover*.

Lawrence was always on the move as if to escape from the darkness of his childhood, his intermittent sense of social inferiority, his anxieties over his wife Frieda, his terrible tubercular illness. It was only while walking all day among the mountains that these anxieties and aggressions lifted. With the healing power of nature he became an imaginative poet and travel writer.

I turned next to E. M. Forster. In the autumn of 1901, at the age of twenty-two, he set out for a year of travel through Italy. And his mother came too. By May 1902 they had arrived at Ravello and, as D. H. Lawrence was to do fourteen years later, they stayed at the Hotel Palumbo. It was in that month that Forster wrote 'The Story of a Panic'. Lily, Forster's mother, reported him as being 'very quiet'. But underneath his quiet exterior something was erupting in Forster's imagination. In the introduction to his *Collected Stories*, he remembered a walk he took near Ravello. 'I sat down in a valley, a few miles above the town, and suddenly the first chapter of the story rushed into my mind as if it had waited for me there. I received it as an entity and wrote it out as soon as I returned to the hotel. But it seemed unfinished and a few days later I added some more until it was three times as long.'

In Forster's story a party of respectable English tourists having a picnic in the chestnut woods near Ravello are suddenly overcome with foreboding and sent into a stampede of 'brutal, overmastering, physical fear' – all except one, a pale, moody, fourteen-year-old boy named Eustace who is afterwards found lying on his back, his hand convulsively entwined in the long grass and rolling in a goat's hoof marks, smiling and seeming so natural and undisturbed, yet unable to say what has happened. It becomes obvious that he has gone through some crucial change. He walks back 'with difficulty, almost in pain'. That evening he throws his arms round a young fisher-boy who is a part-time waiter at the pension, and later that night stands in the garden wearing only a nightshirt marvelling at the power and beauty of nature. Finally he escapes from his aunts and their friends, leaping with a strange inhuman cry, like an elfin creature, down the hillside until at the end of the story, 'far down the valley towards the sea, there still resounded the shouts and the laughter of the escaping boy'.

The story was one of sexual awakening, but in the nature of a dream: and Forster slept on. It had been, to use D. H. Lawrence's word, an earthquake deep in his unconscious, the reverberations of which only gradually reached the surface. 'The Story of a Panic' was a world away in time and language from *Lady Chatterley's Lover*. Lawrence's novel used anger and blatant sexuality to attack the inhibitions and restraints imposed by a rigid artificial class system. It was as if his internal problems, Lawrence's social and sexual unease, grew until they became the problems of England. Though they had a common enemy and similar targets, Forster seems tepid in comparison with Lawrence. What nerved him to begin writing fiction, freeing him somewhat from his inhibitions and enriching his work, was journeying out of England: to Italy and then India. Lytton Strachey was similarly fortified by his love of France. His connection with Italy, which grew gradually over his life, was less obvious. He had crossed the frontier between France and Italy, travelling from Menton to Ventimiglia, in the winter of 1901–2 and soon became aware of a strange sense of danger lurking behind the beauty of the Italian landscape – like a disturbing echo from the Roman past – and this excited him rather as Forster had been excited.

Early in 1913, Strachey set out on a miniature grand tour of Europe lasting some two months, armed with a camera and plenty of film to snap old buildings and young men. From Marseilles he sailed to Naples. 'I try to take snapshots,' he wrote, 'but my hands shake so with excitement that no doubt they're all failures.' He also made an excursion to Pompeii. 'It was an enchanting experience,' he wrote. 'The heat of an English July can you imagine it and the hills all round – and that incredible fossilisation of the past to wander in. What a life it must have been! Why didn't we live in those days? Oh, I longed to stay there for ever – in one of those little inner gardens, among the pillars and busts, with the fountain dropping in the court . . . Some wonderful slave boy would come out from under the shady rooms, and pick you

some irises, and then to drift off to the baths as the sun was setting —
and the night! What nights they must have been!'

Ravello was wonderfully peaceful after Naples. In the precipitous
mountains above Amalfi, with terraced gardens and wild flowers, the
sea smooth and inexhaustibly blue a thousand feet below, he felt he
was in heaven — or as near to it as you could reach on earth. Perhaps
he could reconstitute and even rejuvenate the Bloomsbury Group in
Ravello — Virginia and Leonard Woolf, Virginia's sister the painter Vanessa
Bell, her fellow painter and lover (and Lytton's lover too) Duncan Grant,
who seems to have loved almost everyone at one time or another,
including Maynard Keynes who must certainly come too, and of course
Forster. Finally he would like to invite his brother James — but not
Henry James, he thought, except perhaps for one weekend a year. 'Don't
you think it would do very well?' he asked Ottoline Morrell.

His fantasy of replanting Bloomsbury in Ravello and along the
Amalfi coast was not Virginia's Woolf's 'death colony' but a Utopian
dream in which no one grew old and everyone enjoyed erotic adventures. This influence of Italy may be seen in Strachey's last biography,
Elizabeth and Essex, which has a place in his work equivalent to that of
Orlando in the work of Virginia Woolf. *Orlando* was written shortly after
Virginia Woolf returned from her spring travels in Italy. It is a novel,
subtitled 'A Biography', which covers the sexual and social adventures
of a historical make-believe — a young sixteenth-century nobleman
who is transformed by the time the twentieth century arrives into a
modern woman writer. This biographical pastiche is dedicated to Vita
Sackville West whose son, Nigel Nicolson, was to describe it as 'the
longest and most charming love letter in literature'. The spur to writing
this novel — what Virginia Woolf called her 'overwhelming impulse' —
was to catch the essential fantasy that mingles with the facts of our
lives and follows us like shadows caricaturing our actions. The opening

Rodin's bronze portrait of Eve Fairfax, c.1909.

Eve in her late twenties and
late nineties; Edward Hughes's
portrait of Luie Beckett and
her daughters, c.1890; Ernest
Beckett at Cimbrone, c.1910.

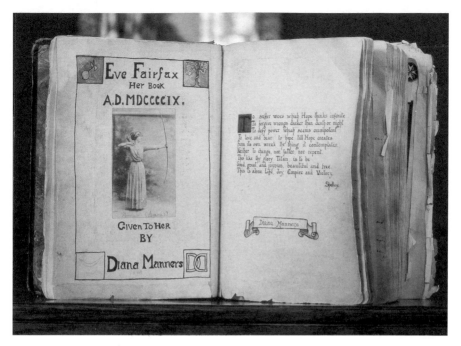

Eve's Book: the frontispiece and Ernest's entry from Swinburne's
'Dolores (Notre-Dame des Sept Douleurs)'.

For the Crown of our life as it closes
Is darkness, the fruit thereof dust;
No thorns go so deep as the roses'
And love is more cruel than lust—
Time turns the old days to derision
Our loves into corpses or wives;
And marriage & death & division
Make barren our lives — Swinburne
Grimthorpe 25 May 1915

The Villa Cimbrone ancient and modern: the pavilion from where I gave my talk
and the new swimming pool.

On Catherine Till's balcony at Cimbrone (April 2000)
and Tiziana Masucci in London (June 2008).

Violet Trefusis on 16 June 1919, her wedding day.

Harold Nicolson and Vita
Sackville-West on the jacket
for *Portrait of a Marriage* and Philippe
Jullian's jacket for *Pirates at Play*.

Poem written on a Monte Carlo hotel telegram form (1918–19):
first 24 lines by Vita, lines 25-55 by Violet, ending 'Tant pis pour moi!'

chapter of the novel is devoted to the overwhelming passion between Vita Sackville-West and Violet Trefusis – the two of them were together in the early summer of 1913 at the Villa Cimbrone.

Strachey had revitalised biography with *Eminent Victorians*. In *Elizabeth and Essex* he tried to transform the genre from a solid craft, built on a platform of factual research, into a poetic drama based on psychological instinct and conveyed in fast-moving narrative prose – rainbow and granite. In Pompeii he had imagined himself wandering in the past: 'What a life it must have been! Why didn't we live in those days?' Writing in the mid-to-late 1920s of Queen Elizabeth I's relationship at the end of the sixteenth century with the Earl of Essex, he saw a way of merging past and present, using human nature as his magic carpet and flying between an intense love affair of his own and that of his biographical subjects. His *Elizabeth and Essex* is an experiment with time – as *Orlando* is with time, gender and identity. Both are constructed round a love affair – Virginia Woolf's with Vita Sackville-West, and Lytton Strachey's with a young scholar 'with a melting smile and dark grey eyes' called Roger Senhouse. 'You seem, on the whole, to imagine yourself as Elizabeth,' Maynard Keynes wrote to him, 'but I see from the pictures that it is Essex whom you have got up as yourself.' Both assumptions are in a sense true: for Strachey tended to fall in love with people he wished to be and, in the act of love, for an illusory moment, he embraced that ideal. Virginia Woolf and others were bewildered by his passion for Roger Senhouse – as we often are by other people's loves. By the time *Elizabeth and Essex* was published Strachey was already ill – he would die some three years later. His love affair with Roger Senhouse was a love affair with youth, an imaginative way of casting off the years and regaining his own youth – a youth he had never experienced in fact until he possessed it in retrospective fantasy.

*

My illness had forced pessimism upon me like a heavy overcoat. To prepare for even a simple journey I found myself making numerous health-and-safety calculations in case cars or trains were late, and everything went awry. I have become ludicrously pragmatic. Otherwise I could be stranded without my travelling companions – the capsules, steroids, syrups and internal equipment I need for what are called 'procedures'. For a journey abroad I had to pack up my troubles rather bulkily, as if for weeks rather than days. But I was reassured by Maggie who has become my memory, my compass, my sense of balance. By the time we finally set out we were both feeling quite excited.

On the plane I showed Maggie some of the material I had collected on my previous journey to Ravello. She read that Vita Sackville-West, 'a friend of one of Beckett's daughters', participated in the planning of the garden. But Vita actually visited the Villa Cimbrone only once, I explained, and that was not to plan a garden but to advance her love affair with Grimthorpe's illegitimate daughter, Violet. It was as if the two girls belonged to the same family – almost as if, Violet conjectured, they were twins. But how could Vita pursue a love affair with Violet at the same time as planning a marriage to Harold Nicolson? Violet seemed to float in an illusory world of romantic ecstasy; Harold belonged to the solid world of facts. And Vita needed both fantasy and fact in her life. Violet Keppel (as she still was in 1913) had a little earlier 'kissed me as she usually does not, and told me that she loves me'. Vita recorded that Violet came to her room one night and 'stayed till I don't know when; she has not repented of our last farewell, and loves me even more'.

Vita sometimes doubted whether she could tolerate giving up her freedom for conventional wedlock. But after returning to England, she felt again the charm of Harold's boyishness, his intelligence, sense of fun and excellent manners. The peace-loving Harold represented her father's influence – and Vita was fond of her less dominant parent. She decided, if decision it was, that 'almost I want to marry this year and get it over'. And having made this almost-decision – like Macbeth's 'if it were done . . . then 'twere well / It were done quickly' – something snapped in Vita's mind and 'I loved Harold from that day'.

Yet Violet still possessed her heart.

Maggie had got this far in the story when our plane landed at Naples. Then we were on our way, skirting Vesuvius and ascending into the dark mountains. We were not staying at the Villa Cimbrone or the Hotel Palumbo, but at a hotel which looked over a ravine to the Piazza del Duomo at Ravello, still alive with children and crowded cafés. We unpacked, looked out of our windows at the fires that were burning higher up in the mountains after a long drought, and decided to wander outside and get something to eat. There were no messages from Tiziana Masucci or her second in command, Valerio Ruiz, whom I imagined to be an elderly civil servant with a heavy moustache. But it was almost eleven o'clock and perhaps they were both safely in their beds.

We went out and were walking through the piazza when there was a movement in the air and something happened – reminding me of those earthquakes D. H. Lawrence sensed. From nowhere two figures appeared in front of us. At first glance I mistook them for schoolchildren. But here were Tiziana Masucci and Valerio Ruiz. How they had discovered us in the middle of so many people I never knew. All I could see was their youth and happiness – not at all those of a retired professor or elderly civil servant I had led Maggie to expect.

Valerio immediately charmed us both – he was so exquisitely polite. Tiziana was a far more mystifying figure. Throughout supper she seldom took her eyes off me ('she adores you,' Maggie remarked later that night). Did she, I wondered, carry within her the spirit of Violet

Trefusis — that 'unexploded bomb' as Vita called her? She was eager for us to see an exhibition she had mounted, celebrating Violet, in the cloisters of the Villa Cimbrone. Dawn would not have been too early for her to take us there, but it had been a long day and we arranged to go there together at noon.

We surprise ourselves by meeting at the agreed time and begin walking up one of the paths to the Villa Cimbrone. It is a hot day and, in the sun, I trudged rather stolidly upwards and even Maggie, who is an agile walker, was moving less quickly than usual. But Tiziana flew ahead; back and forth she went like a miraculous bird, eager for us to reach our destination. And I suddenly found myself thinking of Eustace, the elfin boy in Forster's story, who careers ecstatically into the valley below. But Tiziana flew upwards as if gravity had little hold on her, as if her natural habitat was some high sphere of the imagination. We reach the entrance of the Villa Cimbrone, turn left into the cloisters: and there was her exhibition celebrating Violet Trefusis.

I knew then what I suppose the general reader probably knows of Violet. I had read Virginia Woolf's *Orlando* and remembered from the first chapter of her novel the extraordinary appearance (though not the full reverberating name) of Princess Marousha Stanilovska Dagmar Natasha Iliana Romanovitch, or 'Sasha' as Orlando calls her (echoing 'Lushka', the luscious name Vita Sackville-West used for Violet). *Orlando* was written partly in response to, partly guided by, two books: one by Vita Sackville-West and the other by her husband Harold Nicolson.

Vita's book was *Challenge*, a fictional account of her love affair with Violet who helped her in its composition between 1918 and 1919 — while the two of them were escaping from the conventional world on sexual and romantic adventures (Vita sometimes disguised as a man and transformed into 'Julian' from the novel, Violet evolving into the eternally feminine 'Eve'). At the insistence of Vita's mother Lady Sackville, who feared the scandal this novel would arouse, the British publication was delayed for over fifty years – until Vita and Violet were both dead, and after Vita's narrative of their lesbian relationship had been made available by her son Nigel Nicolson in his famous book, *Portrait of a Marriage*. But *Challenge* was published in the United States in 1924 and it was this edition that Virginia Woolf took up and read during the summer of 1927 by which time she and Vita had grown very close.

Vita's sexual ambivalence changed Virginia Woolf's awareness of her own sexual nature. But her literary imagination was caught the same month (June 1927) by Harold Nicolson's *Some People*. 'I can't make out how you combine the advantages of fact and fiction as you do,' she wrote to him. The day before, she had written to Vita about *Challenge*, politely calling Eve 'very desirable'. She wanted to write her own make-believe pen portrait of Violet Trefusis – with all the freedom of fiction since they had never met. 'I lie in bed making up stories about you,' she had told Vita. She was planning to write a life of her that would be 'all fantasy'. Later on she was to judge Lytton Strachey's *Elizabeth and Essex* a partial failure because it used personal experiences and fictional devices within his biography – and the craft of biography was too intractable to tolerate this. But Harold Nicolson, whom she rated a far less talented and original writer than Strachey, had (as she wrote in the *New York Herald Tribune*) 'devised a method of writing about people and about himself as though they were at once real and imaginary'. This merging of biography and autobiography into a series of semi-fictional stories showed her that she must introduce a sprinkling of historical facts into her fantasy, reinforce it with some granite. Fiction had the suppleness to absorb this and convey sexual ambivalence with subtlety. And she could produce a parody of historical biography, making fun of its inflexible limitations. 'I want to revolutionize biography in a night.'

Harold Nicolson's hybrid of a book became a useful compass for Virginia who saw Vita's novel as a warning against making fiction plod too steadfastly in the shadows of the author's real-life experience. Julian '*is* you', Violet had written to Vita, 'word for word, trait for trait'. As for 'Eve', had Vita not depended on 'much excellent copy' from Violet herself? The result of this self-indulgence was, in Lady Sackville's words, 'brilliantly dull'. As she read *Challenge*, Virginia became aware of a warning. 'I want dreadfully to see you . . . you have become essential to me,' Vita had written to Virginia early in 1927. But Vita was a serial lover, frequently overtaken by these essential sightings – and besides, Virginia was older and more sensitive as to how things might end. 'I have to take my little precautions,' she explained.

Their love affair was nothing like so physically committed as Vita's passionate involvement with Violet, but it gave Virginia as much sexual experience as her nature could accept and withstand. It was unique. In her review of *Some People* she wrote: 'By the end of the book we realise that the figure which has been most completely and most subtly displayed is that of the author.' In her magic mirror of Vita, *Orlando* also gives us a subtle reflection of the author behind her subject – revealing what attracts her and of what she must be cautious.

Many years later, when asked whether Vita had really loved Virginia, Violet replied: 'Not for a minute. Virginia ran after her, and she couldn't get rid of her. She found her so sentimental.' In fact it was Violet who ran after Vita – and Vita eventually got rid of her. Violet's statement was one of jealousy and denial. *Challenge* had been written with what Virginia was to call Vita's 'pen of brass' and, when eventually published in Britain during the 1970s, was eclipsed not only by *Portrait of a Marriage* but also by the enduring fascination of *Orlando*, Virginia's love gift to Vita, in which Violet appears as a phantom that soon vanishes.

Challenge had been dedicated to Violet – but she is not named. The dedication, citing her as an 'honoured witch' whose tormented soul would be changed and made free by reading these coded pages, was itself concealed in the Romany language. Recognising that *Orlando* would be a riposte to her novel, Vita asked Virginia to dedicate it to her. This she did, but omitted the hyphen in her name for the Hogarth Press edition of the book (and future editions in Britain) – perhaps an unconscious sign that a connection was missing.

The opening chapter in *Orlando* focuses on two love affairs. The first shows what danger an older woman risks by loving someone younger. In Sally Potter's film (1992), marvellously enhancing the merging of genders, Quentin Crisp is cast as the ageing Queen Elizabeth who, seeing the 'strength, grace, romance, folly, poetry, youth' of Orlando, 'kept him near her . . . For the old woman loved him.' This is the same theme, the coming together of age and youth, as Strachey had in mind while writing *Elizabeth and Essex*. One freezing day, Virginia Woolf tells us, the Queen catches sight of Orlando in a mirror kissing a girl. The illusion of repossessing youth through her own love of him is suddenly over and, stricken by the evidence of man's treachery, she destroys the mirror that has witnessed this devastating truth.

The girl whom Orlando will be kissing for the rest of this chapter is the ravishing Sasha. Though she will sail over the horizon and out of the story at the conclusion of its opening chapter, she evokes some of the most lyrical passages in the novel. During the Great Frost of 1608, time itself seems to stand still throughout the frozen landscape. Yet in this suspended world, Sasha and Orlando become wonderfully animated. As they skate to King James's coronation carnival, the shoals of fish held in an icy trance below them and above them coloured balloons hanging motionless in the sky, it is as if, 'hot with skating and with love', they alone are alive. Sasha is a creature of many similes.

'She was like a fox, or an olive tree; like the waves of the sea when you look down upon them from a height; like an emerald; like the sun on a green hill which is yet clouded . . .' She speaks in perfect French, which no one but Orlando understands. 'Yet perhaps it would have been better for him had he never learnt that tongue; never answered that voice; never followed the light of those eyes . . .' As Virginia Woolf writes this, perhaps she is wondering if it would have been better for her never to have learnt the language of love, never answered Vita's voice. Sasha's voice, so voluptuous and enchanting, conceals something. There are no facts in her life: she is all fantasy. 'What was her father? Had she brothers? . . . He [Orlando] suspected at first that her rank was not as high as she would like . . . What then did she hide from him?'

The end of their love comes as a performance of *Othello* is given on the ice. Orlando has seen Sasha on the knee of a Russian sailor and is torn with grief and disillusion – as Queen Elizabeth had been on seeing him kiss a young girl. Everything ends in sexual jealousy. 'The frenzy of the Moor seemed to him [Orlando] his own frenzy, and when the Moor suffocated the woman in her bed it was Sasha he killed with his own hands.' Then the rain poured down, the ice cracked and retreated, and the ship of the Muscovite Embassy, released from its frozen moorings, gaining its freedom, sailed over the horizon with the faithless Sasha on board.

How much truthfulness was encased in this fantasy? And would Tiziana's exhibition of Violet Trefusis's life and work at the Villa Cimbrone follow the implications of this story? The exhibition traced the connection between the three Vs – Violet, Vita and Virginia – in their lives and writings. Tiziana argued that whereas Virginia was a writer, tied to no specific time, whose novels might exist for all time, Vita belonged (even in her own time) to the past, and Violet was a

European writer who represented her own time. Partly for that reason, Violet's novels were more modern than Vita's. She emerges like a figure from the pages of Proust.

In her introduction to the exhibition catalogue, Tiziana describes Violet as 'a literary thunderbolt that led me to a long and careful study about the life and works of this writer'. Something that became clear to me, as the three of us left the cloisters and went down to have lunch together in Ravello, was that Tiziana's look of 'adoration' the previous evening had been a reflection of her love for Violet.

I was particularly interested to see in Tiziana's Cimbrone exhibition two photographs of Ernest Beckett, the second Lord Grimthorpe (Violet's father, Luie Tracy Lee's husband, Eve Fairfax's fiancé and Catherine Till's grandfather). In the first photograph, taken in England, we see him clothed in all his dull misleading respectability. He wears a dark suit with heavy imprisoning waistcoat, and carries, as tokens of his probity, a top hat and a walking stick. This is the allegedly reliable Yorkshire banker who harbours extravagant political ambitions. Years later, freed from his abortive career in Britain and looking younger, His Lordship is elegantly perched on a terrace of the Villa Cimbrone. He has blossomed into a rather dashing, bohemian figure with gleaming co-respondent's shoes and a rakishly tilted bow tie.

I was to deliver my talk on Lytton Strachey from a pavilion in the upper reaches of the garden at the Villa Cimbrone, the audience seated among the statues and flower beds before us. Only there was no audience. No one was surprised by this. Italian time is more elastic than English time and there was no urgency in the atmosphere. Above us passed occasional growling helicopters, like monstrous wasps, carrying bags of water to deposit gently on the unresponsive mountain fires. Meanwhile the audience wandered slowly in from all parts of the grounds. Half an hour after I was due to begin, I began.

They do things differently abroad – and so do we. I had never thought of delivering Lytton Strachey's words in a falsetto voice in Britain. But in Italy, who was there to stop me? The answer is that there was Maggie, seated next to a statue of a faun. I looked away, raised my voice and was on my way. Gabriella Rammarione, my translator, had the notion of compensating for this unexpected treble by lowering her voice to a special contralto when translating Strachey's words. And the audience responded, particularly to the more serious passages, with waves of laughter drowning out the periodical growl of the helicopters.

Both Lytton Strachey and Virginia Woolf had momentary dreams of relocating Bloomsbury in Italy. It was up to us, I said, to recreate memories of them here – and hope their spirits looked benignly down on us. I looked across at Maggie and saw her smiling. I had got away with it.

Next day Tiziana and the Italian film director Lina Wertmuller (who was about to celebrate her eighty-first birthday at Ravello) gave a performance dedicated to Violet Trefusis and based on her letters to Vita Sackville-West. It seemed to me that Forster and Lawrence, Strachey and Woolf were all investigating in their books new possibilities of human conduct – which Violet Trefusis also explored. I sat in the garden with Maggie and listened to the talk from the same pavilion I had occupied the previous day. The beauty of the place and their voices, like a serenade mingling old age and youth, were such that I was never bored by my lack of understanding. But Maggie did understand and afterwards told Tiziana how impressed she had been by her advocacy, which made Violet no longer seem merely 'the other woman' but someone of interest in her own right. Tiziana stretched out her arms and hugged her with delight.

6

Women in Love

That autumn, back in London, I set myself to read Violet Trefusis's novels and was struck by their quality. In the public mind these books had been almost wholly submerged by Violet's notorious love story with Vita Sackville-West. There seemed to me two ways of approaching Violet: through her fiction (and the fiction of other writers into which she had been absorbed): or through her autobiography and correspondence. These two routes of fact and fiction, like the two steep paths up to Cimbrone, intertwine and, meeting at the same destination, could be charted together.

Biographers often struggle to escape the prison of chronology before resigning themselves to opening with a birth. Violet Keppel was born in London on 6 June 1894. The most influential figure in her life appears to have been her mother Alice Keppel. In 1952, five years after her mother's death, Violet published a volume of memoirs, *Don't Look Round*, dedicated 'To the memory of my beloved mother'. As a child she had been wrapped in the resplendent warmth of her mother's love – 'luminous . . . like golden armour'. She embellishes this armour with many brilliant accessories: intelligence, humour, courage, style. Above all, her mother 'excelled in making others happy'. Violet omits her greatest achievement, which lay in making the Prince of Wales, King Edward VII, happy. Alice Keppel was a woman of almost obscene discretion; and Violet tailors her book of 'selected moments, hand-picked' to match this discretion. It is deceptively well camouflaged.

Her parents competed in telling Violet stories when she was a child. Her mother's stories were 'a startling mixture of fantasy and realism'; her father's 'intrepid, if orthodox'. *Don't Look Round* is, like her mother's stories, a blend of make-believe and vitality, shaped like fiction, with plenty of dialogue and revelatory omissions.

Alice Keppel was the dominating character in the marriage, its life force. Violet is careful to grant her father some modest abilities: he is kind-hearted, easily pleased, methodical, tidy – a large man of little consequence with a finely waxed moustache and an eye for classical works of art. Nowhere does Violet suggest that he might not have been her biological father. Her mother's lover, Ernest Beckett, finds no place in her book.

Another area of telling reticence is her pen portrait of Vita Sackville-West. *Don't Look Round* was published over twenty years before the love affair between Violet and Vita became known to the public. Vita, with her 'deep stagnant gaze', is depicted as being a somewhat gauche and perpendicular figure. Both girls dream of romantic heroes from the upper echelons of history and literature. And they have one other property in common: powerful mothers.

In her novel *The Edwardians* Vita was to describe Violet's mother, Alice Keppel, as 'a woman who erred and aspired with a certain magnificence. She brought to everything the quality of the superlative. When she was worldly, it was on a grand scale. When she was mercenary, she challenged the richest fortunes. When she loved, it was in the highest quarters. When she admitted ambition, it was for the highest power.' Under the name Romola Cheyne, she is presented as a figure out of grand opera: not the virtuous heroine but an amoral schemer.

It is when describing Vita's mother, the oppressive Lady Sackville, that Violet looks round momentarily and abandons her caution.

> She was as intermittent, yet omnipresent, as the Cheshire Cat. Her daughter, who admired and distrusted her, was, up to a point, the Cheshire Cat's plaything . . . In her too fleshy face, classical features sought to escape from the encroaching fat. An admirable mouth, of a pure and cruel design, held good . . . Her voluminous, ambiguous body was upholstered, rather than dressed, in what appeared to be an assortment of patterns, lace, brocades, velvet, taffetas. Shopping lists were pinned to her bosom. She kept up a flow of flattering, sprightly conversation, not unlike the patter of a conjuror, intent on keeping your mind off the trick he is about to perform.

Lady Sackville was a formidable woman and a noted beauty in her day. She had also sat to Rodin, after meeting him at the dinner party given by Ernest Beckett in 1905, around the time Rodin was embarking on his bust of Eve Fairfax. Despite a number of invitations over the next few years, Rodin was not to visit Lady Sackville at Knole until 1913, when the place so impressed him that, according to her grandson Nigel Nicolson, he 'had fallen in love with Lady Sackville'. Lady Sackville's biographer, Susan Mary Alsop, suggests it was her 'vanity and innocence' that 'led her to believe' he loved her; while Rodin's biographer, Ruth Butler, maintains that he 'allowed himself to be drawn into a friendship with one of the most world-weary women alive'.

Victoria Sackville was then in her early fifties and Rodin approaching his mid-seventies. Their negotiations, to and fro, over the next eighteen months had the exaggerated gestures of a ballet. After his visit to Knole, Rodin suggested that he make a portrait bust of Lady Sackville's daughter Vita. But Victoria Sackville was adamant. She enjoyed having portraits made of her and had in the past commissioned them from John Singer Sargent, Charles Carolus-Duran and others. She looked forward to being 'done' with a boa round her neck, she informed Rodin, since 'at my age being almost a grandmother, one loses a bit of line in the neck'. What she hoped for was the repossession of those handsome classical features that were becoming engulfed in the fleshy casing of middle age. But perhaps it was already too late. She had been spectacularly beautiful when young but, as Violet observed, her famous 'classical features' were now swelling voluminously into an inflated balloon-like shape. Feeling curiously lonely since Vita's marriage to Harold Nicolson (though hopeful it would put an end to her daughter's scandalous relationship with Lord Grimthorpe's daughter Violet Keppel), she sought to shed her world-weariness and enjoy an adventure or two abroad.

Making a daughterly reconnaissance of Rodin's 'nice messy atelier' in Paris at the beginning of 1913, Vita was impressed by the empty room into which she was shown. 'It was rather dark and there were huge roughly-hewn lumps of marble and a chisel left on a chair where he had put it down, and nothing else,' she wrote to Harold, 'and the suggestiveness of it grew on me more and more as I waited.' But when Rodin entered, she saw only 'a rather commonplace French bourgeois . . . rather an unreal little fat man . . . and the whole thing was a reaction and a come-down from the massive white marbles all round'. Then he began talking of his work, caressing the marble, pointing out the lines with a sweep of his thumb: the commonplace old man vanished and there stood a genius.

It was on this genius that Lady Sackville focused her mind as she sat for him that autumn. Over a fortnight during November 1913, she filled her journal with details of these sittings. 'He wears a long cape and a big velvet Tam O'Shanter all the time, and never stops talking,' she wrote.

> . . . I was fully décolletée, and felt quite shy over it! . . . He deplores the fact that I can't always look after him, as I understand him well. He keeps saying I am so beautiful, and yet the bust is perfectly hideous up to now . . . He asked me to chuck everything this winter as he wanted me to come to the Riviera where the vile weather is driving him . . . he would do me all the winter and draw me doing my long hair, which he had heard was wonderful, and he had never had a model with long hair . . . Rodin made me sit on the floor while he was standing on a packing-case doing the top of my hair . . . He is such a dear old creature, so simple, so detached from everything.

Victoria Sackville was a hard-headed woman, yet she was open to flattery and had warned Rodin before the sittings began that she needed his indulgence. So he indulged her and she copied down his compliments: he 'got up and came to me with his hands full of *terre glaise* and knelt in front of me . . . it was very touching'. So the sittings went on, her Ladyship in the nude and the elderly sculptor kneeling before her.

She allowed herself to be taken to his home in Meudon where she met his companion of fifty years, Rose Beuret. The frugality of their life shocked her. 'They generally have some soup and a glass of milk,' she noted. '. . . curious agglomeration of grandeur and of great discomfort.' Rose was 'very much nicer to me than she generally is to other visitors'. As for Rodin, though he never spoke to Rose (and seldom stopped speaking to Lady Sackville), 'he is kindness itself and so gentle.'

Victoria Sackville's reanimated feelings shine through her letters from England. Before the end of February 1914 she joined Rodin and Rose Beuret in a villa they had rented near Roquebrune – 'very dark and tiny'. The bust of her was by now 'a horrible disappointment'. She gave him some money – far less than he usually charged – and Rose was furious 'for some reason or other'. In the hope that he could make it less thick-lipped and unflattering, she agreed to go with him to Cap Ferrat. 'He is utterly miserable,' she noted in her journal. '. . . I had to be very considerate . . . Mme Rose got on my nerves exceedingly.' She was intolerably lower class and did nothing but grumble.

The adventure was almost over. She sailed away for three months in Italy, saw other men, began new adventures. On her way back to England that summer, shortly before the First World War, she stopped in Paris and saw Rodin who complained that life with Rose was now unbearable (he was to marry her in 1917 shortly before his death). 'I was so sorry for him that I forgot to speak about my bust.'

Both Violet and Vita admired yet came to resent their extraordinary mothers. Violet adored what she called 'the unparalleled romance' of Alice Keppel's life as 'La Favorita', the King's mistress. 'I wonder whether I shall ever squeeze as much romance into my life as she has had in hers: anyhow I mean to have a jolly good try!' But in her early years she did not feel that she and her younger sister Sonia were 'as lovable, or as good looking, or as successful as our mother. We do not equal, still less surpass her.' And Sonia, who was much closer to her father, agreed that from earliest childhood their mother stood on a pedestal and was invested 'with a brilliant, goddess-like quality'.

Vita, too, felt she would have 'murdered anyone that breathed a word' against Lady Sackville. 'I would have suffered any injustice at her hands.' And injustice, she came to feel, was what she did suffer.

The old lady was one of the few aristocrats who had refused the Prince of Wales's wish to be accompanied by Mrs Keppel when he came for the weekend to Knole, the Sackville family's three-hundred-and-sixty-five-room ancestral home. Like Queens on a chessboard, both mothers were to exercise much power over the desperate love game their daughters were destined to play.

The game began when they were children. Both of them recorded their early meetings. 'I was twelve, she was two years younger,' Vita remembered, 'but in every instinct she might have been six years my senior . . .'

We met at a tea-party by the bedside of a mutual friend with a broken leg, and she [Violet] made to me some remark about flowers in the room. I wasn't listening; and so didn't answer. This piqued her – she was already spoilt. She got her mother to ask mine to send me to tea. I went. We sat in a darkened room, and talked – about our ancestors, of all strange topics – and in the hall as I left she kissed me. I made up a little song that evening, 'I've got a friend,' . . . I sang it in my bath.

Vita was 'the worst person in the world at making friends'. But now she had one   for life it felt.

In Violet's account there is no counter-attraction of a mutual friend with a broken leg. She omits the darkened room and the kiss in her well-behaved memoirs. The two girls are painfully isolated children, lost in their tediously grand surroundings. Violet notices that Vita seems overwhelmed by the presence of Lady Sackville. 'She was tall for her age,' Violet writes, 'gawky, most unsuitably dressed in what appeared to be her mother's old clothes . . .'.

I asked if I might have her to tea. She came . . . I thought her
nice, but rather childish (I was ten). We separated, however, with
mutual esteem. The repressions of my short life immediately
found an outlet in a voluminous correspondence . . . Our friendship pro-gressed all that winter.

Violet had noticed her 'family's gratification' on seeing her friendship with Lady Sackville's daughter; and when she went to stay at
Knole she understood the reason for their gratification. With its towers
and battlements, its long gallery, its multitude of staircases, its chapel
and courtyards and spacious parks, the Sackville family home was
infinitely more majestic than anything to which the Keppels could
aspire. Violet saw at once how much Vita loved this splendid house
and wanted her to feel that they were both in its loving embrace.
'How I adore that place!' she later wrote to Vita almost in Orlando
fashion. 'Had you been a man, I should most certainly have married
you, as I think I am the only person who loves Knole as much as you
do! – (I do really) . . .'

Over the first half-dozen years of their friendship, Violet and Vita
saw each other fairly regularly in London and Paris, Scotland and Italy.
'Went to tea with Violet, and stayed to dinner,' Vita wrote in her diary
in December 1908. 'The King was there.' The King was an anonymous,
often invisible presence at the Keppels' house in Portman Square, the
empty one-horse brougham waiting patiently outside, the butler
whispering 'a gentleman is coming downstairs' as he steered Vita into
a dark corner. All of which 'added a touch of romance to Violet', Vita
remembered.

Violet continued to visit Knole and Vita came up to stay with Violet
at Duntreath Castle, the ancestral home in Stirlingshire where Alice
Keppel had been born. This was a medieval toy castle, set in a lunar

Scottish landscape with flaming sunsets seen against the hills and peacocks wandering through the grounds. Its exotic atmosphere, heightened with smells of cedar wood and gunpowder, stimulated the girls' imaginations. Vita remembered how they dressed up, how Violet chased her with a dagger down a long passage, how they spent the whole night together talking, talking, 'while little owls hooted outside'; and Violet remembered how, racing up and down the staircases, going from room to room, they 'fled from terror to enchantment'. Duntreath was for her almost what Knole was for Vita.

Both Violet and Vita felt houses to be living entities. But their feelings for Duntreath and Knole were not quite the same. Vita loved Knole all her life, wherever she lived, whomsoever she loved. She had great need of love, an urgent sexual appetite, and she spread her affaires around promiscuously. Her love for Violet was unique: no one else would occupy that special place in her heart; yet she could still take on other lovers who meant less or meant something different. Violet, on the other hand, saw Vita as the single supreme love in her life, someone who outshone even her mother. She could flirt and play and appear to be happy with others, but in fact she was never happy without Vita. To tell their story from Violet's point of view it is necessary to eliminate everyone else except for those who impeded their love and were their enemies — just as she had eliminated her sister Sonia, who was born when she was aged six and immediately seen as a rival for their mother's love. 'I did not fancy her,' Violet remembered. '. . . I did not speak to her until she was ten.' (And Sonia corroborated this: writing that her sister, 'for the first ten years of my life, viewed me with an expression of unmitigated dislike'.) Ten years later Violet would express a similar dislike for anyone she saw as a rival for Vita's love. 'I am primitive in my joy as in my suffering,' she told her. '. . . We are absolutely essential to one another, at least in my eyes!'

But until Vita became her lover 'the lady Violetta amused herself madly at the expense of others. Which is perhaps not altogether a good thing.' It was not a good thing for the many men who, over the years, became entrapped by her seductive games. Gerald Wellesley, later the seventh Duke of Wellington, found himself rather tremendously in love and 'half-engaged' to be married to her; and Sir Osbert Sitwell's engagement was broken off, she told friends, only by his insistence that, once married, they would be obliged to sleep at opposite ends of his gigantic medieval mansion, separated by many haunted rooms and state apartments (an arrangement that should have suited them both equally well). Then Gerald Tyrwhitt-Wilson, the fourteenth Baron Berners, after lunching with Violet in Paris one day, read in the newspapers that he was shortly to marry her. (In retaliation he contemplated printing an announcement that he had 'left Lesbos for the Isle of Man'.) And, among others, there was the handsome poet and athlete Julian Grenfell with whom she was embarrassingly discovered in a cupboard . . . Such escapades would end, she implied, once Vita was permanently with her.

Meanwhile Vita had been the object of several odious proposals of marriage. 'Men didn't attract me,' she wrote. '. . . Women did.' And the woman who first attracted her was not Violet, but Rosamund Grosvenor who had been at the same school in London as them both. Vita sought from her love affairs with women what she had failed to find in her relationship with her mother. 'Mother used to hurt my feelings and say she couldn't bear to look at me because I was so ugly,' she wrote in *Portrait of a Marriage*. '. . . She loved me when I was a baby, but I don't think she cared much for me as a child, nor do I blame her.' Vita saw herself as 'plain, lean, dark, unsociable, unattractive – horribly unattractive! – rough and secret'. And in secret she set about 'writing, always writing', trying to create something beautiful her mother and the world would admire. In Rosamund Grosvenor she met someone of polished and curvaceous beauty, someone who passionately cared for her and whose presence soothed the injuries Lady Sackville had inflicted on her. 'I was very much in love with Rosamund,' she wrote. But though she worshipped Rosamund's beauty, as a companion 'she always bored me . . . she had a sweet nature. But she was quite stupid.' They went to bed, hugged and kissed, 'but we never made love'. Making love was something Vita would learn from Violet. With Rosamund, whom she called 'the Rubens lady', she was so excitingly close to beauty she almost possessed it. But with Violet, who admired her resplendent heavy-lidded looks, her tall strong figure, her peach-like complexion, she felt miraculously beautiful herself. And whereas Rosamund wasn't interested in books, Violet established herself as a literary muse. She appeared to answer all Vita's needs.

And Violet challenged her too. She seemed to have no sense of fear, no apprehension of danger. 'Follow me. Follow me!' she urged. But to follow her meant rejecting everything Vita's mother planned for her. Surely it was better to have everything and reject nothing.

But then what a combative, compelling style Violet had acquired! 'I love you, Vita, because I've fought so hard to win you,' she wrote. '. . . I love you because you never capitulate . . . I love you because you have the air of doubting nothing! I love in you what is also in me . . .' There was no tyrannising over such a woman. They were, in their fashion, equals.

The development of their relationship was delayed by two awkward historical events: the death of the King in 1910 and the outbreak of the Great War in 1914. 'How people can do anything I do not know,' Alice Keppel wrote to her friend Lady Knollys after King Edward VII's death on 6 May 1910, 'for life with all its joys has come to a full stop, at least for me.' In the words of the historian Giles St Aubyn, she had been 'the most perfect mistress in the history of royal fidelity' and now, as the 'unofficial widow', she continued to act with perfect deportment. The King's financial adviser Sir Ernest Cassel (nicknamed Windsor Cassel) had made her a very rich woman and she was able to move her family into an immense eighteenth-century mansion at 16 Grosvenor Street where the atmosphere of luxury suited what Osbert Sitwell called her 'instinct for splendour' – as it suited Violet's too (though not Sonia's). But Alice Keppel's life had suddenly changed. Diana Souhami writes in her dual biography of Alice and Violet: 'Without a role she [Alice] could not publicly parade her grief or continue as part of Palace life. She was cold-shouldered by Bertie's son and rebuffed when she went to sign her name in the visitors' book at Marlborough House.' She had become an embarrassment to the royal family and decided to go abroad for a year or two. She announced this to the children like a character in one of Violet's novels: 'I have news for you, children. I am taking you to Ceylon for the winter. In my opinion no young lady's education is complete without a smattering of Tamil . . . The boat leaves in four days, so you will just have time for your packing.'

Without Vita, Ceylon was in Violet's words 'a completely irrelevant interlude'. And it was full of anxious premonitions. In 1909 Vita had 'come out' and, though still in her 'teens, she was officially on the marriage market. Suddenly realising the significance of Vita being two years older than she was, 'I ought to have foreseen that perhaps at your age [nineteen] a masculine liaison would have come about,' Violet wrote desperately on 12 December 1910 from Ceylon. '. . . I feel that I am about to say improper things . . . Do try not to get married before I return.' She was acutely aware of the difficulty in luring Vita on to what she called 'territory almost totally unknown'. She felt anxious over Harold Nicolson with whom Vita had started what she called a 'rather childlike companionship'. He was such fun: rather shy, a charming smile, sympathetic and exuberant: the perfect playmate. Violet scented danger.

Early in 1911 Violet and Sonia were 'dumped down, like Babes in the Wood, in an exclusively German forest' near Munich to complete their education while their mother hurried off to China. Meanwhile Vita seemed to be sleepwalking into marriage. What could Violet do? Vita was no longer looking into Violet's eloquent eyes, listening to that seductively clandestine voice of hers or feeling her red lips pressed so disturbingly against her own: there were only Violet's letters to enchant her – and they were not enough. In 1912 Violet returned to England. The time was filled by her own debutante dinner parties and a grand coming-out ball at Grosvenor House. It was not a process she appeared to be enjoying. She needed to see Vita all the more emphatically because the only other woman with whom she had felt an intense happiness, her mother, was manoeuvring her towards marriage, preparing to distance herself and lead a separate life. Violet could not bear the prospect of being alone.

For Vita this passage of time apart from Violet was a mere interval in the inevitable drama between them. However baffling and elusive Violet might be, Vita felt confident of repossessing this brilliant, unearthly creature whenever the opportunity arose. 'What that bond is God alone knows; sometimes I feel it is as something legendary,' she later wrote. 'Violet is mine, she always has been, it is inescapable.' She had no 'fear of losing her, proud and mettlesome as she was'. As for Violet, Vita added, 'she knew it too.' But they knew different things. Violet knew that following their love to its ultimate end meant having to renounce all other commitments – including friends, family and a privileged place in society. Vita saw no reason why their choice should be so absolute. Surely it was possible to enjoy a homosexual and hetero-sexual relationship in tandem — had she not in fact done so, up to a point, with Rosamund and Harold?

The year 1913 began brilliantly and ended disastrously for Violet. 'Violet Keppel and I gave a party,' Vita told Harold in late February. 'It was the success of the year . . . Violet and I acted afterwards, and ended up in each other's arms.' But Vita disguised from Harold her sense of proprietorship over Violet; nor did she tell Violet of her deepening sense of attachment for Harold. Forty years later, in *Don't Look Round*, Violet was to write of this time: 'She [Vita] married without letting me know. I had heard rumours of her engagement, but as long as she did not tell me herself, I attached small importance to them. I was stunned by what I took to be a piece of perfidy I did not deserve.'

During the early years of the war they saw little of each other. Vita and Harold bought Long Barn, not far from Knole ('too self-consciously picturesque,' Violet decided, '. . . like living under the furniture instead of above it') and a house at Ebury Street in London (which struck Violet as depressingly middle-class and suburban). Between 1914 and 1917 Vita gave birth to two sons, Ben and Nigel Nicolson (another child was stillborn). The stormy side of her life, she felt, was over. 'I saw Violet from time to time, but she was more alien from me than she had ever been.'

Harold was not an effeminate man but he had a strong feminine strain in his nature, which made him all the more attractive to Vita. But working in the Foreign Office he was increasingly engulfed by a masculine world that was of no interest to her and that Violet posi-tively despised. And then another difficulty arose: after a casual homo-sexual affair in 1917 he caught a venereal infection and was advised against any sexual intercourse until after 20 April 1918. Violet was keeping watch on what she called Vita's 'radiant domesticity'. That spring Harold was away in London where the Zeppelin raids were taking place, working day and night at the Foreign Office during a crucial stage of the war. It was as if he had left a door temptingly open at Long Barn – and Violet walked in.

She invited herself to stay for a fortnight early in April 1918. The first week passed unsatisfactorily, Vita absorbed in her writing, Violet terribly restless. Then, on 18 April (two days before Harold's period of venereal infection ended), Vita put on some new clothes that the land girls were wearing and 'I ran, I shouted, I jumped, I climbed . . . and Violet followed me across the fields and woods with a new meekness . . . never taking her eyes off me, and . . . I knew that all my old dominion over her had never been diminished . . . It was one of the most vibrant days of my life.' That night, while Harold was working in London, the two women talked long and intimately, then went to bed and made love. For Vita it was a sense of extraordinary liberation.

Violet wrote of her not long afterwards: 'I revel in your beauty, your beauty of form and feature . . . I exult in my surrender . . . I love belonging to you – I glory in it, that you alone . . . have bent me to your will, shattered my self-possession, robbed me of my mystery, made me yours, *yours* . . . I exult in the knowledge of how little we have in common with the world.'

At this crucial moment of my research (where Violet and Vita were transformed into Mitya and Lushka), Tiziana Masucci (or Tizy as she had now become in her playful emails to me) arrived from Rome to pursue her research in London.

I ask her how she had first become interested in Violet. She had been given *Portrait of a Marriage* and read it 'when I was feeling very sad', she tells me. The book had fallen from the shelf while she was reorganising her library and on its open page was a picture of Violet.

Those basilisk eyes gazed up at her — and she began to turn the pages. After that she got all Violet's books, shut herself away with them and, when she emerged, started to reorganise her life around them. Violet had made another conquest. But whether *Portrait of a Marriage* had been a gift from the gods or a poisoned chalice who could tell? I ask her what the extraordinary appeal was — and she gives a great gesture of bewilderment. 'Violet is me!' she exclaims; and then, 'I love Violet!' Other people, living people, let you down. Violet is a shield against betrayal.

In a legal-literary sense Tiziana has become Violet. She has bought Violet's posthumous copyrights, lasting another thirty-five years (until 2042), and is full of plans and projects: plans to translate more of Violet's books into Italian, plans to complete a stage play she is writing about Vita and Violet, also to make a film and then (why not?) a musical! She laughs as she says this. And of course she must prepare an edition of Violet's letters, curate a large exhibition and also write her biography. This is a lifetime's commitment. How old will she be when the copyright runs out? It does not bear thinking of — she dreads old age as Violet herself did. Sometimes she looks nineteen, sometimes thirty-five (her actual age). Sonia Keppel wrote that her sister Violet was born old and never became young during her childhood or adolescence. But after her affaire with Vita she began to grow younger and many people who met her in her twenties and thirties remarked on how childlike she was (Harold Nicolson, seeing her in Paris after the Second World War, observed that she looked seventeen). She seemed to defy the laws of age, to ricochet from girl to matron each day — and back again overnight. Then 'nearing forty, she suddenly aged', her friend and biographer Philippe Jullian wrote. It was as if a tragic muse had darkened the romantic spell that enveloped her. I notice something a little similar perhaps in Tiziana. She is part of a film and theatre world in Rome, and meets many people, but 'I don't belong to them', she says. Under her high spirits there is a melancholy. She belongs to a dead woman whom she is bringing back to life. No wonder, in a crowded life, she is solitary. But because I have recently been reading books by and about Violet, we can have vicariously intimate conversations, full of concealed quotations, private jokes and allusions we both recognise. 'I've got a friend,' she exclaims, echoing what Vita wrote after first meeting Violet. But, she adds: 'I'm faithful, Vita wasn't.' It is as if she, and not Vita, is Violet's 'twin spirit'.

It is this strange atmosphere, in which Violet momentarily seems to come alive again, that Tiziana values even more than practical discussions as to how she might advance her crusade in Britain. But we do speak about registering her copyright, acquiring an agent in England and finding out if there are at the BBC Written Archives Centre any copies of some broadcasts Violet made from London to France during the war. Tiziana longs to hear her voice. She already has, on her mobile telephone, a recording of Vita's voice reading an excised passage from *Orlando* – and also Virginia Woolf's voice, both from the British Library.

We are invited to supper by Carmen Callil who, while chairing Virago Press, was one of the few British publishers to take an interest in Violet's writing, bringing out her novel *Hunt the Slipper* in 1983 as a Virago Modern Classic, with an introduction by Lorna Sage. She tells us she had hoped to add several other titles to the Virago list (*Pirates at Play* was added thirteen years later) but there were copyright difficulties – and she welcomes Tiziana's acquisition of Violet's copyright. Over supper we talk about Violet's talent and reputation. Carmen says she is tired of the Violet–Vita affaire and more interested in Violet's writing. Tiziana agrees. I take a somewhat different line. Violet's novels would not have been the disturbing light-and-dark comedies of manners they are, I argue, had she not lived in the shadow of grief amid all the bright lights of European society after her love affair ended. Tiziana then speaks out against Vita and the Nicolson family – those whom she blames for having caused that grief. Vita, she says, was a coward. She had threatened to scandalise well-dressed conventional London, but then put her dubious literary reputation, her gardening and the family (to which she was so regularly and in such a trivial manner unfaithful) before a unique and profound relationship. As for Harold Nicolson, Tiziana dislikes him for having written in 1918 that he wished Violet were dead. But if she denigrates Vita and Harold and reduces their worth, I reply, she will be left with a very one-sided drama; and besides, if Vita was so worthless does this not reflect badly on Violet for having singled her out as the love of her life?

Maggie disagrees with this. If we are to be judged by the people we have loved during our lives, none of us would come out so well. It is not a valid way of appraising anyone. Each of us, I feel, agrees with the other's opinions without quite renouncing our own. Tiziana reminds us that Violet wrote to Vita saying that they were like two people who had been caught stealing, and that one was put in prison and the other was not. The time has come, she declares, for Violet to be liberated. This sounds melodramatic, but it may be true that Violet has been immured in other people's books – Vita's and Virginia's, Nigel Nicolson's, Cyril Connolly's, Nancy Mitford's and Harold Acton's books.[6] Violet's own novels are scattered over Europe like a leaderless and dispersed army. They are written in French or English as if she is vainly trying one key, then another, to set herself free. Can Tiziana free her? Can she give what Lorna Sage called Violet's 'sardonically lightweight, accomplished and comic' novels a secure place in literature? She has extraordinary determination. But the thought comes to

[6] See A History of the Books, pp. 233–241.

me that, while seeking to liberate Violet, she might be imprisoning herself.

During these days, which are given over to the Tiziana–Violet phenomenon, you would not guess that Maggie is a novelist. She never mentions herself or her books – and she has taken care to read one or two of Violet's novels beforehand and likes them. When we do talk of other things, Tiziana sometimes falls silent as if the world beyond Violet is a desert.[7] Of course, English is not her first language. She is at the beginning of a quest to recover someone who is uniquely precious to her. After she has left for Rome, handing us both a heartfelt letter of thanks, I go up to her empty room. It is all precisely as it was before she arrived, so neat and tidy, almost untouched, as if no one has been there.

'It is a tremendous story,' Victoria Glendinning wrote of the Violet and Vita romance. But it 'needed a new slant on old material'. Mostly it had been told from Vita's point of view, and I wondered whether I could get a new slant by illustrating the effect it had on Violet's writings. 'We love only once, for once only are we perfectly equipped for loving . . . And on how that first great love-affair shapes itself depends the pattern of our lives.' Violet marked this passage from Cyril Connolly's *The Unquiet Grave* in red crayon. Her novels were the negotiations she made between this love and the rest of her life.

In the opinion of Harold Nicolson's biographer, James Lees-Milne, Violet's letters to Vita are 'stupendous'. Most love letters bored him, 'but not Violet's', he conceded. 'For sheer ruthless, persistent passion I have never come upon their equal.' In his diaries he admits that he did not really like Violet. But there is a grudging note of admiration when, in a review, he likens her correspondence to 'those flaming

---

[7] But in 2009 Maggie's novel *The Red Queen* was published in Italy, translated by Tiziana.

yellow bulldozers which one meets tearing up road verges, hedgerows, concrete walls, asphalt roads and any and every obstacle that lies in their path . . .' And for Vita's biographer, Victoria Glendinning, she is troubled by 'the flamboyant and brilliant' figure of Violet and can't help feeling pain on seeing her handwriting, which reminds her of the unhappiness she inflicted. Nevertheless, in the *Times Literary Supplement*, she acknowledges that Violet's 'letters to Vita, even as a young girl, are fluent, fanciful, multilingual, inspired. Vita's, in comparison, are dull.'

'For sixteen nights I have listened expectantly for the opening of my door, for the whispered "Lushka" as you entered my room, and tonight I am alone. What shall I do? How can I sleep?' Violet wrote in the summer of 1918. '. . . I don't want to sleep, for fear of waking up, thinking you near my side, and stretching out my arms to clasp – emptiness! . . . we must once and for all take our courage in both hands, and go away together.'

At the end of April 1918, the two of them had left Long Barn and gone to stay at the novelist Hugh Walpole's house at Polperro, in Cornwall, for ten days. 'They have a sudden desire', Harold obligingly explained to Walpole, 'to see the sea.' Here Vita began writing her novel *Challenge* (which Harold later nicknamed 'Smuts'). They went again to Polperro for three weeks in July. 'I hadn't dreamt of such an art of love,' Vita wrote in *Portrait of a Marriage*. It was seductive and sinister. Violet 'let herself go entirely limp and passive in my arms', Vita remembered. '(I shudder to think of the experience that lay behind her abandonment.)'

They also saw each other in London that summer and began a bold transvestite experiment, Vita dressing as a rather untidy young man called Julian and staying the night at a lodging house as Violet's (or 'Eve's') husband. 'I felt like a person translated, or re-born,' she wrote. It was fun, it was exciting, and it all seemed extraordinarily natural. Their escapade acted as a spur to Vita's novel and a rehearsal for their adventures abroad. But it meant something more for Violet – not simply a passionate episode in their lives, but the promise of an entirely new life. All that August she advanced on Vita with those 'flaming yellow bulldozers' that were her letters.

> Oh, Mitya, come away, let's fly, Mitya darling – if ever there were two entirely primitive people, they are surely us . . . I have never told you the whole truth. You shall have it now: I have loved you all my life, a long time without knowing, 5 years knowing it as irrevocably as I know it now, loved you as my ideal, my inspiration, my perfection . . . And the supreme truth is this: I can never be happy without you . . . My days are consumed by this impotent longing for you, and my nights are riddled with insufferable dreams . . . I want you. I want you hungrily, frenziedly, passionately. I am starving for you . . . I will have you all to myself or not at all, so you can choose.

Violet likened herself and Vita to two gamblers, both eager to win, each nervous of playing a card 'unless the other throws his at the same time'. But this was not quite true. Violet had only one chip to hazard; Vita (though her capital may have been no greater) had several smaller chips and could play a more tactical and patient game. Violet tried to unsettle Vita's patience by provoking her jealousy – telling her of the love letters she was receiving from a romantic officer in the Royal Horse Guards named Denys Trefusis, handsome, golden-haired and piratical, a decorated war hero with whom she had been flirting and whom her mother wished her to marry – it was rumoured that they were unofficially engaged. She insisted that Vita was jealous of Denys Trefusis because he 'is like you'. And it was true that when Vita met him she liked him very much: 'I see his tragedy – for he is a tragic person,' she recorded in *Portrait of a Marriage*. In case Vita was not sufficiently jealous of Denys, Violet also told her of a dreadfully attractive young lady she met who had 'long almond-shaped eyes, the aquamarine colour I'm so fond of, sometimes blue, sometimes green . . . and quite the loveliest red mouth I have ever seen'.

But in truth it was Violet who felt penetrated by jealousy because, unlike Vita, 'it is impossible for me to care for more than one person at a time. You will never know how jealous I am of you till the Day of Judgement.' She was even jealous of 'the insurmountable Nicolson' who she had felt confident would have politely disappeared by now; and she made Vita promise never to have sexual relations with him again. Even then she hated having to address her letters to 'Mrs Harold Nicolson', a conjugal label that was prematurely investing Vita with middle-aged habits. Vita had sacrificed her freedom, it seemed, for this diplomatic nonentity and was in danger of sacrificing her love for Violet whose resentment was developing into a disease that 'will kill our love as surely and remorselessly as cancer gets its victim in the end'.

Realising, to his surprise, that Violet wanted to destroy his marriage, Harold went and complained to Lady Sackville. At about the same time Violet also had a long talk with Lady Sackville, confiding to her that Vita was not at all attached to Harold now that she was beginning a serious literary career – and speaking of her own excitement over the prospect of marrying Denys Trefusis. It seems she was imagining a magical trinity in which she and Denys should share their lives with Vita – he as a good friend to them both, they as lovers (Harold in this dream was nowhere to be seen). But her conversation with Lady Sackville took an unexpected turn. On the point of separating from her unfaithful husband, Lady Sackville had grown fond of scatological stories and coarse sexual anecdotes of horrifying male lust. What she said opened Violet's eyes to what married life with Denys might entail.

For though emotionally so alert, Violet seems to have been ignorant of the facts of heterosexual intercourse – until Vita's mother made the details of men's sexual habits 'dirty and hideous' to her. 'Thank goodness, I have been spared this horrible knowledge for much longer than most people,' Violet wrote. 'No wonder I have always lived in a world of my own – or as much as possible . . . no wonder I have always preferred fairy-tales to facts.'

To keep alive her fairy-tale life, she needed to escape abroad where (she presumed) they ordered things differently. 'O Mitya, come away with me! Let's go to Paris, the Riviera, anywhere. What do I care, so long as we are out of England!'

Their flight became more practical after 11 November, Armistice Day. 'I am so busy getting peace terms ready,' Harold informed Vita from the basement of the Foreign Office in London. 'It is rather fun, though I feel oddly responsible.' He also made himself oddly responsible for getting Vita and Violet passports and spent 'a tiresome day' on 24 November trying to explain to Lady Sackville why her daughter – his wife – was suddenly leaving for France with Violet. He was finding some difficulty in explaining it to himself.

The two women arrived in Paris a couple of days later. Denys Trefusis also happened to be there and he was allowed to take Violet out to meals during the day, while Vita, dressed as a wounded soldier with a bandage round her head, attracted heart-warming compliments as she roamed the streets. Sometimes the three of them would dine together and it must have seemed to Violet that her dream of a magical trinity was coming true. But for Harold it was becoming a nightmare. 'You have been in Paris nearly a week without a word to me as to when you were going south or where,' he complained to Vita. '. . . I put it all down to that swine Violet who seems to addle your brain.' As if spurred on, Vita and Violet set off for Avignon the next day and then went on to Monte Carlo. They were to spend some twelve weeks there dancing tête-à-tête, losing money gambling (Harold forwarded Vita £130 to help out) and continuing to write *Challenge*. 'Monte Carlo was perfect, Violet was perfect,' Vita wrote. Rumours of these adventures, including their 'scandalously indiscreet caresses' in public, soon reached England. 'Damn! Damn! Damn! Violet. How I *loathe* her,' exclaimed Harold who had gone with the British Delegation to the Peace Conference in Paris. But though he deplored anything 'vulgar and dangerous', he was so busy pursuing peace it grew difficult for him to sustain his anger and he was soon apologising for his 'cross letter'. The fact was that he could not comprehend the strength of the two women's feelings for each other and attributed everything to Violet's flattery. 'Every silly ass woman is bowled over by flattery,' he told Vita. 'How I *hate* women.'

Vita had given Harold to understand that she would not be gone for long; and when she eventually did leave Monte Carlo, she let Violet believe that their separation was temporary. This habit of telling them both what they wanted to believe was like two sides of a coin made from what she called her 'duality', which continued to spin in the air, turning up now one side, now the other, displaying her divided loyalties.

It was at this stage that the two mothers, Victoria Sackville and Alice Keppel, re-entered the story. Both were determined that there should be an end to these embarrassing escapades. Lady Sackville gave Vita a long lecture about Violet's sexual perversion, insisting that she break off her relationship with 'that horrible girl'. Mrs Keppel meanwhile insisted that her daughter make the engagement to Denys Trefusis official – and on 26 March 1919 an announcement appeared in *The Times*. It seems Mrs Keppel believed that once her daughter was married, all this nonsense would cease – and if it didn't altogether cease there would at least be a fig leaf of respectability to hide it. As for Violet, she found it almost impossible openly to defy her mother.

Perhaps she still had dreams of a *mariage blanc* and a magical trinity with Vita. 'All three of us are young,' she told Vita, 'absolutely indifferent to the world's opinions, equally intolerant of treasured conventions.' But the truth, as she began to discover, was that, though in many ways a romantic personality and physically frail after his war experiences, Denys Trefusis was far more conventional than any of them (he appears never to have heard of lesbianism). So Violet's main hope appears to have focused on the belief that Vita would rescue her – perhaps sensationally at the door of the church. The two of them would then begin a new life together as nature intended.

Violet's letters to Vita during the spring and early summer of 1919 grow increasingly painful. 'In giving you up, I am giving up my whole life,' she wrote. '. . . Are you going to stand by and watch me marry this man? It's unheard of, inconceivable. I belong to you, body and soul . . . My life – what is left of it – is just one raw, limitless bitterness . . . I am flooded by an agony of physical longing for you . . . All my life I have been lonely. I never knew what it was to have companionship till I met you . . . I feel trapped and desperate.'

Denys Trefusis was to destroy Vita's letters to Violet over this period (those that Violet did not destroy herself), so there is no record of what exactly she wrote. But from Violet's side of the correspondence it appears that she was being cautious, balancing Harold's claims on her and those of her family and home, against Violet's appeals to live permanently with her. The inadequacy of these letters filled Violet with rage and horror. 'My God, Mitya, if I could kill you I would,' she wrote. '. . . The depths of duplicity in you make my hair stand on end . . . If I can't have you, I'll have my revenge . . . do you wonder I mistrust you? . . . Are you really only heartless and a coward?' Violet was on the edge of a breakdown and in her state of depression began to loathe herself – her ungovernable anger, misery, vindictiveness.

'Make allowances for great unhappiness,' she telegraphed after one of her bleakest days.

The target for her most extreme anger was Denys. Her plan seems to have been to force him, if Vita failed her, to call off the marriage. But he was silent, inscrutable, a sphinx of a man. What Violet did not understand was the shocking effect of the war upon him – that was the tragedy Vita had seen. 'He cares for me drivellingly,' Violet wrote. She told him that her love for Vita was greater than any love she might have said she felt for him. But he did not really understand her, thinking this was premarital nerves and promising 'never to do anything that should displease me – you know in what sense I mean'. But copying this to Vita was a mistake. On reading of their engagement in the newspapers, she had almost fainted, believing that Violet, like herself, must be to some degree bisexual. Now it seemed to her that if both their husbands agreed to do without sexual relations, then they would be free to go on further holidays as Julian and Eve. But Violet wanted more than holidays.

In mid-April 1919 Violet spent three days with Vita at Knole. Then, feeling 'terribly unhappy', Vita went off to see Harold in Paris. With whom should she spend the rest of her life? The answer seemed to be with Harold – and Violet. 'Oh darling I have suffered so, this long dark year,' Harold appealed to her on 22 May, 'have I got to go through another?' The answer to this was yes: another year and then another. He promised to love and understand her 'and let you do whatever you like'. And that is what she attempted to do. She agreed to Violet's plan that they would bolt shortly before the wedding; and then arranged to be with Harold in Paris on the day of the wedding, and for him 'to keep me under lock and key'.

Denys and Violet were married at St George's Church, Hanover Square, on 16 June 1919. Nellie Melba sang Gounod's 'Ave Maria' as the two of them signed the register, and among the many wedding presents was an alabaster head of Medusa from Vita. That day Violet sent her a note in pencil: 'You have broken my heart, goodbye.'

And surely that must signal the end.

But of course it did not. Vita knew that Denys and Violet were spending the first days of their honeymoon in Paris, and she knew that Harold would soon release her from custody and go back to work. So, once it was too late, she acted with fierce resolution, turning up at their hotel and carrying off Violet for an hour or two. 'I treated her savagely, I made love to her, I had her, I didn't care, I only wanted to hurt Denys . . .' Next day there was another opportunity for hurting him when the three of them met at the hotel. 'I can't describe how terrible it was – that meeting . . .' Vita wrote in *Portrait of a Marriage*. The two of them humiliated him, calling him impotent, telling him how they planned to elope. Then Vita joined Harold in Switzerland and Violet and Denys continued what was left of their honeymoon in the South of France.

Alice Keppel had thought it wise to rent a house for her daughter and son-in-law some twenty miles from Vita at Long Barn. Violet's life there was one of quiet banality – she and Denys were scarcely on speaking terms. 'I could kill myself, Mitya. I don't know what prevents me,' Violet insisted. What prevented her were Vita's promises to elope again – this time for ever. But could Violet trust her? Or Vita trust Violet?

An element of farce was now entering the drama (wonderfully enacted by the two Nicolson children's nanny striding into the village one afternoon attired as 'Julian' in one of Harold's suits). Harold's own position in all these negotiations was slightly compromised by an affaire he had begun with the couturier Edward Molyneux: 'a funny new friend – a dressmaker with a large shop in the Rue Royale'. If only Vita could have taken her affaire in such a pleasant light-hearted manner. But what this showed her was not how extramarital, same-sex relationships should be conducted, but how disastrously Harold had misunderstood her devastating passion for Violet. 'I don't think you realise except in a very tiny degree what's going on or what's been going on,' she apprised him. 'I don't think you have taken the thing seriously.' In his fashion, he did take it seriously. But by convincing himself that Violet 'has all the weapons and I have none', he disarmed himself.

Alice Keppel was shocked by the appalling weakness of the two husbands. She herself was not weak and she refused to listen to her daughter's pleas. Either Violet remained married to Denys and led a reasonably discreet and respectable life, or Alice would leave her penniless (or as Violet described it 'jewel-less'). Only when mother and daughter went up to Duntreath Castle, the family home in Scotland, did they find any peace together. Here, where she had been happy in her childhood, Violet seemed to become a child once more, shedding the complexities of adulthood.

In her dual biography, *Mrs Keppel and her Daughter*, Diana Souhami writes that 'Vita could neither commit herself to Violet nor reject her'. This is true. But she could do both. Violet was also in two minds. 'I want adventure . . . I am completely reckless,' she wrote to Vita in September 1919. They planned to go abroad on another adventure that autumn. But four days before they set off, Violet cautioned Vita. 'I must absolutely implore you not to go unless you are unmoveably sure . . . This time you would absolutely do me in, and I swear I don't deserve it at your hands.'

Nor did Harold deserve being done in. 'If you think you can treat me like V[iolet] treats D[enys] T[refusis] you are wrong,' he suggested to Vita. 'I shan't allow my life to be wrecked.' Nevertheless he consented to their going off to Paris and Monte Carlo again and, to reassure him, Vita left a letter 'packed with love'.

Violet was unaware of this. But she became aware that her mother was determined to put a stop to this scandal before it imperilled her daughter Sonia's marriage. Incredibly Alice Keppel had rented another house even closer to Long Barn and then dispatched Denys Trefusis to the Riviera to bring back his wife to live in it. Vita persuaded her to return with Denys while she herself went back to Long Barn so that they could both prepare for their future together. Having told Harold that she and Violet were giving each other up for ever, Vita now notified him that their elopement had been the prelude to a life-long commitment. He wept, begged her to change her mind: and she felt dreadful. 'I hate myself,' she told him. '. . . I wish I were dead.' Fifteen miles away Violet was telling Denys much the same thing.

And at this point, reader, I throw up my hands in despair at any of these characters behaving with proper consideration for their biographers — Victoria Glendinning, James Lees-Milne, Diana Souhami, me. A tragic love story — for this is what it is — has been made chaotic and incredible by the tumult of contradictions. Lady Sackville, who was threatening to cut Vita out of her Will and come to the aid of 'little Harold', could not help observing (with a tinge of admiration) that it was 'quite like a sensational novel'.

Early in February 1920, the two women headed erratically for Dover. On the way Violet tried to tell Vita that on their last night together she had allowed Denys some degree of sexual intimacy. But Vita shut her ears to this. The very suspicion drove her crazy. The choreography of their story then grew wildly complex. Violet (who hated travelling alone and had never done so before) nervously crossed the Channel by herself and proceeded to Amiens. Vita, preparing to follow her next day from Dover, sent telegrams to her parents and Harold so that they should know her plans and be able to rescue her. Instead she was unexpectedly joined by Denys whom she hadn't telegraphed. The two of them, who had recently wished each other dead, got along surprisingly well as they travelled to Calais together where, another surprise, they met Violet who, unable to be alone any longer at Amiens, had found her way back to Calais. The following day, after an evening in Violet's hotel bedroom discussing French literature, the three of them hurried on by train to Amiens from where Denys, his entreaties all rejected, travelled back in despair to England.

Denys was suffering from tuberculosis, but to Alice Keppel's way of thinking this was hardly an excuse for his abysmal retreat from France – she had expected better from a decorated war hero. Quickly taking command, she procured an essential ingredient in a modern novel of sensation – a small aeroplane – and instructed Denys to fly back to Amiens. This development was much to the liking of Lady Sackville who enquired whether there was room in the plane for little Harold. There was: and the two husbands flew off together.

The confrontation between Denys and Harold and Violet and Vita at the ruined town of Amiens was truly dreadful. Vita appeared shocked by the appalling abuse Violet kept shouting at Denys, who remained silent and pale as a ghost. 'To my dying day I shall never forget the look on his face,' she wrote. '. . . If he had slipped down and died at our feet I should scarcely have been surprised.' But it was what Denys had confided to Harold on their plane journey, and which Harold now whispered to Vita, that suddenly changed the direction of events. Vita already had her suspicions – though she had tried to stifle them. Had Violet allowed Denys to have sexual intercourse with her? Did she 'belong' to him? Denys refused to answer these questions even when Vita promised never to 'set eyes on Violet again' if the answer was yes. And when she questioned Violet herself she saw a look of 'absolute terror' pass over her face. That look gave her the answer and it was obviously yes. Yet she knew how limp and docile Violet was in bed, how passive she could be in someone's arms, how she permitted anything being done to her, how her abandonment suggested masochistic tendencies. Could Denys have done to Violet some of those very things Vita herself had done? 'I was half mad with pain,' she wrote. Violet, now in tears, held ferociously on to her. 'I couldn't get away till Denys helped me,' Vita remembered. Guarded by Harold, Vita began packing – then suddenly dashed through to kiss Violet before hurrying off with him. They took a train to Paris from where Vita was to continue her journey home. But Denys and Violet, travelling separately, unfortunately took the same train to Paris . . . And Denys, seeing Vita in hysterics 'perjured himself' (in Harold's opinion) by assuring her that there had been no sexual relations between Violet and himself after all.

Even a sensational novelist would end the story here . . .

There is, at any rate, an interval here for the second coming of Tiziana. I arranged for the two of us to give a presentation, 'Rediscovering Violet Trefusis', at the Charleston Summer School in Sussex and then at the Oxford Festival. Tiziana prepared a small publication, similar to her Ravello exhibition catalogue, containing pictures, poems, epigrams, two or three passages from Violet's novels and occasional writings, for our audience.

Tiziana shows me the printout of an academic eulogy she wishes to deliver. It is lovingly done. How can I persuade her to put aside something she has worked on so devotedly? I explain that the audience is expecting a conversation between the two of us into which, for the last fifteen minutes or so, they are invited to enter. They will not be won over by a monologue. She offers to reduce it to fifteen minutes or so. 'Fifteen minutes!' I cry. Is she absolutely merciless? Five minutes at most. We are both laughing now, but this is a real test as to whether she believes I have Violet's best interests at heart.

I suggest that we introduce Violet through three women: Alice Keppel, Vita Sackville-West and the Princess de Polignac under whose patronage in France she wrote her novels. Tiziana agrees to the first two women but not the last – possibly because there is something in the relationship she does not like, I cannot tell. But I agree. We will sketch out Violet's emotional life, then discuss her novels showing to what extent they began autobiographically and developed into imaginative chamber pieces.

The small lecture room at Charleston is crammed with an international audience, many from America. We are speaking from a slightly raised platform and, sitting in chairs for our conversation, the front rows of our audience can see us and the back rows merely hear us – as if we are on television for some and on radio for others. I introduce the event by telling everyone that Tiziana is someone who exemplifies very powerfully the effect Violet's life and work can produce on a new young generation of readers.

Our discussion is both serious and light-hearted. The audience laughs and listens, listens and laughs. What do they make of us? We seem to present something like a father-and-daughter exhibition match, full of jokes, quotes and references to the family of Bloomsbury in this Bloomsbury house. Then Tiziana stands to give her address. It lasts four minutes and I feel a stab of guilt at curtailing her so severely. But what she says is charming and leaves a sense that there is much more to be discovered. The audience claps enthusiastically. Maggie, one of our radio listeners at the back, chimes in with some pertinent questions and we come to an end. Tiziana is smiling. 'We were a perfect match,' she says delightedly.

Back in London on the Sunday evening we have invited Primo Levi's biographer, Carole Angier, to dinner. She and Tiziana break into rapid Italian – stopping occasionally to explain to me and Maggie (who understands much more than I do) their helter-skelter discourse. I can see that Tiziana is something of a puzzle to Carole who feels the pattern of Italian life to be somewhat rigid. The family protects its children, especially its daughters, until they are no longer children, until they are adolescents and even in their twenties or thirties if need be, protects them until they marry and can start protecting their own children to the same extravagant degree. Many Italians, in Carole's view, fall into two categories: the protected and the protectors. But Tiziana does not fit neatly into either of these categories. She is not closely protected by parents, she has no children to protect. She has a circle of admirers but is obliged to protect herself. When she speaks of Violet, speaks of London, England and Scotland, she seems extraordinarily young and romantic. She has some liberal-aesthetic views, but also holds the retaliatory judgements of someone who may be quite vulnerable within Italian culture. She has the apprehension of an old person who sees contemporary life as unattractive and possibly dangerous. Her optimism and sense of romance come alive when she takes on the virtual existence of Violet and assumes a life that has been renewed in the novels she is translating.

She has brought her beautifully printed monograph, 'Violet's Rhapsody', and gives us copies. 'With a degree in English Literature and an MA in scriptwriting, her main interest is Violet Trefusis,' a career note at the back informs readers. Above this is a description of Violet Trefusis as 'a precocious romantic enfant terrible who felt alienated from English society [and] found her true place in artistic and literary Paris . . .'. There is an obvious crossover with Tiziana who feels alienated from Italian society and wishes to find an acknowledged place in English literary society. She wants to improve her written English, she tells us, up to publishable standards. Meanwhile there is this little book.

It is a love token: 'Violet and I: a *coup de foudre*'. That is her opening statement and in a sense it tells the reader everything.

The book contains two of Violet's poems: one is a call to her ally, Nature, to 'Fight for me'; the other an invitation to 'Come with me!' followed by what she promises those who do — as if she herself is a force of nature. Tiziana does not quote the poem I particularly like which, its last line echoing Yeats, Violet wrote shortly before her death:

> My heart was more disgraceful, more alone
> And more courageous than the world has known.
> O passer-by my heart was like your own.

Elizabeth Barrett Browning's sonnet 'How do I love thee?' is printed as the book's epigraph and reading it I silently count the ways that bind Tiziana to Violet. There is an intense emotional need as well as a sense of purpose — almost the pull of destiny. I see her searching for a new identity, a reinvention of herself, a rebirth and transformation: all this to be achieved through a dedicated pattern of work — the 'passion put to use / In my old griefs, and with my childhood's faith'. Tiziana has already testified that she first came across Violet at a time of grief, and it was love at first sight. She uses the sonnet to affirm that it will be love everlasting: 'I shall but love thee better after death.' This is an all-consuming commitment, an imaginative ideal. Her ambition, she says, is to 'write a biography that could survive me after my departure from this silly world'. This silly world is a dark place, but the possession of Violet's novels, her rekindled life, has become a luminous source of happiness. And this part of my book is now part of her world.

7

Ultraviolet

'As soon as one had left her one wanted to go back to her,' Vita wrote in her novel *Challenge*, 'thinking that this time, perhaps, one would succeed better in seizing and imprisoning the secret of her elusiveness.' And so, after a few weeks apart, they met at Avignon and travelled on together to Bordighera, San Remo and Venice. They were quarrelling now, promising one thing, threatening another – and then Violet fell ill with jaundice, 'a most unromantic complaint'. They could no longer be happy together or apart. 'We are invited to Happiness,' Violet wrote, 'and we don't answer the invitation.' But the invitation date had passed, Vita believed. 'We weren't happy – how could we be?'

'We hardly see each other now,' Violet complained after they returned in the spring of 1920. This was partly the result of severe policing by Alice Keppel. The scandal circulating round her elder daughter was by now extreme and the family was in danger of becoming, Mrs Keppel feared, 'the laughing stock of the country'. Already decent families were refusing to invite Violet to their houses. It was essential that no further odium be added to the wretched business before Sonia married the affluent Hon. Roland Cubitt. As the date of Sonia's marriage approached, and afterwards the news came of her pregnancy, Alice Keppel's treatment of Violet grew harsher. 'Her undis-guised hatred of me is a terrible thing,' Violet told Vita. '. . . She says that her affection for me is dead, and that after Sonia's baby is born, I may do what I like.'

Might Vita even now rescue her? 'I can't live any longer without seeing you,' Violet wrote. She tried to jump out of a window but was prevented by Denys, though he had advised her, since she set no value on life and was making everyone wretched, that suicide might be the 'most decent thing one can do'. Mrs Keppel was inclined to agree. 'Mama made me cry and cry last night,' Violet wrote to her friend Pat Dansey. 'She said that if she had been me she would have killed herself long ago!'

Feeling there was no one else who cared what happened, she still relied on Vita. 'I want to reconquer all I have lost,' she declared. The correspondence between them was crowded with resolutions, evasions, misgivings, sadness. Violet paraded her helplessness and appealed to Vita's sense of power. It was an awful year with short haphazard meet-ings that opened up old wounds on parting. 'We wanted far too thirstily to be uninterruptedly together,' Vita explained. And so, defying everyone, they absconded one more time, staying in Hyères and Carcassonne from January to March 1921. It was, as it always had been, like 'two flames leaping together'. But this journey was, in the words of Harold Nicolson's biographer Norman Rose, 'the last flickering of a blazing fire'. The fire never quite went out. Meeting again some twenty years later, Vita warned Violet that 'we must not play with fire again'.

When they got back from France, Violet was escorted to Italy, guarded like a prisoner by a 'garrison-governess' and forbidden to write to or receive letters from Vita. She had vaulted over such obstacles before, but there were two factors this time of which she was unaware. The first was Vita's confessional, which she finished writing at the end of March 1921. It was as if the writing of this love journal gave her control over events and a release from them.

It was not easy for Violet to get letters to her. To outwit her jailers and keep the forbidden correspondence half alive, she had chosen her friend Pat Dansey as a go-between. 'I have been more than touched by her efforts to bring us together,' Violet confided to Vita. '. . . She has been an absolute angel . . . the most forgiving and generous person I know . . . Pat has placed herself unreservedly on our side.' Pat Dansey was apparently Violet's closest friend during this period. A lesbian herself, she had been fascinated by the passion between the two women, not liking Vita at first but being carried towards her by the fierce current of this passion. With Violet's letters, which she addressed and forwarded to Vita, she inserted her own unseasonable messages. 'She [Violet] is such a monkey . . . I was working entirely on your side . . . Please, Vita trust me . . . I think she will get round you . . . I hate the way she tricks and deceives people . . . I simply fail to see why people don't see through her. Love from Pat.' Instead of bringing them together as Violet believed, Pat insisted that 'the best way of helping Violet is to make a complete break'. In this belief she may have been sincere. But there was another agenda. 'If you happen to be in London and have a spare second, do come and see me,' she invited Vita. '. . . I spent the whole night dreaming about you. I expect it was because I had taken your poems to read in bed. Queer dream it was too . . .' At the beginning of 1922 Vita had a brief fling with Pat Dansey – the sort of passing intimacy that did not disturb Harold (who had been enjoying an undisturbed relationship with Comte Jean de Gaigneron, a society wit and aesthete whom he used for his pen portrait of 'the Marquis de Chaumont' in *Some People* – and who in later years became an escort of Violet's in Paris).

'I think we have got something indestructible between us . . . a bond of childhood and subsequent passion, such as neither of us will share with anyone else,' Vita wrote to Violet over twenty-five years later. Violet had always believed this to be true. But by March 1921, when Vita was finishing her narrative of their affaire and wondering in 'great unhappiness' whether she might 'never see Violet again', Violet already knew the answer: 'You have chosen, my darling; you had to choose between me and your family, and you have chosen them.'

Reading *Challenge* you can feel Violet's presence as Vita herself experienced it. She describes the drowsy tone of her voice, her irresistible red mouth, her strange shadowy eyes, deep-set and slanting upwards, alive with mockery yet sometimes inexpressibly sad. Spoilt, childlike in many ways, she seemed destined to 'grow into a woman of exceptional attraction, and to such women existence is packed with danger'. She used secrecy, the provocative mystery of her person disguised under a superficial expansiveness, as a 'shield and a weapon', sensing that 'existence in a world of men was a fight, a struggle, a pursuit'.

Vita had more difficulty in portraying herself as Julian who is described in the British publisher's blurb as 'a young, Byronic Englishman who led a group of islanders in revolt against their masters in the mainland'. Violet was unremittingly helpful. What about those 'heavy-lidded eyes, green in repose, black in anger'? Could he not also be likened to a young Hermes, the god of eloquence and good fortune, the patron of travellers and thieves? (A bronze copy of *Hermes at Rest* stood in the garden of the Villa Cimbrone.) And surely there should be more about his grace, strength and sensuality – all fine pagan virtues. '"Julian was tall," let us say, and "flawlessly proportioned",' she suggested. '. . . Julian's hair was black and silky. Eve found herself wondering what it would feel like to stroke, and promptly did so; she was amazed to feel a sensation akin to pain shoot up her fingers and lodge itself definitely in the region of her heart.'

In his foreword to the novel, Nigel Nicolson likens Julian to Sir Philip Sidney, the Elizabethan poet and adventurer. Had she been born a boy (and she always regretted not being born a boy), this is the person Vita would have wanted to be – also the son she would have liked and (Nigel Nicolson wryly adds) never did have. Of Eve, she writes: 'Whatever she touched she lit.' The other characters inhabit the shadows. Rosamund Grosvenor, who appears as Fru Thyregod, is a blatant young woman, without any of Eve's instinctive shrewdness, whose conversation is a petulant 'babble of coy platitudes'. The politicians and diplomats who worked with Harold in the Foreign Office are seen as a pretentious and unattractive crew who enact foreign policy as if it were part of their family business.

Over fifty years later, when the book was finally published in Britain, there appeared to be 'nothing here for the prurient', Paul Theroux wrote in a review for *The Times*, '. . . one is left wondering why it was suppressed for reasons of delicacy.' But it would have shocked Lady Sackville's friends because they knew the dramatis personae. Had Vita made the protagonists two women, the novel might have gained a place in the history of lesbian literature as a predecessor to Radclyffe Hall's *The Well of Loneliness* (which Vita thought 'loathsome'). When it was eventually published in 1974, it sold well as a romantic pendant to *Portrait of a Marriage*. But the social climate had changed from one of deference before the aristocracy to one of incredulity. 'The literary merits of the book are strong,' Nigel Nicolson stated in his foreword. But reviewers were unable to discover this literary merit. Today *Challenge* merely emphasises the contrasting achievement of *Orlando*. It is an inanimate book – with an interesting subtext.

Violet meanwhile had been struggling with a novel called 'Battledore and Shuttlecock'. In June 1919, four days before her marriage, she had made a resolution to use her unhappiness as a spur to writing:

both an assuagement of grief and a weapon raised against her enemies. 'I will write the most mad, obscene, relentless book that ever startled the world,' she announced. 'It shall be more than a book. It shall be all passion, insanity, drunkenness, filth, sanity, purity, good and evil that ever fought and struggled in human anguish . . .' But she could write only when she was comparatively happy and she could not be happy when she was alone — and she had to be alone in order to write. This was a complicated knot to unravel. It seemed unlikely that she could sustain a narrative beyond the length of a novella or reach beyond the *roman-à-clef*. Her chief limitation, she believed, was her single-mindedness. 'I only see my side of the question; I am blind to the other person's . . . If it turns out to be rotten it will really break my heart,' she admitted. 'I have so little confidence in myself.' But though writing was 'so difficult it makes my brain reel' her desire to write grew. And in 1922 she began another novel.

This was a romantic tragedy called *The Hook in the Heart*. 'It's an awful temptation to make books end badly,' she had written to Vita in the summer of 1920. *Challenge* had ended badly with Julian's betrayal by Eve who drowns herself on the final page. That novel had been their stillborn 'love-child'; Violet's novel was a lamentation. Cecile, a young and innocent girl, who is Violet's portrait of herself, finds that 'her love of love had bred disgust of love . . . she cursed passionate love, the hook in the heart that you cannot tear out without tearing out the heart also'. The melancholy plot is manipulated by a sinister mother figure — an amalgam of Lady Sackville and Mrs Keppel. Rejected by everyone, Cecile is confronted at the end by what Violet most feared: solitude.

The Hook in the Heart reflects Violet's bitter state of mind between 1922 and 1923. The manuscript is fluently written and has the vitality of her letters. But she has not yet clothed herself in the dark comedy of manners that could subtly convey what she needed to say. She did not try to get the novel published, probably because it was too nakedly self-revealing. In 1923, however, her life was to change dramatically.

At the end of her journal, on 28 March 1921, Vita wrote in great unhappiness of 'Violet's doom, which she herself has consistently predicted'. But in Violet's polite volume of memoirs, written thirty years later and distinguished by the skill with which she interweaves her omissions like lace depending on the pattern of its spaces, she covers this time with ease. She had not been the only girl, she tells us, to 'set her cap' at the slim and elegant figure of Denys Trefusis. It was impossible to withstand his charm. Once they settled down in France, 'we were able to establish a modus vivendi . . . Denys was given a job in Paris . . . we were by no means unhappy there . . . In 1923 we found the home we had always longed for; a diminutive house in Auteuil, facing full south . . . I tried to pick up the threads of the life I had lived as a jeune fille.' There had been some arguments between them, she recollects, but 'we both rather enjoyed these Noel Coward episodes'. This is a framework of their lives: the frame without a picture. Violet's novel contains more truth than this 'non-fiction'; Vita's journal more truth than her fiction. There are no rules in these matters.

But scattered through Violet's memoir are glimpses of her frustration: 'I liked many of Denys's friends, but cared not for their nocturnal peregrinations.' He was, she adds, 'the darling of the Caveau Caucasien and other night-clubs and . . . I was jealous . . . the wasp-waisted Caucasian dancers had probably more in common with him than I had . . . I had no intimate friends . . . No, I had no intimate friends.'

Violet and Denys occupied the same house but led separate lives. 'No one loves me or lives with me,' she wrote to Vita. '. . . I should not lead the life of chastity.' The interim modus vivendi they established was her agreement not to object to his affaires or his long journeys into Russia; and his agreement to encourage her writing (she began attending lectures at the Sorbonne).

It was Alice Keppel who arranged for Denys's job at a bank and bought their house at Auteuil. She would continue to support them financially so long as they remained married and lived in exile with at least a patina of respectability. And that patina is what Violet gives the readers of the memoirs she dedicated to the memory of her mother. What she did not know was that her mother was using Pat Dansey to report on her way of life in Paris and that Pat Dansey was forwarding stories about her to Vita. In Violet's memoirs, Pat Dansey is described in terms of a quirky animal: 'small and quick and done in various shades of brown, her hair was the colour of potato chips, her eyes like bees, her face had the texture and hue of a pheasant's egg. I have made her sound edible, but she was too brittle and furry to make really good eating. She had a stutter that sounded most incongruous in her small neat person, for it gave one the impression she was slightly intoxicated.' This was the deprecating camouflage under which Pat Dansey plotted her manoeuvres. In her letters to Vita she attributed secret amours to Violet ('her falseness simply appals me . . . She's a hopeless woman'). She wished to make sure that Vita would not become attached to her again and impede Pat's own relationship – which nevertheless ended explosively in the winter of 1923–4 after Vita told her she had fallen in love with the writer Geoffrey Scott.

'Russia was his Holy Land,' Violet was to write of Denys. But for Violet herself the Holy Land was France. On her first visit to Paris at the age of eleven she had announced: 'When I'm grown up, I'm going to live in Paris.' Her technique of living, she believed, was acquired in France. Now, at the age of twenty-eight, she decided to reinvent her life there. Paris must make up for everything: love abandoned, friendships fallen into disuse. 'I was intimate with Paris, which replaced them . . . Paris, failing people, could give me all I craved.'

It was Denys who helped her find a new beginning. He was 'extremely, and, a trifle pedantically, musical', Violet explained. '. . . His Egeria was Princess Edmond de Polignac.' In 1923 he introduced Violet to the Princess who became the third significant woman in her life.

Violet described this immensely rich and remarkable woman as being 'inscrutable'. She 'hung over life like a cliff; her rocky profile seemed to call for spray and seagulls; small blue eyes – the eyes of an old salt – came and went; her face was more like a landscape than a face, cloudy hair, blue of eye, rugged of contour. . . . Like all fundamentally shy people, she was infinitely intimidating. People quailed before her.' She had been born Winnaretta Singer, one of the many children of the American sewing-machine multimillionaire Isaac Singer. Her first marriage, a distressing experience involving an umbrella, had to be annulled. Her second, to the homosexual Prince Edmond de Polignac, was a marriage of convenience uniting their passion for music and aligning his great social position with her great wealth. His tremendous funeral in 1901 was used by Proust to describe the funeral of Saint-Loup.

Edmond de Polignac had been thirty years older than his wife; his widow (aged fifty-eight) was almost thirty years older than Violet when they met. Violet gives a sketch of the spectacular salon for musicians, writers and artists which the Princess had created at her house in the avenue Henri-Martin and which Proust describes in *A la Recherche du Temps Perdu*. She mentions some of the writers she met in the 1920s: the elegant, crane-like Giraudoux; Anna de Noailles so 'tiny, brilliant, restless'; Paul Valéry 'mumbling almost unintelligible epigrams beneath his chewed moustache'; and, perhaps her favourite, Colette whom she called 'a genius in the art of loving, and in the art of living and of describing those arts'. According to Colette's husband Maurice Goudeket, the two women understood each other well but were very different – 'one of them earthy, always in direct contact with everything; the other ethereal, seeing everything through a prism'. Certainly Violet does not follow Colette's example in her writing. She does not tell us that the Princess fell in love with her, or reveal that she was an implacable lesbian with sadistic tastes. There is a story Duff Cooper told his wife Diana of a friend who was mistaken one morning for 'the lady who was expected' and shown to a room 'where she was greeted by the old Princess in a dressing gown and top boots. On a sofa in another part of the room she saw Violet Trefusis with another woman, both stark naked and locked in a peculiar embrace. She ran from the room in terror.' According to Harold Acton, Princess 'Winnie' taught Violet discretion – 'it was rumoured with a whip – so her subsequent liaisons with ladies were less advertised'.

The attraction between Violet and the Princess was strong and instantaneous. 'From the start the two women exercised a hypnotic fascination for each other,' wrote Michael de Cossart. '. . . Winnaretta was bowled over by Violet's beauty, vivacity and apparent availability.' (Denys had left for a prolonged visit to Russia shortly after introducing them.) It is easy to understand her attraction for the sensuous twenty-nine-year-old Violet – for what Sylvia Kahan calls her 'dramatic dark looks', her 'quick wit' and 'alluring spontaneity'. But Violet's attraction to the rough-cast Winnaretta was, as Arthur Rubinstein observed, more 'complicated'. She admired her strength, gained entry into her wonderful court of musicians and writers, and abandoned the life of chastity.

The Princess's majestic patronage was welcomed by Mrs Keppel. For both women the appearance of social respectability was essential to their way of life, and Winnaretta always invited Violet's parents and husband to her soirées. This arrangement was a variation of Mrs Keppel's own discreet, extramarital arrangements with Ernest Beckett and later the Prince of Wales. They were a distinguished group: the Princess and her good friend Denys Trefusis with his wife and her mother and father. During the 1920s and early 1930s they travelled together to Egypt, Italy, Greece, Algeria, Cuba, the United States (where they were invited to the White House) and Spain (where they met King Alfonso XIII).

In 1924 Alice Keppel left Britain (though keeping a furnished suite at the Ritz) and bought the Villa dell'Ombrellino, an imposing fortress of a house on the Bellosguardo overlooking Florence. This new home, with its spacious view, its formal terraced garden, was Mrs Keppel's version of Ernest Beckett's Villa Cimbrone: a place she could fill with memories of a royal past and revive a grand epoch of England that no longer existed. She never learnt Italian – she did not need to. There were her servants to do that for her and there was her daughter who picked up languages with the ease of an accomplished mimic.

Violet acquired a new house too. In *Don't Look Round* she writes of a luncheon party at which she met Proust not long before his death. He advised her, she remembers, to visit St Loup de Naud, on the road to Provins some eighty kilometres from Paris. He had used the name for Robert, Marquis de Saint-Loup-en-Bray, the effeminate woman-ising career officer in his novel, who marries Gilberte Swann, is killed in action and buried at Combray. Violet adds that rereading Proust a few years later, the name Saint Loup 'smote me like a reproach' and she set out to find the place. Asking the patron of a restaurant where she had lunch if there was any property to be bought in the neigh-bourhood, she was told that there existed 'an ancient tower, but it is very dilapidated'. She bought it.

In Violet's memoirs the truth is located in hidden places: the people are concealed within them. With its haunted bedrooms, its Gothic atmosphere, St Loup was 'not a reassuring place', Philippe Jullian wrote, 'beneath the dining room are many oubliettes.' The picture of St Loup that Violet gives is a form of self-portrait. The house could 'lay claim to a certain magic spell of its own', she wrote. '. . . It was passive, immutable, like sensuality – a climate, not an episode. It lay coiled within the massive walls like a snake, which only rears its head when trodden on . . . the character of St Loup cannot be described as "nice". It is sensuous, greedy . . . ruthless, vindictive. If it takes a dislike to you, you are done . . . If, on the other hand, you have the good fortune to please St Loup, it is equally unscrupulous. No *scène de séduction* is too crude, no posture too audacious. It beckons, importunes, detains.'

What she does not tell the reader is that St Loup was actually bought for her by her lover, the Princess de Polignac, who restored the fifteenth-century tower with its big rooms containing canopied beds, tapestries and vast looking glasses 'whose mottled depths turned anyone who gazed into them into an old portrait'. She also added a more comfortable wing (where Violet slept) and helped to furnish it for her.

'I was not the only one to have le coup de foudre for St Loup,' Violet writes. 'Denys was also subjugated: it was exactly the kind of house he could understand and appreciate; it was in keeping with his Shakespearian character. He came there often and willingly, but he was fundamentally restless.' She does not reveal which Shakespearian character she had in mind – he should rightfully belong to Shakespearian tragedy. There was little understanding and appreciation over his last restless years, less coming often and willingly than Violet's pages suggest. She did not detain him long.

But she did detain Winnaretta Polignac at St Loup. They were able to 'pursue their relationship in tranquillity', wrote Sylvia Kahan, 'away from the watchful eyes of society'. Winnaretta's pet name for Violet was 'Mouse', suggesting a provocatively timid lover. But Violet was far from timid in society as if, by rebelling against this mother substitute, she was gaining revenge for battles lost against Mrs Keppel. Winnaretta feared the sort of gossip that Duff Cooper and others were picking up. At the start Violet's flirtations with men (which had so misled Pat Dansey) helped to draw attention away from their liaison, but when the flirtations turned more aggressively towards married men and also other women, Winnaretta grew exasperated and finally lost patience.

The end of the affaire came after a stormy voyage to Morocco in 1933. Maybe Winnaretta had 'trodden on' Violet too much and, after ten tumultuous years together, she wished to escape. Her indiscretions certainly resembled a struggle for independence. Like a bored child, her 'moaning and groaning defies description', Winnaretta wrote. '. . . Her mother scolds her uselessly'. By the time they returned to France the affaire was over.

Denys had been teaching in Russia before the Great War and had seen it then as a 'land of mystery and enchantment'. Returning in 1926 with a friend who 'was being sent to Russia on a mission', he found the enchantment had vanished. Moscow was sunk in Dickensian squalor, its streets full of ragged child thieves 'with the sly, furtive look of wild animals in search of prey'. In an unpublished narrative he wrote called 'The Stones of Emptiness', he deplored the new Bolshevik regime and the philosophy of communism: 'Wealth has flown but poverty lingers.'

These post-war journeys into Russia are mysterious. 'He knew he was suspect,' Violet wrote. But of what was he suspected? Was he there on behalf of the bank that employed him? He seems to have spent little time in its office. Was 'The Stones of Emptiness' read by the British Government? 'I have never taken any part whatever in espionage of any sort or kind,' he insisted. But he would not have classed his patriotic duty as spying. When he went there again in 1927 (meeting Vita at the British Embassy in Moscow) he was arrested and fined for 'contravening the Labour Code'. He escaped over the border to Poland travelling under the seat of a train, convinced that if found he would be brought back to court and imprisoned.

Still suffering from chronic tuberculosis, it was unlikely he would have survived long in a Soviet prison. Nevertheless in 1928 he went back to Russia once more 'at the risk of his life', Violet suggested. On his return he stayed for a time in England recovering from a chest infection. Then he rejoined Violet in France. But his health deteriorated. 'All day long,' she remembered, 'Denys lay gasping for breath.' She wondered if it might be appropriate to carry him off to Switzerland. 'But he was too ill to be moved.' Denys's sister came over and moved him into the American hospital at Neuilly. 'One of the people whose visits he seemed to enjoy most was Madame de Polignac,' Violet remembered. '. . . I was not encouraged to be present.'

Denys died on 2 September 1929. He was thirty-nine. Violet had not liked to trespass into his thoughts and feelings during these last weeks of his life (she ignored a young Australian nurse who fell for him and later kept in touch with his family). Three weeks after his death she wrote to Cyril Connolly whom she had recently met in Florence: 'I have been living in a sort of mist . . . D[enys] was a curiously sumptuous element in my life, like a tapestry brought out on fête days, precious because intermittent. I never got tired of him, he had all the freshness of a chance encounter. More than anyone I know, he liked to live dangerously, his life was spent in impossible crusades.'

Twenty years later, when the mist had cleared and she was writing her memoirs, Violet refined this draft obituary. 'He had all the ballad-like qualities I most admire,' she wrote, 'I, all the defects it was most difficult for him to condone. Nevertheless, there was a great link between us, we both loved poetry, travel, being insatiably interested in foreign countries. We were both Europeans in the fullest sense of that term. The same things made us laugh, we quarrelled a lot, loved not a little. We were more to be envied than pitied.'

Alice Keppel would certainly have approved of this poetic union — one of adventure, laughter and affection overcoming small domestic differences. A less enviable glimpse of the marriage may be seen in a novel published in France shortly before Denys died.

8

Emergency Exits

In her memoirs, Violet described *Sortie de Secours* as 'a mediocre little book, a patchwork affair, aphorisms, maxims, annotations, loosely woven into the shape of a novel. It . . . was a loophole, an outlet, above all, a piece of blotting paper which absorbed my obsessions.' She looked round at her life through this novel and, not liking what she saw, decided to purge her past. 'I am forced to admit that I do not have any good or bad qualities which make love flourish,' says the central female character Laure. 'Happiness comes to me from things, not people.' It is as if Violet has floated up from one of those dark oubliettes at St Loup and decided to pass the rest of her life giving parties in the dining room above. 'In every person there is an emergency exit; a self-interest which in its various forms allows one to escape . . . The disadvantage is that one cannot always come back.'

Laure is a comparatively wealthy young woman whose charming and handsome lover Drino is growing increasingly distant. Diana Souhami neatly summarises the painful games of love Laure plays: 'Because she loves him so much he withdraws. Because she fears betrayal she finds it . . . Because she finds someone else Drino is jealous.' Finally, when she believes she has found true love, she is let down.

Violet juggles aspects of her life in this story: but however she plays her cards, the game comes out badly.

Sortie de Secours was never translated into English. An early draft was dedicated to Denys, but Violet removed his name leaving no dedication in the published volume. She would not have wanted it read in Britain for fear of arousing unpleasant memories in her mother (with whom she was now on good terms).

Sortie de Secours cleared the ground for her more sophisticated novels. In her forlorn days, while writing 'Battledore and Shuttlecock', she had admitted to an inability to express herself. 'I don't know English well enough, I can't analyse, I can't reason, and am altogether too stupid,' she had confessed to Vita. She found more encouragement in France and was soon to discover more oblique methods of orchestrating her thoughts and feelings in the French language. There is a recurring tension between the social life these novels describe and their emotional under-current, a battle between past and present, culture and morality.

'*Sortie de Secours* led to *Echo*,' Violet noted briefly in her memoirs. This second novel came within one vote of winning the Femina Vie Heureuse Prize (it was awarded that year to Antoine de Saint-Exupéry's *Vol de Nuit*). It is a miniature Gothic story, which culminates in a fatal seduc-tion. The formidably uninviting Scottish castle called Glendrocket where it opens is sparsely populated by a comic opera cast of Scottish char-acters. Since the death of her sister, the sixty-five-year-old Lady Balquidder has been nervously bringing up her untutored orphan twins, Malcolm and Jean. They are Rousseau's ideal primitives.

Into this wild and anachronistic world comes the twenty-eight-year-old Sauge de Cervallon: a great beauty and a very French Frenchwoman, she is well married, often silent, always mysterious, the subject of much speculation. Each year she feels an urgent need to leave Alain, her husband, and travel abroad for a few weeks. When the story opens she is feeling sweetly disposed to him because she is about to leave for Glendrocket where she is to meet her cousins. Never having been to Scotland, she imagines it as the dream of someone who has been reading Walter Scott and sees around her the antique world of *Rob Roy* or *The Heart of Midlothian*: 'a completely different planet'.

Echo is cleverly told by means of letters between Sauge and her husband in France – letters sent and not sent. The unsent letters tell a disturbing psychological truth, the sent ones are largely pragmatic. The novel is full of dark omens. Sauge remembers a fairy tale she read as a child in which, as at Glendrocket, the interior and exterior *mises en scène* are in conflict. In this story 'the trees grew almost into the windows; the man encouraged them, called them to him; a branch from his favourite tree, a horse-chestnut, climbed inside the room; encroaching ever further, its arms approached nearer and nearer to his bed. One morning he was found dead from strangulation.' The lesson Sauge learns from this story is a recurring one in Violet's novels: 'Objects seemed so much more alive than people in this weird place.' This was the condition Violet sought, the condition she criticised in her novels and celebrated in her memoirs. In *Echo* the landscape of Perthshire and the rooms within the castle have become extensions of the characters: of the twins and Lady Balquidder. The danger lies in bringing the twins indoors and encouraging them to lose their innocence.

A more potent omen is suggested by a dream that Sauge has in which she meets again her long-dead first love. 'She could hardly breathe; her heart was in her mouth. Expecting only to feel the shadow of her love, she was staggered to see him in the flesh, rising from his bed, as active and vigorous as the day she had first met him. And then little by little, all faded . . . She awoke in deathly sadness.' The predicament in which Sauge finds herself would be familiar to those who knew the Violet–Vita story, especially Vita's side of it. 'Sauge was prey to constant unease . . . The more she felt attracted to others, the more she needed Alain . . . Did she love Malcolm? Yes, if she could keep Alain; no if she had to lose him . . .'

We have been warned of the danger Sauge will create if she wakes from the torpor of Parisian society. The twins who adored each other before she came to Glendrocket are soon made bitter rivals and the plot is hastened to its tragic end by a series of inevitable accidents. What had begun as comic opera concludes as a tragic ballet, a version of *Petrushka* in which Sauge becomes the magician and the twins puppets who succumb to her experiments.

By giving her novella the title *Echo*, Violet invites the reader to find a lingering note in it of her intimacy with Vita. 'The whole of humanity finds its echo in me, brought through pain,' she had written to Vita. Then she had been unable to express any person's point of view other than her own. In *Echo* she ingeniously sidesteps this problem by discovering aspects of herself within several of her characters and sometimes merging them with memories of Vita. The identical twins, who may be seen as androgynous aspects of a single bisexual person, encounter Sauge at a place reminiscent of Duntreath Castle in Scotland where the sixteen-year-old Violet had first invited the eighteen-year-old Vita. She had gone to Vita's bedroom, they had heard the 'incessant tick-tick of pigeon feet upon the roof, and the jackdaws flying from turret to turret' and afterwards Violet had declared her love. 'I am primitive in my joy as in my suffering.'

Ghosts from the past rise up from time to time and haunt the story. It is they, as it were, who render the anonymous Scottish ballad, repeating two of its lines:

> For me and my true love
> Will never meet again

And on hearing this, 'sudden intense pain made her close her eyes . . .'

Echo belongs to island literature in which sophisticated travellers, their baggage full of knowledge and culture and apparently excellent intentions, spread disease through the noble islanders – those Johnsonian inhabitants of the 'Happy Valley' also sought by Melville's characters in *Typee* and idealised by Rousseau in his *Discours*.

Ideally this is a novel for younger readers: but I first read it in my seventies and it has imprinted itself on my imagination as if I had known it all my life.

'*Echo* brought a lot of new friends in its wake,' Violet wrote in *Don't Look Round*. 'I realised I was a self-made woman and also, in spite of appearances, a lonely one.' Having two older women, Winnaretta Polignac and Alice Keppel, to look after her in Italy and France seems to have made her doubly childlike and she flirted with the notion of having a man to protect her. In her memoirs she presents herself, after Denys's death, as being besieged by male admirers. Max Jacob 'called on me one afternoon, dressed, he imagined, for the part of suitor. A small dapper Punchinello, he wore a top hat, white spats, gloves the colour of fresh butter. He hung his hat on a stick which he held like a banner between his legs.' He told her that he had waited forty years before proposing to anyone and that he possessed the great advantage, in a husband, of being twenty years older than Violet. 'He was irresistible,' she writes. And she had no difficulty in resisting him. Like so much else, it was a charade. She tells us that Max Jacob was a 'poet, painter, libertine, dandy, wit', but not that he was the current lover of the writer Maurice Sachs.

Don't Look Round gives a superficially accurate impression of Violet's social life during the 1930s. St Loup became a theatre and Violet 'a stage director', in Philippe Jullian's words, who used her rooms there as 'sets

against which she could act out the luxurious scenarios' of transfer-
ence and surmise. These scenarios became sinister parodies of her
mother's Edwardian career: both a homage and satire of Alice Keppel's
way of life. Mother and daughter were by now almost unnaturally
close to each other. 'You are all the world to me, and I could not live
without you,' Violet confided to her mother. And Mrs Keppel
reassured Violet ('precious Luna' as she called her – a name not so
very different from Vita's 'Lushka'): 'You know you are the person I
love best in the world.'

Violet's gift for mimicry and love of costume balls made her social
life at St Loup and the Villa dell' Ombrellino a camp version of hetero-
sexual games-playing. She entertained many improbable fiancés:
princes, counts, knights, prime ministers were her escorts but none of
them her lovers. They were for decoration and also perhaps camouflage for loves of another order – though by the time Philippe Jullian
met her after the war 'Violet had conceived a positive distaste for
Sapphic circles'.

'I had been put into the world to write novels,' she declared. Her
novels explore individual loneliness and the search for close attach-
ments within privileged circles of society. The success of *Echo* had given
her fresh confidence and she wrote her next novel in English, taking
it in the autumn of 1932 to Virginia Woolf with the intention of getting
the Hogarth Press to publish it. Virginia Woolf makes no mention of
meeting Violet in her diary and later on, after her own relationship
with Vita had ended, she confided to Ethel Smyth that she 'didn't take
to Trefusis'. But at the time she wrote excitedly to Vita: 'Lord what
fun! I quite see now why you were so enamoured – then; she's a little
too full now, overblown rather; but what seduction! What a voice –
lisping, faltering, what warmth, suppleness . . . like a squirrel among
buck hares – a red squirrel among brown nuts. We glanced and winked

through the leaves; and called each other punctiliously Mrs Trefusis and Mrs Woolf – and she asked me to give her the Common R[eader] which I did . . . And she's written to ask me to go and stay with her in France, and says how she enjoyed meeting me . . .'

But the Hogarth Press did not publish Violet's novel and 'I think she's been rather silly about it', Virginia confided to Vita. *Tandem*, as it was called, was published by Heinemann in 1933. Graham Greene in the *Spectator* noted that almost all the characters had titles, sometimes spelt in the English way, sometimes in the French, and there was a strong period atmosphere conveyed 'in a prose rather consciously spangled with felicities'. The motive for writing it he thought was 'indiscernible, but it has wit and is easily read'.

'There is in this book a great resemblance to the true course of people's lives,' the blurb of Putnam's American edition reads. But this social pageant bears no great resemblance to Violet's life. In order that it could be safely read by her mother (to whom it is dedicated), she was at pains to remove the characters and plot from anything that would prompt awkward memories. There is one significant minor figure from that period: a witchlike mischief-maker, the contriver and exploiter of love affairs, called Nancy, who is clearly based on Pat Dansey – though her origins are well concealed. The blurb informs readers that the author 'is the daughter of the Honorable Mrs George Keppel'. Who her father was we are not told.

It is called *Tandem* because, as the *Times Literary Supplement* reviewer explained, 'though Madame Demetriades had three daughters, Marguerite whose perfect digestion was considered a little vulgar did not count'. Marguerite is a stolid, healthy, uninteresting woman married to a wealthy nonentity and devoted to her recipes and her children (reflecting Violet's view of her sister Sonia).

The other two sisters show us alternative lives Violet might have lived: one wholly in France, the other in England. The brilliant Penelope marries a French duke, and becomes with miraculous rapidity a successful writer and a grande dame famous for collecting books and admirers (though being sensuous rather than sensual, and not caring for physical relationships, all her 'lovers' — save of course the King — are merely social companions). Her gentler sister Irene marries Mr Gottingale and is carried off to England where she tries hard not to be afraid of horses but is thrown and killed while hunting. Her story is mainly told through letters and journals. 'They know how to write, but no one has taught them how to live,' says their mother.

But Penelope lives on. 'Her nose had been bobbed, her eyes had been slit, and subsequently "taken in" again, her eyebrows had been plucked, her eyelashes had been artificially prolonged; her hair had been dyed over and over again . . .' She is lonely: her literary reputation has become a thing of the past, her husband is dead, her only comforts are food and the Légion d'honneur.

The Hogarth Press refusal of *Tandem* was a stimulus for Violet's novel, *Broderie Anglaise*. As *Orlando* had evolved from Vita Sackville-West's *Challenge*, so *Broderie Anglaise* took its origins from *Orlando* — the three interconnected novels woven round the love affairs of the three women. 'The balance between truth & fantasy must be careful,' Virginia Woolf had noted in her diary while working on *Orlando* in 1927. There is a different balance in *Broderie Anglaise*. It is a contemporary novel, disquisitory and domestic. There are no outrageous tricks with time, though tremors of human drama reverberate from the past and disturb the present. The character of Alexa Harrowby Quince (rather a sour fruit — it is a surname given to a servant in one of her later novels) is Violet's representation of Virginia Woolf. She is a bluestocking, well-known for her 'gastronomic incompetence', writing novels in a fussy Bloomsbury study, which contains an expensive counterfeit primitive from Siena and a genuine Roger Fry that 'would have been all the better for being a counterfeit'. Aspects of Violet herself are present in Anne Lindell, a legendary figure from the past, the two women, like their originals, having the same first letter of their initial names.

The novel is in part a branch of literary criticism (like Fielding wrote of Richardson's *Pamela* or Cervantes's *Don Quixote* was of *Amadis of Gaul*) and it contains some astute observations on *Orlando*. 'From a comfortable anonymity,' Alexa [Virginia] had used her novel to 'focus on Anne [Violet] the spotlight of her lucidity . . . She already knew her as if she had created her – every feature, every tone of voice.' But, we are told, Alexa 'was sometimes afraid truth might hamper her imagination, which used to get on so well on its own'. Her book exhibited Anne (that is Violet dressed in the exotic plumage of Sasha, the Russian princess) as a 'brilliant, volatile, artificial creature, predictably unpredictable, a historical character'. Alexa's novel became a whimsical success. 'The general public, with its taste for the romantic, loved the book. It also won enthusiastic praise from the critics, astonished to see Alexa depart from her usual austerity.'

As Violet had collaborated in the writing of *Challenge*, so she imagines the first chapter of *Orlando* arising from stories Vita had told Virginia about their romance (Vita may also have shown Virginia some of Violet's letters). In *Broderie Anglaise* it is upon a similar one-sided account – an account given to Alexa by her lover, the young Lord Shorne – that she based her book.

Lord Shorne is the male equivalent of Vita Sackville-West. He is a taciturn young man, disdainful, self-assured, a Prince Charming with heavy dark eyelids and full prominent lips – 'a hereditary face which had come, eternally bored, through five centuries' of one of his country's most illustrious families. A languid, sombre beauty, he has 'a latent fire which turned this picture of idleness into a figure of rhetoric'. Both Anne and Alexa believed they could bring this latent fire alive, give content to his rhetoric and rescue him from himself – and his mother. For he is a man divided against himself. The good John Shorne, we are told, 'was his father's son; the bad John Shorne was the son of his mother'.

His enormous castle called Otterways, 'at once a palace and fortress', is a fairy-tale setting with theatrical similarities to Knole. Alexa (now aged thirty-seven) had fallen in love at first sight with John Shorne (who is some eight years younger). This is her one-and-only love, her first sexual encounter. She is presented as a highly successful writer and 'one of the most distinguished women in England'. But despite being so sure of herself on the page, under her monastic reserve she is still socially inept and sexually apprehensive: all mind and little body. Her manner with Lord Shorne is arch, sentimental, helpless. She seems determined to prove a victim. Several times Violet plays with Virginia's name to emphasise Alexa's lack of femininity. 'It's not a question of virginity,' she protests, 'nothing so simple. It's an attitude.' Something chosen.

In her introduction to the first English-language edition of *Broderie Anglaise*, published in 1985, Victoria Glendinning makes the point that Violet uses her characters' hair as a symbol of their sensuality. Lord Shorne's name suggests that his hair has been closely sheared. Alexa's hair is thin, scanty and 'unenterprising'. She is a narrow angular figure with an elderly neck, contemplative, colourless, but with youthful eyes and beautiful hands.

There was not one detail of her person that was not famous from her nostalgic hats, medieval hands and timid expression to her little handbag that always ended up looking like a half-plucked chicken. The vagueness, or, rather, the limpness, of her clothes lent her movements the undulation of a sea-anemone. She was fluid and elusive; a piece of water-weed, a puff of smoke.

Lord Shorne is in love with Alexa's literary reputation; Alexa loves his aristocratic status. Violet parodies the historical romance of *Orlando* by leading the two of them into the Charles II bedroom at Otterways where (thinking they are unseen) they make love for the first time. Alexa is conscious of being 'awkward as a mistress and incomplete as a woman' and Lord Shorne wearily exploits her insecurity. 'Why won't you ever surprise me?' he chides her. It is the business of this novel to show how eventually she will surprise him.

Alexa's transformation comes about as the result of a meeting between her and Anne. Before their meeting, Alexa had hated the spectre of Anne, like an absent intruder who seemed all-powerful because wholly inaccessible, a ghost who could never be banished. Anne is a decade younger than Alexa, and was the childhood sweetheart of Lord Shorne. She has become a figure cloaked in legend: 'the only one that mattered', and is a ravishing beauty, says Lord Shorne. She is also the woman who mysteriously left him on what was to have been their wedding day and escaped to France (a re-enactment of Violet's dream of being rescued at the altar and carried off abroad by Vita).

Yet the woman who comes to tea and eats Alexa's chocolate éclairs is no great beauty after all. She is plumpish, with a turned-up nose, a large Asiatic red mouth and small eyes 'full of veils'. But she has 'a mass of thick springing hair, curly as vine tendrils, [which] stood up like a trodden-down bramble'. And then there is her voice: 'soft, full of hidden depths, crepuscular'.

Violet entertainingly develops a surreal conversation that took place between Alice Keppel and Virginia Woolf. She uses this source to emphasise the empty talk of her two protagonists. But as soon as the two women are left alone they say what's on their minds. Both of them have 'managed to breathe a semblance of life' into Lord Shorne: and as such this handsome puppet lives in their imaginations. Anne confesses that she still loves him. Why then did she abandon him? She did not abandon him. The villain of their story is Lord Shorne's mother.

'There was something not quite right about this great lady,' Alexa feels. She is ridiculous when seen 'clad in a dirty old flannel dressing-gown [and] covered with jewels from head to foot'; but sinister and dangerous when likened to 'a big spider in a web' hanging over the plot of the novel, terrifying her son and frustrating the women who love him. This corpulent, calculating, inquisitorial character is Violet's fictional portrait of Lady Sackville (more devastating but still recognisable as her description in *Don't Look Round* where she is not mentioned by name or listed in the index). In *Broderie Anglaise* she joins Violet's cast of matriarchal villains. She has room in her antique dealer's heart for only one love: Otterways, a castle to which she is fanatically attached.

Having gained a measure of feminine understanding, Alexa emerges as a more sympathetic person. Anne has offered her insights about the politics of love, which is what she knows best. But what can Alexa exchange for this knowledge? It is a promise to help with Anne's literary career — the sort of help that Violet had vainly hoped to gain from Virginia.

In the final paragraph, after Anne leaves with a present of Alexa's flowers, Violet makes a silent play on her own name by having Alexa think of 'the flower whose name must never be mentioned again because its scent was too powerful'. She breathes in the powerful knowledge she has been given. 'People only love those things they're never sure of,' Lord Shorne told her at the beginning of the novel. He will never again be sure of Anne.

Broderie Anglaise is an ingenious and original link to *Orlando* though there is no evidence that Virginia Woolf read it. Unlike *Orlando*, unlike *Challenge*, this novel has no dedication. It is a postmodern work, the work of a writer in exile. It was not translated into English for fifty years when, as Victoria Glendinning writes, it joined 'those other books that celebrate, satirize, justify, construct and deconstruct' the life and work of Virginia Woolf, Vita Sackville-West and Violet Trefusis herself. These associations enrich a narrative that is nevertheless strong enough to stand on its own.

Violet had now liberated herself from the *roman-à-clef* and wrote in English what is my favourite among her novels. *Hunt the Slipper* contains three traditional characters: the husband, his wife and her lover. Sir Anthony Crome is the dry, over-refined, good-looking husband, a man who leads 'the negligently luxurious life of the British aristocracy' and treats any display of natural emotion as vulgar. The critic Lorna Sage likened him to Meredith's egoist Sir William Patterne, or even Henry James's Osmond in *Portrait of a Lady* insofar as 'he shares their deadly capacity to translate art and sexuality into the stuff of lists, objects ordered and paid for (preferably, of course, by previous generations)'. To Violet's mind this habit was intellectually and spiritually embedded in the English aristocracy.

Five years before the novel opens Sir Anthony has married the young Caroline Trude, choosing her because she comes from a good county family, is presentable and, he believes, obedient. She will look well, he thinks, wearing the family jewels and will go well with the furniture in his Georgian house. He is essentially a curator and his house a museum. Caroline is part of his collection. But she is beginning to feel dismay at the prospect of spending the rest of her life opposite this desiccated man.

To her astonishment, she falls in love with a friend of her husband, the stocky, snub-nosed, forty-nine-year-old Nigel Benson who, to his dismay, falls in love with her. His character, with its limitations and potential, is cleverly delineated. He belongs to another sort of Englishman, one easily bored with men and dominated by women. He is not quite of the whole blood, his powerful grandmother having been French (he sometimes refers to himself as being 'half-French', which in Violet's dictionary means half-sympathetic). He has never married and lives with his sister Molly who has also never married because 'there would be no one to look after him' if she did. Both of them still love their dead mother, preferring her to anyone else dead or alive. Nigel 'passionately loved Caroline, but her love for his mother was different'. It is mothers like this who see to it that their children never grow up. None of the three main characters in the novel is really adult: not Anthony who collects furniture and pictures as a boy collects stamps or lead soldiers; nor Nigel who has been brought up 'amongst photograph albums, potted palms and gushing little trifles' and is helpless 'to the point of genius' in a larger world. His love for Caroline is his chance of growing up.

Caroline is also immature: but discontentedly so, like an unhappy child eager to get to the next stage of her life. She is one of Violet's most adventurous heroines, longing for risks, exposure and a hardening of the muscles, as she plots her escape from a world that, as Lorna Sage observes, bows to the 'power of places and things to collect the people who think they collect them'. Her brothers and her mother, like her husband and her lover, are all collectors of things: coins, keys, birds' eggs, Venetian glass. But Caroline is a changeling and the treasure she hunts is love. Will she find Cinderella's glass slipper? And if she does, will it fit? Anthony does not have the capacity for loving, but Nigel may have. Violet expertly guides him through the uneven landscape of love. (A masochistic feature, mentioned several times, may derive from Violet's relationship with the Princess de Polignac. 'Never you fear, you'll get beaten right enough,' Nigel assures Caroline, but she fears he is too kind for beating her, too conciliatory, too familiar with compromise.)

As in *Echo*, Violet uses letters sent and unsent, read and not read, to hide and then expose layers of this landscape. Caroline possesses all Violet's intransigence – she has no qualms about leaving her daughter as well as her husband to be with her lover. She wants, so she says (not very convincingly), to have Nigel's child. One can overhear the insistent ring of Violet's early letters when Caroline tells Nigel: 'I want to throw everything away for your sake. I wish you weren't so well-off. I could easily dispense with luxury.' Can Nigel meet the challenge Caroline sets him?

In a letter to Vita, Violet had written of the difficulty in finding an authentic happy ending to a serious novel. In the final two pages of *Hunt the Slipper* she reproduces the text of a letter that Nigel has delayed opening – a letter that gives a fertile twist to the plot and hands the ending of this tragicomedy to us, its readers.

In the second part of her memoirs called 'Youth', which reaches into the early 1940s covering her mid-forties, Violet is seen writing a series of articles for *Le Temps*. She is always on the move but obstructed by a series of accidents signalling the end of youth – 'I seem to be what is called "accident-prone",' she wrote, after having nearly drowned in the Seine, broken her hip, fractured her leg and been left 'with a slight limp for life'.

But she was becoming recognised as a novelist, publishing four novels in France within nine years, while her fifth, *Les Causes Perdues*, was due from Gallimard in 1941. There was a rumour that she was moving away from the politics of love to politics itself – a rumour occasioned by her frequent companion during the late 1930s, the Minister of Finance, Paul Reynaud (a rumour revived during her last years by her friendship with François Mitterrand). According to Violet, Paul Reynaud 'had a charming tenor voice; a quizzical eye, a caustic wit . . . He resented being short, and practically walked on tiptoe. His clothes were always ostentatiously neat . . . his wavy black hair was parted down the middle, and nearly rejoined his Mongolian eye-brows . . . What were his real convictions? He was, in point of fact, an *homme du Centre*, with little or no political backing. Excess was both alien and suspect to his frugal, fastidious mind.' This is not a description by someone who has entered the political world. But by 1939 everyone was caught up by the overwhelming tide of European politics. Violet's views were simple. 'I, who have never been anything but a pessimist by nature . . . knew the Germans . . . It is fatal to give in to a bully, or a bluffer. The Germans are both. I knew we were "in" for it.' (A dislike of Germany had been imprinted on her when she had been dumped down with her alien sister in Munich to complete her education far away from her mother and from Vita.)

'I was at St Loup when war was declared,' Violet wrote. 'There was not much excitement; rather, a sombre resignation, an air of fatality, anti-climax . . . My home was on the direct line of the invasion . . .'

She joined the ambulance brigade of the Red Cross – 'a somewhat quixotic gesture in view of the fact that she didn't know how to drive,' Philippe Jullian observed. She had finished *Les Causes Perdues* at the end of January 1940 and was in Paris when the German army pierced the French defences near Sedan and advanced towards Amiens and Arras. Paul Reynaud, who had become Premier in March, wanted to transfer the Government to North Africa but, none of his colleagues supporting him, he handed over to Pétain when the Germans entered Paris and was later imprisoned.

Violet was incensed when she heard that Pétain had petitioned for an armistice. 'I could not believe my ears. France! It wasn't credible. Of all countries the least compliant, the most refractory, the only country which takes itself for granted! . . . And this enfant terrible among nations, this spoilt child of Europe, with its impudence, cussedness, spunk, is to be surrendered without a murmur to the spirit breaker, the giant bully, the ostracised gatecrasher of Europe . . . What had possessed Reynaud to send for Pétain? Why hadn't he tried a *levée en masse*: it was not too late?' France appealed strongly to Violet – she identified with the country and felt it had much in common with her. But it would have been impossible for her to have joined the *levée en masse* she wished Paul Reynaud to lead, for she had already left St Loup and, wearing a mass of jewels like a covering of exotic armour, joined the hasty exodus from Paris.

'I was anxious about my parents.' Mrs Keppel was anxious about her money. 'My darling, we must discuss our finances,' she wrote. The Keppels left the Ritz in London during the spring of 1940 to negotiate with their bankers in Florence and Monte Carlo, and to place in safe storage many of their possessions at the Villa dell'Ombrellino. By the time Mussolini declared war on Britain, and under the protection of the British Consul, they had reached Biarritz. Violet gives a spirited account of what she did on behalf of her parents and herself to gain a safe passage to England. It shows all her stamina, initiative and determination, and also the complete uselessness of her desperate chase after Spanish and Portuguese visas compared with her mother's superior influence in securing them all places on a Royal Navy troopship sailing from St Jean-de-Luz in July 1940.

There are over thirty pages in *Don't Look Round* describing the five years Violet lived in England during the war and they are among the most charming and generous pages in her book. She wishes 'to do justice' to all those who were kind to her — for she was on the edge of a breakdown and 'looked upon England as exile'. It was a place of double exile: a country from which she had been expelled in the 1920s and where she was now incarcerated. Her melancholy surfaces in single sentences, or half-sentences, which appear within the telling of amusing anecdotes. '. . . It was as though I were in mourning for an unmentionable relation . . . longing for some kind of outlet, someone with whom I would not have to conceal my yearning for France as though it were an unsightly disease . . . I was fundamentally sad and homesick . . . My nights were tormented . . .'

James Lees-Milne observed that she was losing her good looks, but people still fell under her spell, including the royal biographer Doreen Colston-Baynes, who confessed to being hopelessly in love with her.

Violet sought intermittent isolation in Somerset. 'I have always loved the English countryside,' she wrote, 'its drowsy, hypnotic charm . . . like a cool hand on my brow . . . [but] what had I done to deserve the relative calm of the country? . . . I seemed singularly useless.'

She attempted to pick up old friendships where they had left off fifteen or twenty years earlier. It was an exercise in *le temps retrouvé*. 'In the summer of 1941 I visited lovely Sissinghurst for the first time; was amazed to discover in Sissinghurst a contemporary pendant to St Loup. *Chacun sa tour*.' After a passing reference, there is no further mention of Vita's world.

She longed to summon back the happy days of her childhood, the loving days and nights with Vita. But the past plays terrible tricks on us. Alice Keppel was no longer the resplendent figure of the Edwardian age. Who would have guessed that this substantial, overdressed, antique woman, now in her seventies, with her backache, bronchitis and bottles of gin, had been the famous 'Favorita' of the Prince of Wales? Nor was she any longer the wonderful mother who had illuminated Violet's early years, but simply 'your old sad Mor' who was being punished, she thought, for the abuse of 'too much' privilege in her youth. The gods give, and the gods take away. Little of this is examined in *Don't Look Round*, though Violet's awareness of it was to give the book its title. One never recovers from one's childhood. 'Too happy, as in my case, it exhaled an aroma with which the present cannot compete,' her epigraph reads, 'too unhappy, it poisons life at its source. In either case, it is wiser *not to look round.*'

Momentarily, she did look round at Vita. Meeting again in their mid-forties, each felt nervous of the other, coming together, moving apart, hopeful, hesitant, like shadows of their past selves performing a ghostly dance. Might they, Violet wondered, write a book together, recalling past days? But the naive days of *Challenge* were long gone. Vita does not seem to have mentioned the secret love journal she had written, which would be published only after they were both dead. Violet does not appear to have given her *Broderie Anglaise* — there was no copy in her library at Sissinghurst. One danger was that they might disturb the past and damage their living memories of it. Another danger was that the past might be rekindled and consume the present. Violet feared that seeing Vita again would renew her mother's antagonism. Vita feared seeing Violet might reignite feelings that would imperil her settled life with Harold and her successful literary career. She wrote of 'her absurd happiness of having you beside me in the car . . . I was frightened of you . . . I don't want to fall in love with you again . . . You and I can't be together . . . You have bitten too deeply into my soul.' And Violet had to be content with that.

Writing came to her rescue: but at a cost. She joined a society called the Fighting French and, feeling useful at last, gave talks for *La France Libre* at the British Broadcasting Corporation. She spoke of her travels while writing for *Le Temps*, of her love of France, of her literary friends there and her Francophile friends in England: Osbert Sitwell, Duff Cooper, Raymond Mortimer. She also brings in Harold Nicolson (whose first book had been a biography of Paul Verlaine) stressing his 'services to France' and describing him as the 'most eloquent of its interpreters who, by his temperament, his culture and his spontaneous spirit, is better able than anyone to understand the French'. Despite her embarrassing habit of repeating his jokes and getting them wrong in her attempts to improve them, she had become 'a good old sort', Harold confided to an astonished Vita (who was describing her, rather invitingly, in a letter to their son Ben as 'one of the most dangerous people I know'). Much of what Violet broadcast overlaps with a collection of autobiographical pieces called *Prelude to Misadventure* dedicated to the 'faithful French who have left their families in order to fight on our side'. The book was published by Hutchinson in 1942 and reviewed by Raymond Mortimer in the *New Statesman*. 'She is remarkably sensitive to the genius of place,' he wrote. '. . . She has lived for twenty years in France; she evidently thinks more naturally in French than in her native tongue . . . [but] she remains incorrigibly English.'

Violet did little imaginative writing during these years in England. But she contributed two short stories to *Horizon*, Cyril Connolly's review of literature and art. 'The Carillon' which appeared in June 1943 is a grim and powerful story set in the late winter of 1940. In her moth-pale room the Duchess goes through the list of those she most despises as she waits impatiently for death. She is 'dying of rage, of humiliation, of despair, and frustration; also, incidentally, of the hereditary tumour, that had almost acquired heraldic significance'. The Duchess dies: and those whom she despised gather, like a swarm of black termites, for the funeral. There is a slight anti-German flavour to the story. How will France emerge from this darkness? 'The carillon was like the soul of France, icily aloof, impregnable, enduring' – all qualities Violet would need in the 1940s. Again Time passes: Violet's world is vanishing and comfort slips away. She feels the rage, humiliation, despair and frustration of her Duchess whose fate foretells her own.

Her second contribution to *Horizon*, which appeared in November 1943, was 'Triptych': three paragraphs listing, thesaurus-fashion, the qualities of England, France and Italy – something she enjoyed composing. It gave her licence to play with the similarly spelt and similar-sounding words she always liked to handle: 'snubs and snobs' (England); 'forms and formality' (France); 'bells and smells, Quirinals and urinals' (Italy). Perhaps it is a fiction, but it is not a story. 'I could not work regularly,' she admitted in her memoirs. 'I had lost the rhythm.'

Published not very long before the Germans began moving into unoccupied France, her novel *Les Causes Perdues* itself seemed something of a lost cause. It is a sombre book and it had come before the public in unhappy times.

The novel is set in a small town near Poitiers. Each of the characters has a lost cause, which must have seemed something of an indulgence during the German occupation. The ageing coquette, Solange de Petitpas, has Violet's juvenile outlook. 'If this aged little girl has the stubborn cult for her childhood,' she writes, 'it is because it is the only thing that cannot be taken away from her. She shuts herself up in it more and more.' The novel has many subplots and is full of violence. Mme de Norbières, the owner of a priceless collection of snuffboxes, is murdered in her bed. Solange's maid shoots and kills her mistress mistaking her for an intruder. Adieu old age; adieu solitude. The pain of lost causes spreads through all the characters. Love itself is a lost cause and doing good to others the height of folly. No one is worth it; no one is lovable. This is Violet's darkest book. The critic and translator Judith Landry likens it to Daisy Ashford's

'*Young Visiters* for adults'. Raymond Mortimer had written of Violet as having the wit to enjoy her privileged social life and the ability to make her readers share her enjoyment. *Les Causes Perdues* shows what bleakness underlies that patina of enjoyment. It was the last novel she wrote in French and it has not been translated into English.

'My English friends would not like me any the less if I gave up writing (for some, it would be, if anything, rather a relief),' Violet wrote. '. . . had I lived all my life in England, not France, it is very doubtful whether I would ever have published anything.'

Nevertheless she began another novel while in England, an early draft of which was typed by Harold Nicolson's secretary ('Well the pattern of life is odd,' Vita remarked).

Pirates at Play is a moral history of young women of Violet's social class in England and Italy during the 1920s. It does not belong, as initially seems probable, to the romantic tradition of Charlotte Brontë, but follows the lead of Jane Austen, being a courtship novel, which plots a similar course to that of *Pride and Prejudice*. The watchword is patience ('*pazienza*'), a quality that had been dramatically absent from Violet's youth. We are shown how foreign culture, so superficially attractive when first encountered, acts on our instincts like a magnet on a compass, steering us away from 'everything that makes life worthy living'. That seems a strange phrase for a reader expecting the words 'worth living' and it stirs a suspicion that Violet, who sprinkles French and Italian words so lavishly into her English narratives, might be suffering from the difficulty experienced by a minor French character in the novel: that of having 'lived so long in England, that she could speak neither English or French'. And yet 'worthy living' is not an inappropriate phrase for a moral history.

Using a comic dexterity similar in some respects to Dryden's

Marriage-à-la-Mode, Violet manipulates her two overlapping plots so that they both arrive simultaneously at a happy ending – the first and only absolute happy ending in all her novels. The story involves two families and two heroines, Ludovica (Vica), the only daughter among six children of the Pope's dentist; and Elizabeth (Liza), the daughter of insular fox-hunting English parents, Lord and Lady Canterdown. They send their daughter to complete her education in Florence (instead of Taunton), though naturally they will not countenance having 'an ice-creamer for a son-in-law'.

Both girls are appallingly good-looking. Vica, with her topaz eyes and hypnotic voice, is a frightening beauty – likened to a runaway horse. She has the ability to play many roles ('One day I am Lucrezia Borgia, another day I am Isabella d'Este') and has begun to sense the power her beauty brings, finding it 'fun to carve one's initials on people's hearts': then 'give them no further thought'. She is not, as she confides in a moment of unhappiness, 'a nice person'.

Liza is less sophisticated. She does not suspect the poetic licence given to beauty, but has at her command a disarming directness, inter-rupted by bursts of boyish laughter (though no marks of humour crease the solemn beauty of her face). 'Everything about Liza shone; her hair, eyes, teeth, skin. She was made of gold.'

Vica and Liza belong to different worlds and in this comedy of errors both look on the other as 'a necessary stage in her education'. The two girls, 'so different, yet completed each other'. Their education takes a turn on the amorous merry-go-round of Violet's novels: it is fuelled by jealousy and malice; by idealised snobbery and subtle miscalculation; and exploitation by the powerful, the apprehensions of those exploited, and also the dangers of sibling love. And what they learn is how to separate powerful secondary considerations from what is primary and genuine. Violet's melancholy is represented by the one ugly, unappreciated brother in Vica's handsome Florentine family. Rigo is the jester at court, a wise fool who is licensed to speak the truth, a creature resembling Caliban, dwarf-like, freakish, lovelorn and lonely, with exuberant gifts as a comedian and an imaginative musician who plays from behind a curtain as Cyrano de Bergerac speaks from behind a tree.

The Violet Trefusis who wrote this novel is no longer in the shadow of Vita. In a letter to Pat Dansey written at the beginning of May 1921 when, exiled from England and under constant surveillance in Italy, she was prevented from communicating with Vita, she described Florence as 'a pestilential place'. Again, in mid-June, she writes: 'As for Florence – !!! I have never hated a town so much . . . One day, if I'm still alive, I shall write a book about Florence. It will be vitriolic.' *Pirates at Play*, published almost forty years later, is that book. Violet's early memories have not entirely faded, particularly her memories of the ageing English governess who, under Mrs Keppel's instructions, kept watch on her in Florence all those years ago (a governess referred to as Miss and pronounced 'Mees' by the Italians). She hands down her long-delayed sentence of justice, the justice of revenge, on the British colony of Florence.

The ancient flower-maidens, wedded to Florence since they first saw the light, nearly half a century ago, making do on a miserable pittance, cutting down everything except their tea! Year by year as they grow older, their hats get younger, more floral, more desperately girlish . . . they continue to admire what they were told to admire when first they came to learn, or to teach . . .

. . . Every indigent Florentine family keeps a tame 'Mees', like some curious pet. The ever-increasing children are taken to see her, as they would be shown a giraffe in the Zoo. They gape at her . . . Never have they seen anything so flat, so barren, so limitless . . .

... Sometimes letters would arrive bearing the postmark of Bournemouth or Sevenoaks. For a few minutes, the voluntarily exiled blue eye is reclaimed by the memory of a certain herbaceous border in June, or a windy walk on the pier, then she catches sight of the ubiquitous Duomo from her window, and all else is blotted out. She sinks back reassured. Yes, it was worth it!

Such passages on the pitiful English expatriates exhibit what Tiziana Masucci calls Violet's 'eye for frailties, her sarcastic tongue'. But her tirade is not wholly aimed at Italy. 'What do they know of Italy who only Florence know?' Violet asks. Her contempt for this English detritus washed up on the smug little hills round Florence is outstripped by her diatribe against the English at home: an effete and undeveloped race without virility or imagination.

... Everything is like English cooking, neutralized, asepticized, castrated. All the good natural juices have been squeezed out. Though they have the richest vocabulary in the world ... they only use about five hundred words ... Their vocabulary is not only restricted, it is cowardly. They refer to diseases by their initials, as though they were old schoolmates, T.B., V.D., etc. They cannot bring themselves to say someone is dead, they say he has 'passed away' or 'gone over' . . . . Infantilism is carried to incredible lengths.
... They are too lazy to hate, it is too much of an effort. The climate is one of affectionate indifference, they are not particularly interested in you, but neither are they particularly interested in themselves.

This is Violet's verdict on those English patriots who had gossiped about her and helped to throw her out of the country – though 'revenge is dead sea fruit'. What is more remarkable is Violet's concealed criticism of herself and her mother. Reading of the Princess Arrivamale's preparations for a great dinner party at the Palazzo Arrivamale, we may catch a glimpse of Mrs Keppel's social life at the Villa dell'Ombrellino (Arrivamale meaning the opposite of a welcome). The part the Princess most enjoyed, we are told, was 'placing the cards on the dinner table. While submitting to the dictates of protocol, she was able nevertheless to distribute rewards and punishments; promoting Y, abasing Z. It gave her a delicious sensation of power.'

The Princess's cynical manipulation of the characters as she plots their unsuitable marriages is Violet's version of her mother's manipulation of her two daughters (Sonia Keppel had by now parted from her husband). The old lady reveals, too, some of the least attractive characteristics that Violet herself was acquiring in her late fifties, including the offhand treatment of servants.

Pirates at Play is a subtle and crowded book. We are introduced in the first few pages to a bewildering number of characters who, after a few lines, seek their fortunes outside the novel — though these fortunes, when eventually revealed, contribute to its theme, which is kept steadily in focus. The style is orchestrated by that clash of similar-sounding nouns and adjectives which Violet loved to put together: anonymous/unanimous; muddler/meddler; monastic/scholastic.

Lisa St Aubin de Teran describes Violet as a social pirate who specialised in the 'constant sand-papering away of hopes and aspirations' within *Pirates at Play*. 'As the author schemes and the characters scheme, each to deceive, disturb or betray, the effect is of a world in microcosm, ruled by prejudice and by misconception which produces various states of alienation.' But Violet has now gained the confidence, skill and authority to rescue her two heroines from the machinations of the plot, bringing them in from their outposts of alienation, manipulating her readers and making her characters too 'enjoy being manipulated', Lisa St Aubin concludes, 'which is no easy task'.

The autobiographical references in the novel are like request stops in a helter-skelter progress, which delighted Proust's English biographer George Painter. 'Her prose is as pure and glittering as an icicle shining in the sun,' he wrote. 'But it moves us in a smoothly hurtling course, with swift lurches and recoveries into slang, internal rhyme, one-word epigrams: so shall I compare the experience of reading it to being driven at 90 m.p.h. over an icefield, by a driver who knows how to skid for fun? . . . The beauty of the girls and the prose style introduce what might have been in total effect a cruel novel, a saving poignancy.'

9

Looking Round

It was the best of times. 'I have no hesitation in saying it was the happiest day of my life,' Violet wrote, remembering the day in 1946 she travelled back to France. 'Sight by sight, sound by sound, the Past was returning; it was really like a reincarnation . . . I was back in Paris! . . . France had been restored to me.'

She dreaded finding out what had been done to St Loup by the occupying German army. 'Nothing is more unpleasant than the knowledge that one's home has been occupied by the enemy.' Their favourite game, she was told, had been dressing-up in her underclothes and strutting up and down the catwalk of her dining-room table – a pornographic parody of Violet's fancy-dress parties. Although some of the furniture had been crippled, many of her books were gone, several pictures damaged, the walls covered with graffiti, 'the place gave the impression of vitality increased, rather than diminished'. Over the year St Loup was 'patched and painted [and] began to recall its past'.

In Paris, too, she set about recapturing the past. She stayed at the British Embassy as the guest of the Ambassador Duff Cooper and his wife Lady Diana Cooper (who, as Lady Diana Manners, before the First World War had presented Eve Fairfax with her extraordinary visitor's book). She had given Violet money to live on during the war and Violet was to repay her in various ways, leaving her son (much to his surprise) a handsome sum of money in her Will, and then another sum by making it a condition, in the event of St Loup's new owner John Phillips selling the house, that he pay Lady Diana or her heir half the sale price.

Diana Cooper gave a grand party for Violet at the Embassy to which she invited 'my friends before the war'. She also entertained Alice Keppel and her husband when, more cautiously, they returned to Europe. In Florence, Alice Keppel soon began renovating the Villa dell'Ombrellino and 'my mother and I made lovely plans for the future'.

But Mrs Keppel had no future. She was suffering from cirrhosis of the liver and had only a few months to live. 'The terrible routine of illness set in,' Violet wrote. The contrast between the sunlight of Florence and the hushed climate of her mother's bedroom (like the interior and exterior scenes in *Echo*) grew unbearable. But Violet was impressed by her mother's serenity and the way in which the lines on her face, those channels of old age, were mysteriously fading. 'She will make a success of her death, was my involuntary thought,' Violet remembered. She stayed in her mother's bedroom reading to her as long as she could – far longer than she had been able to stay with Denys Trefusis. Mrs Keppel died on 11 September 1947. 'Yet, I wasn't with her when she died . . . When I came in, her head, with its blunt white curls, was buried like a child's in her pillow.'

In the account of her mother's last illness in *Don't Look Round*, Violet wrote of having bent over her despairingly towards the end, asking if there was anything she wanted, and hearing the whispered answer: 'You. You.' The final chapter of her memoirs is a eulogy of her mother. She has greatly changed. 'My mother never tried to influence me,' she writes; 'the result was that, in point of fact, she was the only person who did.' She recalls her mother's religious sense, her charity, unselfishness, humility. In all her life, Violet tells us, she had never 'let anyone down'. And she concludes: 'there is no limit to my debt.' It was no surprise that her father consented to die soon afterwards. Violet, too, had no strong wish to survive. 'What has happened to me since is but a postscriptum.'

'Something comparable to a landslide took place in me,' she wrote. In this fallen and infertile landscape she lives a postscriptum life in the sense that it is not a novel-writing life. She can no longer look round and use aspects of her past to create imaginative fiction. So much of her fiction had, by implication, been a criticism of her mother's way of life – and that is no longer permissible. There is almost no mention of her novels in *Don't Look Round*. But she had another twenty-five years to get through. In 1960 the mildly amusing *Memoirs of an Armchair* written by Violet and Philippe Jullian (who also illustrated it) was published. It is a device that enables the authors to escape from the present and give us intimate glimpses of what-ever events in history they choose. This aristocrat among chairs was made in Paris in 1759 and takes us on adventures from the royal apartments at Versailles (where it supported Louis XV) to episodes in Regency London and 'the roaring twenties' in the United States. We have brief encounters with Voltaire, Talleyrand, Balzac, Byron, Lady Hamilton, Diaghilev and others. It is a party-game book.

Violet's last book was *From Dusk to Dawn*. It has her name on the title page though it was also written by Frank Ashton-Gwatkin, a retired diplomat (who added a hagiographic introduction), and it carries a dedication to him ('my companion, my guide and my own familiar friend'). It is a not very amusing mock-Gothic novella and was published a few months after Violet's death.

Violet's memoirs take her up to her fifty-ninth year when *Don't*

Look Round was published. 'By craning a little, I can see into the sixties,' she wrote. She saw herself: 'rich and blue of hair, hostessy, successful'. But at another level they were 'less successful' years, indeed awful, these 'secretly obscene sixties . . . hiding their revelatory passports like a crime . . . Haggard, hunted sixties, terrified of missing some-thing, rubbing themselves superstitiously against the topical, the fashionable, men and women of the day . . . this sad crowd . . . rich in experience and indulgence . . . Extreme old age is as lonely as God. It has no one to talk to . . . Survival is the ultimate satisfaction' – unless, like Solange in *Les Causes Perdues*, you can make yourself believe that you will see your loved one after death.

Coming at the end of a great tradition of the novel as social tragicomedies of manners, Violet had added a penetrating and authentic minor variation to the genre, which might be called flir-tatious tragedy. She combined French wit with English seriousness and relied, not simply on customs belonging to a social milieu that no longer exists, but on the way human nature operates in highly mannered and amoral circumstances. She was a chronicler of the human heart. The writer who worked alone for two or three hours each morning went about her business ruthlessly dissecting the woman who would occupy the rest of the day so emptily in smart society 'not caring a damn for anyone'. Unable to write by the end, she is stranded: 'utterly lost, miserably incomplete, condemned to leading a futile, purposeless existence', as she had predicted in one of her letters to Vita.

'Is St Loup a comfort?' Winnaretta Polignac wrote to her. 'I hope so. I don't like to think you are sad and dépaysée [disenfranchised].' But this is how she was. Alice Keppel had left Violet a lifetime's tenancy of the Villa dell'Ombrellino, but none of the furniture, almost all of which her sister Sonia insisted on selling. Violet would spend the spring and autumn in Florence, and the rest of the year at St Loup, being chauffeured between the two houses, the car rattling with acquisitions. In 1958 she added a new complication to her life by buying an apartment in Paris. It was the wing of a mansion in the rue du Cherche Midi that had once belonged to the Duc de Saint-Simon (and was later bought by Andy Warhol). She decorated the enormous drawing room, the conservatory and bedrooms with marble busts, Aubusson rugs, Louis XV chairs and eighteenth-century portraits. From here it was no distance to London where Violet would stay, as her mother had done, at the Ritz Hotel. Wherever she went she travelled with her chauffeur and her maid. She could not be alone and yet, however chaotically crowded her life, 'I was the cat that walked by itself.'

At one place and another she commanded an army of servants: cooks, gardeners, butlers ... She treated them unceremoniously, seldom letting them know how many people were coming to lunch or whether she was going out for dinner. She would dismiss them, employ others, then sack them and engage more. But there was one exception to this disorder. Madame Alice Amiot, her chic flirtatious maid, was, so Violet claimed, Proust's cousin. She had been the mistress, it was rumoured, of a grand duke. And she had the same first name as Violet's mother. Her presence became very necessary to Violet who behaved like a tremulous and demanding child, often going to Alice's bedroom and waking her at night. Vita visited St Loup after Mrs Keppel's death and was shocked by the way Violet spoke to this maid. 'It's really more than a little mad,' she told Harold. Alice complained that her health was breaking down under this treatment and Vita predicted that 'Alice really will go' after which Violet would be miserable. But Alice did not go. It was a strange game they played. Alice treated Violet as if she were royalty, though, at a practical level, she herself was in command of everything. She became 'her surrogate mother, nursemaid, confidante and lady-in-waiting', Diana Souhami writes.

Over these last years Violet entered ever more deeply into a make-believe world. When young she had been carried into a fancy-dress party in a carpet which, suddenly unrolling, revealed her as Cleopatra. Now she made her entrance with solemn grandmotherly tread as Queen Victoria. She was hedged about with the illusions of royalty. Lord Grimthorpe had faded in her imagination and the Prince of Wales, King Edward VII, took his place as her father. She told everyone, in strict confidence, that she was thirteenth in line to the English throne. Her royal identity, she confided to her friend John Phillips, was the reason for her sister's sense of inferiority, which 'in a way poisoned her life'. Sonia 'cannot accept my being who I am'. But the un-mentionable fact was that if anyone was the illegitimate daughter of the Prince of Wales it had been Sonia, born in 1900 while he and Alice Keppel were conducting their famous affaire. As if to lend credence to this hypothesis, it was Sonia's granddaughter Camilla who, after another clandestine relationship, went on to marry Charles, her Prince of Wales, early in the twenty-first century.

After the war, Violet continued collecting 'fiancés', one of the most daring, a celebrated bullfighter, enabling her to assume the role of Carmen. Many of her closest friends were homosexual men who, according to Vita, 'all dislike each other'. (Vita herself had shown contempt for Harold's 'cheap and easy loves . . . Those rank intruders into darkest layers.') It was to Vita, many years before, that Violet had declared how much she preferred heterosexual to homosexual men. Over homosexual men she had no power. But after her mother's death she attained the power of wealth. She gathered round her people who dedicated their lives to amusing and admiring her. And she played games with them, turning their speculations and investments of time into charades. Who would inherit her apartment in Paris, her house at St Loup de Naud, her pictures and, above all, her parade of jewels? The wheel spun and the distribution changed, spun again and changed again. The game never ended till it came to a halt in a chaos of contra-dictory Wills.

She had become a subversive snob. Strict rules of precedence and attire were observed at the Villa dell'Ombrellino. Everything was correct; everything mocked. Like royalty, she would approach the dinner table, once everyone had reached the appropriate place. She advanced, leaning on a stick and the arm of an elderly butler or some promoted favourite of the evening, and attended by Alice darting back and forth behind her with whispered instructions about handbags and handkerchiefs. During dinner she would, like an actress, make up her face a dozen times while her guests were eating (between meals she liked to touch up the photos of herself by Cecil Beaton and others – though she never took a paintbrush to her portraits by James Lavery, Jacques-Emile Blanche, Ambrose McEvoy and others). When she rose from dinner she would spread a cascade of crumbs around her. She liked to take aside some retired Italian diplomat or elderly member of the English aristocracy to express her political concerns: 'China worries me,' she would murmur. She kept alive the hostility her mother had formed with Bernard Berenson and made a new enemy of Harold Acton. But on bright days she was playful, generous, alert, amusing and irrepressibly flirtatious with the men she liked – her friends (who included her sister's granddaughter Annabel, an art student in Florence) all used these words to describe her.

Vita died in 1962, and Violet's health deteriorated. It was the worst of times. All was waste: 'waste of love, waste of talent, waste of enter-prise'. In the Gothic atmosphere of St Loup, its great tower visited by migratory birds rising from the mist, traces of vanished lovers seemed to linger, their shades not entirely dispelled, registering unmitigated passions like distant cries from the dungeons. There is an evocative description of these last years by Philippe Jullian:[8]

> At l'Ombrellino she wandered beneath the cypresses like an exiled queen who could entrust her confidences only to the statues lining the terraces. At St Loup, she climbed the tower to make sure all was in order in those charming rooms which sheltered charming friends but never, alas, the valiant lover . . . for whom she had longed . . . her faithful friends were part of the décor, walk-ons in the plays of the imagination in which Violet took the leading roles. With the onset of age, insomnia and illness, these roles became harder for her audience to follow, despite the fact that they were rehearsed again and again. They concealed the real Violet behind the clown's make-up applied by a blind man. Her friends suffered as they watched . . . Approaching seventy, Violet looked eighty.

In 1970 Alice Amiot died and Violet, appearing at parties as a ghostly and a ghastly figure (as she herself might have written and as Vita had foreseen), endured the humiliations that afflicted the Duchess in her *Horizon* story 'The Carillon'. Ravaged by infirmities, treated with blood transfusions, almost incapable of walking, waiting for death, she sat among her audience of guests at St Loup like a damaged relic from a

---

[8] After Violet's death, Philippe Jullian's life went into a decline. Some eight months later, his home caught fire destroying many of his possessions including his pictures. He grew increasingly dependent on his Moroccan servant and companion Hamoud who helped him settle into an apartment in Paris. On 23 September 1977, Hamoud was stabbed to death by a stranger and, five days later, the police found Philippe Jullian's body hanging from a hook inside the front door of his new apartment.

distant past, unable to eat yet still greedy for gossip, a living skeleton at the head of her table, fiddling with the bread – a more horrific version of Dickens's Miss Havisham. Charades and fantasies made life bearable, kept her alive. 'I do not cling to life,' she insisted; but cling to it she did – she could not help herself. Arriving at the Villa dell'Ombrellino at the end of 1971, its fountains empty, dead flowers bent over the flower beds, she retired to her bedroom (once her mother's bedroom), her Fabergé animals and jade statuettes round the walls – and starved to death on 1 March 1972.

Epilogue

Time Regained

This book has its origins in the Villa Cimbrone from where I set out to rediscover some of the women in the life of its owner Ernest Beckett. In retrospect it appears in my dreams like a mirage, a place that exists but not quite where it seems to be. It belongs now to my imagination. As I was writing this book, the villa came to represent a challenge and an opportunity – an opportunity to meet the challenge to biography, in particular its intractability, set by Virginia Woolf's *Orlando*.

Cimbrone is a place of beauty and relaxation; it is not a centre for archival research. Working on one of the terraces there in the evening sunlight, I came across a photograph of Eve Fairfax taken at the time she was engaged to Ernest Beckett (and was sitting for Rodin). But none of the love letters Ernest had written to her then, and which she had many years later given to Ernest's daughter Lucille, has survived. Nor was there any record at Cimbrone of Ernest's American wife Luie who had died so young – long before he retired to the villa (though he had transported other mementoes from his past). I did find a signature by his daughter Violet, but none of her books was in the library and I saw no evidence of her mother, Alice Keppel's, love affair with him. And yet, though the villa provided me with almost no facts, no information, none of what Virginia Woolf called 'granite', my days at Cimbrone somehow increased my determination to reach these women and write, not so much a traditional 'biographical' narrative, as a set of thematically related stories. Of necessity there are many empty spaces marking what has been hidden or forgotten, lost or misunderstood – mysterious spaces, which have themselves become part of a recurring pattern in this recreation of their lives.

In her novels, Violet Trefusis warns her readers against giving priority to places above people – as if falling in love with a place will protect you against the agony of grief. Cimbrone contained nothing that was obviously useful for Ernest's granddaughter Catherine Till in her attempt to solve the problem of her parentage. But the spirit of this place had intensified her love for someone absent. There is nothing definitive at the villa, but the atmosphere appears to prompt speculation and bring back the past. And it seems to me that an intense involvement with absent people from the past is what moves biographers to write.

As for Tiziana Masucci, there could not have been a better frame for her exhibition, dedicated to Violet Trefusis, than the cloisters of the Villa Cimbrone. And when she turned her hypnotic gaze on me it was not on her own behalf, but on behalf of someone who had taken possession of her. Nowhere else, I think, would I have been so receptive to her appeal to bring Violet and her writings into my book.

This book has no settled agenda. I do not insist that women are superior to men or claim that the past was more glorious than the present – indeed the word 'illegitimate' is mercifully fading in our time and we content ourselves by expressing our moral indignation over other people's behaviour with the bureaucratic and impotent word 'unacceptable'. That, too, will fade.

Go to the Villa Cimbrone today and you will see a rather different place with a helicopter landing pad, a swimming pool, a cocktail party lawn, polite teas and all the lavish paraphernalia of a five-star hotel. But it commands the same view over the Gulf of Salerno as it did for Ernest Beckett in 1905. Some of the garden remains as it had been and you may be confronted round any corner, behind any tree, by some Beckett eccentricity. The reclining golden statue of a plump and naked Eve, which D. H. Lawrence covered in mud, is still protected by its cage in the rock as it was when I first went there.

At the villa I visited more than ten years ago there were no paying guests and, in those bright pretty rooms with their terrific furniture, it was easier to conjure up the Beckett family who had intermittently lived there for over half a century. It was as if the fire that broke out on the top floor had only recently consumed their troubled past and that the palazzo and its gardens were still occupied by shades from that past. I stood in the temple where Ernest Beckett's ashes had been buried and thought of Luie and Eve and José and Alice and others who had for a time belonged to his world — as he did to theirs. On my second journey I delivered my talk in one of the garden pavilions summoning the spirits of Bloomsbury — Lytton Strachey, Virginia Woolf and by association Vita Sackville-West, who had all played with time, fantasy and the transfer of identities.

Now, as in a film, I can bring back the characters who occupy the pages of this, my last book. I can imagine them arriving at the Villa Cimbrone I recognise, and hear them filling all those empty spaces in my narrative that I could not complete. Finally they will all meet one another, explain what had been inexplicable and learn with much amazement and the shaking of heads what they never knew before: and then, after a silence, the sound of laughter. So everything will be understood and what had been grief, and the avenging of grief, will at last be transmuted into the comedy of life.

Afterword

A History of the Books

In 1973 Nigel Nicolson published *Portrait of a Marriage* and the name Violet Trefusis, which had been largely forgotten in England, surfaced again and re-acquired its notoriety.

As he read Vita Sackville-West's hidden love journal after his mother's death in 1962, Nigel became convinced that she wished it to be posthumously published. 'She could have destroyed it,' he wrote. 'It presumed an audience.' But Violet Trefusis and Nigel's father, Harold Nicolson, were both still alive. He was chiefly concerned about his father and, when Harold died in 1968, only Violet stood in his way. He had lent Vita's precious manuscript to a number of his friends, most (though not all) of whom advised him to publish it. 'It is one of the most remarkable things that your mother ever wrote,' Peter Quennell answered. 'You need not fear damage to her reputation. It might have been so in 1950 or 1960. But not now. And don't worry about V[iolet] T[refusis]. She is among the stupidest and most conceited women I have ever come across, and I suspect that she would be highly flattered.'

Nevertheless Nigel decided that he should not publish the journal while Violet Trefusis was alive. He was encouraged in this postponement by Violet's sister, Sonia, who wrote to him coldly about 'this distasteful book' and was to cause him 'great trouble with her [Violet's] intellectual friends' such as Cyril Connolly who 'cut me dead'. But Connolly considered Vita Sackville-West 'a damned outmoded poet' — so perhaps this was no loss. He had met Violet Trefusis in the late 1920s, describing her as 'very attractive, rather heavy and vicious-looking and the only person here [Florence] who one feels is really modern'. Later he used her for the 'wicked . . . fat red-head' Geraldine in his novel *The Rock Pool* (1936), representing her as having a 'rakish musical voice, a babyish prettiness' and 'the wide sensual mouth of a Rowlandson whore'. Connolly's Geraldine is made for mischief and, though sometimes charming, she had the 'trick of leading people on till she could make them in some way ridiculous'.

After Violet died in 1972, Nigel began preparing Vita's journal for publication. He did not alter or suppress anything his mother had written, but the thirty thousand words he added to the book as co-author placed the Vita–Violet love affair, which in his estimate lasted hardly more than three years, against a marriage that lasted fifty years. And to make his agenda clear he called the book *Portrait of a Marriage*. His is the single name on the title page and he dedicates the book to someone he had greatly loved, S[hirley] A[nglesey]. The one event he concealed in his commentary was the venereal infection Harold Nicolson had caught in 1917 which, Nigel believed, had prompted Vita's affaire with Violet. But 'the crisis in the marriage made it all the more successful and secure,' he wrote. His book demonstrated 'the triumph of love over infatuation'.

Though he accepted that later in her life Violet Trefusis had changed in character and become the author of 'some clever novels', he hated the thought of her remorseless campaign to take Vita away from his father and the family. In his autobiography *Long Life*, he wrote that nothing could excuse Violet's youthful selfishness. 'She had attempted to destroy the happy marriage of her closest friend, and herself married a decent man, Denys Trefusis, with the sole intention of humiliating him. She despised marriage, thinking it a hypocritical façade for infidelity, like the marriage of her own mother, Alice Keppel . . .' And, it is only reasonable to add, not unlike Vita's infidelity-ridden marriage to Harold.

Vita had always put others before her sons in her emotional priorities. If her unsatisfactoriness as a mother, her awful absences, were to be traced back to any single person, it was not to Violet Trefusis but to Vita's mother Lady Sackville who, being illegitimate, had to contend with her own difficulties – which became part of Vita's inheritance. Under the cover of celebrating her marriage to Harold, the reader of *Portrait of a Marriage* is led into believing that their happy if unconventional union was seriously threatened by one person – and that person was Violet. Vita's love for Violet was certainly the most intense passion of her life, and so perhaps Nigel was right to see her as a threat. But his motives in deciding to publish his mother's manuscript were made more complicated by his knowledge that the book might be seen as a form of filial revenge. People who had liked Vita and knew little or nothing of her love for Violet would read *Portrait of a Marriage* and think less of her. (Lord Sackville, for example, who had 'great admiration for your mother', wrote to say that 'these feelings have been tarnished by your book).'

Nigel Nicolson was as remote a parent as his mother had been. 'My sisters and I orbited around the sad and central absence of our father,' Adam Nicolson writes in *Sissinghurst: An Unfinished History*. Nigel had many sterling attributes, talents and virtues, yet there seemed some human quality lacking in him. 'He is a cold man who wants to be warm,' James Lees-Milne wrote, 'and cannot be.' And now he was about to risk embarrassing his children by opening a secret cupboard and letting out the family skeleton to dance for public entertainment and, as Violet's sister Sonia accused him, 'for profit'.

Yet who would have thanked him or felt he had acted nobly if he had simply destroyed his mother's hidden manuscript? Would that not also have been construed as revenge? Whatever he did, guilt would descend on him.

But there was another motive for publishing *Portrait of a Marriage*. The way he had constructed the book was highly original: it evolved into an extraordinary hybrid like his father, Harold Nicolson's, *Some People*. Each book has a secure place in the history of non-fiction and semi-fictional literature. *Some People* was praised highly by Virginia Woolf and influenced her writing of *Orlando*. *Portrait of a Marriage* provides an associated narrative, like a key to a secret language used in several interrelated stories including Violet Trefusis's novel *Brodérie Anglaise*, originally published in French in 1935 as a riposte to *Orlando*.

Nigel Nicolson, who was a publisher, appointed James Lees-Milne as his father's biographer. Lees-Milne had had a brief amorous fling with Harold Nicolson and felt an enduring affection for him (his wife Alvilde had affaires both with Violet Trefusis and her two principal lovers, Vita Sackville-West and Winnaretta Polignac). More simply, Nigel chose Victoria Glendinning to write the life of his mother. They were excellent biographies (I reviewed them both) and by the beginning of the 1980s these formidable vessels sailed into publication while to one side, like a pirate boat, a television film by Penelope Mortimer appeared.

It was in the wake of all this commotion that the novels of Violet Trefusis were introduced into Britain – *Echo* and *Brodérie Anglaise* were translated from the French for the first time. There were two reasons for this revival: the fact that Violet's story was in the news; and a feeling that the recent non-fiction publications had come too exclusively from Vita Sackville-West's side of the story. The books that set out to sea from the Trefusis anchorage were scattered and ill-assorted – and they had begun their journey in what seemed to be atrocious weather. 'The "great affair" was surely one of the most absurd episodes in English literary and social history,' wrote a reviewer in the *Literary Review*. He was reviewing one of Violet's novels, not *Portrait of a Marriage*, which nevertheless dominated the climate in which these books were received. On collision course were two published versions of Violet's letters to Vita. Both were packaged with short biographies and, in an unsuccessful effort to steer away from 'the great affair', one of these volumes changed its title between America and Britain, starting out as *The Other Woman* and ending as *Violet Trefusis: Life and Letters* (though carrying the subtitle: *Including correspondence with Vita Sackville-West*). A plan to reissue Violet Trefusis's novels as Virago Classics with new introductions by contemporary novelists was interrupted by copyright complications. Her memoir *Don't Look Round* was introduced in America by Peter Quennell (no friend of Violet's to judge from his letter to Nigel Nicolson) – and he also wrote an entertaining if somewhat derisive picture of her in his volume of contemporary portraits, *Customs and Characters*. Victoria Glendinning contributed a good introduction to *Broderie Anglaise*, but surely she belonged to the Vita camp – Nicholas Shakespeare suggested in his *Times* review that 'it was a story which packs much greater charge than Victoria Glendinning allows'. Whatever vessel set hesitantly out from the Trefusis harbour appeared to her enthusiasts to be immediately captured by the enemy: Sophia Sackville-West writing an appalling review of *Echo*, James Lees-Milne reviewing Diana Souhami's fine double biography of Alice Keppel and Violet Trefusis, and Victoria Glendinning giving a kindly but understandably modest review of Henrietta Sharpe's *Life of Violet Trefusis* in 1981 – which was greeted more aggressively by Harold Acton. 'She [Violet] had a pathological dread of being left alone with her conscience,' he wrote, adding that 'Madame Trés Physique', as she was nicknamed, reminded him as she grew older of 'a poodle'.

Over the years Harold Acton had grown remorselessly hostile. At the beginning of one of his short stories called 'Codicil Coda', which appeared in a collection of his stories, *The Soul's Gymnasium* (1982), we see Muriel, his fictional portrait of Violet, making her Will. Since her doctor told her she was ill, she has passed her days and nights renegotiating this Will. But her friends keep tiresomely dying – a coronary here, a fatal accident somewhere else – and Muriel is obliged to alter her codicils again, filling in the gaps. Muriel's only other distraction is the writing of a sensational autobiography. 'It was my vocation to become a legend,' she informs her secretary. '. . . I forget our precise connection with Charlemagne . . . Even in the cradle my cheeks were tickled by a royal moustache.' But the pointlessness of this book, like the pointlessness of her life, eventually overwhelms her. By the end of the story all her friends are dead. She orders her maid to lay out the trays of jewels once more and painfully plants them all over her fragile anatomy, lying back in her bed 'panting from the effort of her transformation'. She stares in the mirror at the barbaric idol she has become. 'The wreck of her features amid the glitter of jewels was intensely dramatic.' Her maid exclaims how beautiful she looks. And Harold Acton concludes: 'Yes, Muriel made a beautiful corpse.'

Acton's story focuses on Violet Trefusis's last years. His memoir of Nancy Mitford, published in 1975, covers intermittently a longer period of Violet's life. 'Make allowances for great unhappiness,' Violet had appealed to Vita. Harold Acton, usually a courteous writer, makes no allowances. He pities her and not her grief, seeing her as if she has always been what she became in her final, sad, postscriptum phase. The memoir contains a photograph of 'Mrs Violet Trefusis, with her maid', which shows an elderly figure, like a superannuated ballet dancer, poised on the pavement as if waiting for a bus, with her maid Alice Amiot a couple of paces behind looking directly at the camera as if, with a confiding wink, inviting us to laugh. Acton writes that there had been 'a definite estrangement' between Violet Trefusis and himself 'owing to Violet's extreme rudeness'. The book shows her as being socially unnegotiable. But this 'need not have been commemorated', Rebecca West observed, 'in so many merciless passages'. We hear of her wearing 'the ribbon of the Légion d'honneur night and day', of her 'supercilious ostentation' and 'fat independent income' and are told that her writing was 'no more than an exhibitionist exercise'. He adds that it was 'fitting that Philippe Jullian, author of *The Snob Spotter's Guide* [*Dictionnaire de Snobisme*], should write the biography of this super-snob for whom literature was a mere hobby'.

Acton's book has no reference to earlier days when Nancy Mitford enjoyed going to Violet's parties. Nancy had likened her to Hilaire Belloc's Matilda 'who told such dreadful lies, it made one gasp and stretch one's eyes'. And yet, she added, 'one can't help being fond of her'. This fondness is wholly absent from Harold Acton's memoir. The Violet Trefusis we are shown is 'quite off her old head' and irritates Nancy Mitford so much with her tiresome telephone calls when she is trying to work that 'I'm really beginning to quite hate her'. Acton believed that this hateful figure regarded Nancy Mitford as a literary trespasser on her private property. Yet in *Don't Look Round* Violet gave an admiring pen portrait of her, praising her for having 'the courage to break with the familiar paraphernalia [of the novel], the decor, family jokes, even the vocabulary'. She describes her as 'France's wittiest conquest'. But there were to be few reciprocal civilities. Nancy suggested that *Don't Look Round* should have been called *Here Lies Mrs Trefusis*.

Nancy Mitford used Violet Trefusis as the basis for Lady Montdore in her novel *Love in a Cold Climate* (Violet is 'Lady Montdore exactly' she told the bookseller Heywood Hill). She had been born Sonia

Perrotte, the handsome daughter of a country squire 'of no particular note'. But her marriage to the cardboard figure of Lord Montdore had raised her unexpectedly high in a society she pretended to despise but which 'gave meaning to her existence'. By the time we meet her in the novel she is aged sixty and has become known for her rampant vulgarity and proverbial rudeness. She is much disliked by people who have never met her and long to do so. Royalty she adores and she also has a weakness for bankers who may not be much to look at but 'one can't get away from them'. Whoever invented love, she believes, 'should be shot'. Everything is coated with a superficial charm and conveys what Nancy Mitford came to regard as the cold climate of the Keppels.

Lady Montdore has one daughter, the beautiful and unfeeling Polly Hampton. Scattered between the two of them are a number of Keppel characteristics enveloped by clouds of gossip (there is even a popular rumour that 'Polly isn't Lord Montdore's child at all. King Edward's, I've heard'). Both mother and daughter are indifferent to children and when Polly's child is born dead, Lady Montdore remarks: 'I expect it was just as well, children are such an awful expense, nowadays.' Polly's long-held secret love for her lecherous uncle by marriage to whom she proposes as soon as his wife 'is cold in the grave', is considered as 'unnatural' as Violet's love had been for Vita – she is described by one of the characters as an 'incestuous little trollop'. Polly had fallen in love with this 'uncle' when she was aged fourteen, not knowing that he had previously been her mother's lover. This secret love for a much older man made her indifferent to other men. She was an unresponsive debutante, unable to provoke eligible suitors to duels or play the game of stirring unsatisfied desire in married men and breaking up her friends' romances – everything her mother had done before settling down to make a socially desirable marriage.

The dramatic surprise of the plot comes with the arrival of 'the awful offensive pansy Cedric' hitherto dependent on the whims of barons and the temperament of a drunken German boy. He transforms Lady Montdore 'from a terrifying old idol of about sixty into a delicious young darling of about a hundred'. And with this fate, the satire is complete.

Violet's lesbian relationship with Vita has been well vindicated by Diana Souhami in *Mrs Keppel and her Daughter*. But she did not make it her business to examine Violet's novels. These novels have been described as period pieces in which the characters step directly out of her address book. Her style is sardonically lightweight, high, comic and faintly camp, veering in places between the influence of Ronald Firbank and Angela Thirkell – and with a French ingredient taken perhaps from Paul Morand. She has been criticised for holding up her narrative with school essays on national characteristics, cluttering it with unnecessary cultural references, with travelogues, commentaries and vivid descriptions of furniture, food and buildings that advance from the background of her novels and take over the foreground. But these 'faults' are part of an original tapestry.

A reassessment of her writing was begun by Lorna Sage whose study of twelve twentieth-century women novelists, in the posthumously published *Moments of Truth* (2001), contains a fine essay on *Hunt the Slipper* and places Violet Trefusis in the company of Edith Wharton, Christina Stead, Jane Bowles and others. In her introductory note to this book, she wrote that Violet Trefusis 'is mainly now remembered as a character in others' books'. Her aim was to extract some of her novels from this punishing incarceration; and she hoped to publish a new translation of Violet's dissenting *roman-à-clef*, *Broderie Anglaise*. I have tried to pick up the baton Lorna Sage left and run a further lap of that course, showing the value of Violet's best novels – *Echo*, *Broderie Anglaise*, *Hunt the Slipper*, *Pirates at Play* – before handing over this baton to a new generation of readers.

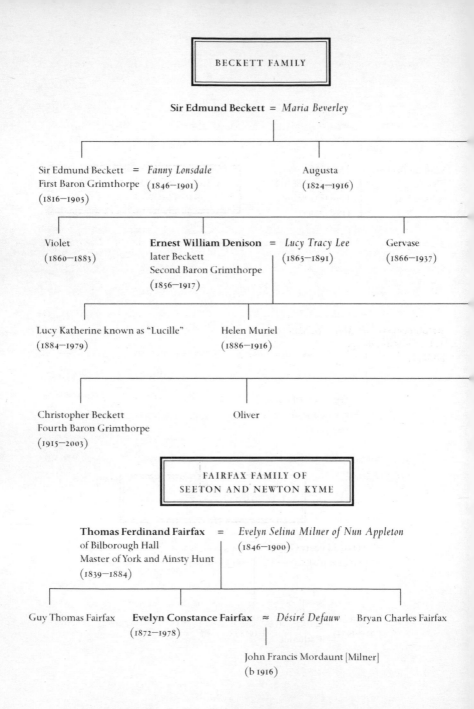

BECKETT FAMILY

Sir Edmund Beckett = *Maria Beverley*

Sir Edmund Beckett = *Fanny Lonsdale*
First Baron Grimthorpe (1846–1901)
(1816–1905)

Augusta
(1824–1916)

Violet
(1860–1883)

Ernest William Denison = *Lucy Tracy Lee*
later Beckett (1865–1891)
Second Baron Grimthorpe
(1856–1917)

Gervase
(1866–1937)

Lucy Katherine known as "Lucille"
(1884–1979)

Helen Muriel
(1886–1916)

Christopher Beckett
Fourth Baron Grimthorpe
(1915–2003)

Oliver

FAIRFAX FAMILY OF
SEETON AND NEWTON KYME

Thomas Ferdinand Fairfax = *Evelyn Selina Milner of Nun Appleton*
of Bilborough Hall (1846–1900)
Master of York and Ainsty Hunt
(1839–1884)

Guy Thomas Fairfax **Evelyn Constance Fairfax** ≈ *Désiré Defauw* Bryan Charles Fairfax
(1872–1978)

John Francis Mordaunt [Milner]
(b 1916)

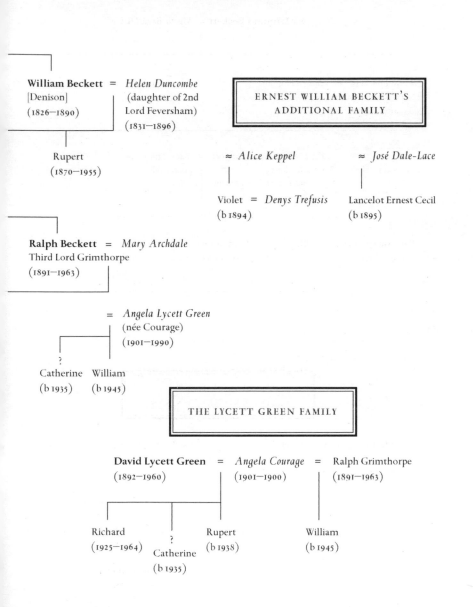

William Beckett = *Helen Duncombe*
[Denison]   *(daughter of 2nd*
(1826–1890)   *Lord Feversham)*
                          (1831–1896)

Rupert
(1870–1955)

≈ *Alice Keppel*   ≈ *José Dale-Lace*

Violet = *Denys Trefusis*   Lancelot Ernest Cecil
(b 1894)   (b 1895)

ERNEST WILLIAM BECKETT'S
ADDITIONAL FAMILY

Ralph Beckett = *Mary Archdale*
Third Lord Grimthorpe
(1891–1963)

= *Angela Lycett Green*
    (née Courage)
    (1901–1990)

?
Catherine   William
(b 1935)   (b 1945)

THE LYCETT GREEN FAMILY

David Lycett Green = *Angela Courage* = Ralph Grimthorpe
(1892–1960)   *(1901–1900)*   (1891–1963)

Richard   Rupert   William
(1925–1964)   (b 1938)   (b 1945)
              ?
           Catherine
           (b 1935)

Select Bibliography

Acton, Harold, *More Memoirs of an Aesthete* (London, Methuen, 1970)

Acton, Harold, *Nancy Mitford* (London, Hamish Hamilton, 1975)

Alsop, Susan Mary, *To Marietta from Paris, 1945–1960* (London, Weidenfeld & Nicolson, 1976)

Alsop, Susan Mary, *Lady Sackville: A Biography* (London, Weidenfeld & Nicolson, 1978)

Asquith, Lady Cynthia, *Diaries 1915–1918* (London, Hutchinson, 1968)

Beauman, Nicola, *Morgan: A Biography of E. M. Forster* (London, Hodder & Stoughton, 1993)

Beckett, Lori (ed.), *City of Leeds Training College: Continuity and Change 1907–2007* (Leeds, Leeds Metropolitan University, 2007)

Blanche, Jacques-Emile, *Portraits of a Lifetime* (London, Dent, 1937)

Bloch, Michael, *James Lees-Milne: The Life* (London, John Murray, 2009)

Brewster, E. and A. Brewster, *D. H. Lawrence: Reminiscences and Correspondence* (London, Secker, 1934)

Briggs, Julia, *Virginia Woolf: An Inner Life* (London, Allen Lane, 2005)

Brittain, Vera, *Testament of Youth* (London, Gollancz, 1933)

Butler, Ruth, *Rodin: The Shape of Genius* (London, Yale University Press, 1993)

Churchill, Lady Randolph, *Reminiscences* (London, Edward Arnold, 1908)

Connolly, Cyril, *The Rock Pool* (rev. edn, London, Hamish Hamilton, 1947)

Connolly, Cyril, *The Unquiet Grave* (London, Hamish Hamilton, 1945)

Cornwallis-West, G., *Edwardian Hey-Days* (London, Putnam's, 1930)

Cossart, Michael de, *The Food of Love: Princess Edmond de Polignac (1865–1943) and Her Salon* (London, Hamish Hamilton, 1978)

DeSalvo, Louise and A. Mitchell Leaska (eds), *The Letters of Vita Sackville-West to Virginia Woolf* (New York, William Morrow, 1985)

Eden, Timothy, *The Tribulations of a Baronet* (London, Macmillan, 1933)

Ferriday, Peter, *Lord Grimthorpe 1816–1905* (London, John Murray, 1957)

Forster, E. M., *Selected Short Stories* (London, Penguin Books, 1954)

Forster, E. M., *Selected Letters: Volume One 1879–1920*, eds Mary Lago and P. N. Furbank (London, Collins, 1983)

Furbank, P. N., *E. M. Forster: A Life* (New York, Harcourt Brace Jovanovich, 1978)

Glendinning, Victoria, *Vita: The Life of V. Sackville-West* (London, Weidenfeld & Nicolson, 1983)

Grunfeld, Frederic V., *Rodin: A Biography* (London, Hutchinson, 1988)

Gutsche, Thelma, *No Ordinary Woman: The Life and Times of Florence Phillips* (Cape Town, Howard Timmins, 1996)

Hare, Marion J., *The Sculptor and His Sitter: Rodin's Bust of Eve Fairfax* (Johannesburg, Johannesburg Art Gallery, 1994)

Harrison, Marjorie J., *Four Ainsty Townships* (Appleton Roebuck, Ainsty Books, 2000)

Jullian, Philippe and John Phillips (eds), *Violet Trefusis: Life and Letters* (originally published as *The Other Woman: The Life of Violet Trefusis*) (London, Hamish Hamilton, 1976)

Kahan, Sylvia, *Music's Modern Muse: A Life of Winnaretta Singer, Princesse de Polignac* (Rochester, University of Rochester Press, 2003)

Keppel, Sonia, *Edwardian Daughter* (London, Hamish Hamilton, 1958)

Lamont-Brown, Raymond, *Edward VII's Last Loves: Alice Keppel and Agnes Keyser* (Stroud, Sutton Publishing, 1998)

Lawrence, D. H., *The Letters: Volumes VI and VII*, eds Keith Sagar, James T. Boulton and Margaret H. Boulton with Gerald M. Lacy (Cambridge, Cambridge University Press, 1991 and 1993)

Leaska, Mitchell A. and John Phillips (eds), *Violet to Vita: The letters of Violet Trefusis to Vita Sackville-West, 1910–21* (London, Methuen, 1989)

Lees-Milne, James, *Harold Nicolson: A Biography* (London, Chatto & Windus, 1980, 1981)

Lees-Milne, James, *Ancestral Voices* (London, Chatto & Windus, 1975)

Lees-Milne, James, *Prophesying Peace* (London, Chatto & Windus, 1978)

Lees-Milne, James, *Caves of Ice* (London, Chatto & Windus, 1983)

Leslie, Anita, *The Fabulous Leonard Jerome* (London, Hutchinson, 1954)

Masucci, Tiziana, *Violet, Vita, Virginia: Passagi a Ravello* (Rome, Mephite, 2007)

Masucci, Tiziana, *Violet's Rhapsody* (Rome, Mephite, 2008)

Masucci, Tiziana, *D. H. Lawrence: A Trespasser in Ravello* (Rome, Mephite, 2008)

Mitford, Nancy, *The Pursuit of Love* (London, Hamish Hamilton, 1949)

Morrell, Lady Ottoline, *The Early Memoirs*, ed. Robert Gathorne-Hardy
     (London, Faber & Faber, 1963)

Mosley, Diana, *A Life of Contrasts* (London, Hamish Hamilton, 1977)

Nicolson, Adam, *Sissinghurst: An Unfinished History* (London, HarperCollins,
     2008)

Nicolson, Harold, *Some People* (London, Constable, 1927)

Nicolson, Nigel, *Portrait of a Marriage* (London, Weidenfeld & Nicolson, 1973)

Nicolson, Nigel, *Long Life: Memoirs* (London, Weidenfeld & Nicolson, 1997)

Nicolson, Nigel (ed.), *Vita and Harold: The Letters of Vita Sackville-West and
     Harold Nicolson, 1910–1962* (London, Weidenfeld & Nicolson, 1992)

Pearson, Hesketh, *The Pilgrim Daughters* (London, William Heinemann, 1961)

Pullar, Philippa, *Frank Harris* (London, Hamish Hamilton, 1975)

Quennell, Peter, *Customs and Characters* (London, Weidenfeld & Nicolson, 1982)

Rose, Norman, *Harold Nicolson* (London, Jonathan Cape, 2005)

Sackville-West, Vita, *The Edwardians* (London, The Hogarth Press, 1960)

Sackville-West, Vita, *All Passion Spent* (London, The Hogarth Press, 1965)

Sackville-West, Vita, *Challenge* (London, Collins, 1974)

Sage, Lorna, *Moments of Truth: Twelve Twentieth-Century Women Writers*
     (London, Fourth Estate, 2001)

Saul, Daphne, *Bird of Paradise: José Dale Lace* (Johannesburg, Parktown and Westcliff Heritage Trust, 1993)

Sebba, Anne, *Jennie Churchill: Winston's Mother* (London, John Murray, 2007)

Sharpe, Henrietta, *A Solitary Woman: A Life of Violet Trefusis* (London, Constable, 1981)

Sitwell, Osbert, *Great Morning* (London, Macmillan, 1948)

Souhami, Diana, *Mrs Keppel and her Daughter* (London, HarperCollins, 1996)

Squires, Michael, *D. H. Lawrence and Frieda: A Portrait of Love and Loyalty* (London, André Deutsch, 2008)

St Aubyn, Giles, *Edward VII: Prince and King* (London, Collins, 1979)

Stein, Gertrude, *The Autobiography of Alice B. Toklas* (London, John Lane, 1933)

Strachey, Lytton, *Eminent Victorians* (London, Chatto & Windus, 1918)

Strouse, Jean, *Morgan: American Financier* (New York, Random House, 1999)

Trefusis, Violet, *Sortie de Secours* (Paris, Editions Argo, 1929)

Trefusis, Violet, *Echo,* trans. Siân Miles (London, Methuen, 1988)

Trefusis, Violet, *Tandem* (London, Heinemann, 1933)

Trefusis, Violet, *Broderie Anglaise,* trans. Barbara Bray (London, Methuen, 1986)

Trefusis, Violet, *Hunt the Slipper* (London, Heinemann, 1937)

Trefusis, Violet, *Les Causes Perdues* (Paris, Editions Gallimard, 1941)

Trefusis, Violet, *Prelude to Misadventure* (London, Hutchinson, 1942)

Trefusis, Violet, 'The Carillon' (*Horizon,* June 1943)

Trefusis, Violet, 'Triptych' (*Horizon*, November 1943)

Trefusis, Violet, *Pirates at Play* (London, Michael Joseph, 1950)

Trefusis, Violet, *Don't Look Round* (London, Hutchinson, 1952)

Trefusis, Violet and Frank Ashton-Gwatkin, *From Dusk to Dawn* (London, Tom Stacey, 1972)

Trefusis, Violet and Philippe Jullian, *Memoirs of an Armchair* (London, Hutchinson, 1960)

Wajsbrot, Cécile, *Violet Trefusis* (Paris, Mercure de France, 1989)

Webb, Gerry, *Fairfax of York* (York, Maxiprint, 2001)

Woolf, Virginia, *Orlando* (London, The Hogarth Press, 1928)

Woolf, Virginia, *The Diary of Virginia Woolf: Volume III* 1925–1930, eds Anne Olivier Bell and Andrew McNeillie (London, The Hogarth Press, 1980)

Woolf, Virginia, *The Letters of Virginia Woolf 1923–1928; 1932–1935; 1936– 1941*, eds Nigel Nicolson and Joanne Trautmann (London, The Hogarth Press, 1977, 1979, 1980)

Index